Aurea Vidyā Collection*

——— 24 ———

* For a complete list of titles see Publications on page 307.

SHORT WORKS

This book was originally published in Italian as
Śaṅkara *Opere Brevi*
by Associazione Ecoculturale Parmenides
(formerly Edizioni Āśram Vidyā) Rome

Āśram Vidyā - Via Azone 20 - 00165 Roma

ISBN 978-1-931406-71-0

On the cover: Statue of Śaṅkara, Amrita Vishwa Vidyapeetham University, Ettimadai, Tamil Nadu, India. Photograph by Shivapratap Gopakumar.

Śaṅkara

SHORT WORKS

Treatises and Hymns

Edited by the Kevala Group

Aurea Vidyā

CONTENTS

Introduction 13

Hymn for morning recitation 21
(*prātahsmaraṇastotra*)

Knowledge of the *Ātman* 25
(*ātmabodha*)

Hymn of praise in ten verses 59
(*daśaślokīstuti*)

The ocean of bliss of one liberated in life 65
(*jīvanmuktānandalaharī*)

Five verses on the ascetic 75
(*yātipañcakam*)

Eight verses on the blessed 79
(*dhanyāṣṭakam*)

Hymn to *Dakṣiṇāmūrti* 87
(*dakṣiṇāmūrtistotram*)

The exposition of the sentence 93
(*vākyavṛtti*)

The five-faceted jewel of instruction 111
(*upadeśapañcaratnam*)

The sacred reproach for the non-self 117
(*anātmaśrīvigarhaṇa*)

Worship Govinda (*bhaja govindam*) 125

The way of Being (*sadācāra*) 137

The song of the knowledge of the *Brahman* (*brahmajñānavālī*) 155

I am Śiva, I am Śiva (*Śivo 'ham Śivo 'ham*) 163

Quintuplication (*pañcīkaraṇa*) 167

Commentary to 'Quintuplication' (*pañcīkaraṇavarttika* of Sureśvara 173

The fivefold conviction (*manīṣāpañcakam*) 191

A hymn in ten verses (*daśaślokī*) 197

The teaching on knowledge of the *ātman* (*ātmajñānopadeśavidhi*) 203

The fivefold realisation of Śiva (*śivapañcākṣram*) 233

A short exposition of the sentence (*laghuvākyavṛtti*) 237

Sanskrit text 247

prātahsmaraṇastotra 249

ātmabodha 250

daśaślokīstuti 256

jīvanmuktānandalaharī 258

yātipañcakam 261

dhanyāṣṭakam 262

dakṣiṇāmūrtistotram 264

vākyavṛtti 266

upadeśapañcaratnam 271

anātmaśrīvigarhaṇa 272

bhaja govindam 275

sadācāra 279

brahmajñānavālī 284

śivo 'ham śivo 'ham 286

pañcīkaraṇa 287

pañcīkaraṇavarttika 288

manīṣāpañcakam 293

daśaślokī 295

ātmajñānopadeśavidhi 297

śivapañcākṣram 304

laghuvākyavṛtti 305

INTRODUCTION

Śaṅkara, considered to be one of the most representative philosophical minds that India has ever produced, realised the most complete synthesis[1] and harmonisation of all Indian philosophical thought. His 'method' in the search for truth, which essentially consists in freeing it from the layers which cover it, has made a very valuable contribution to the philosophical/metaphysical[2] thought of the whole world.

He dedicated his short but intense life (788-820) to the noble purpose of 'revitalising' the Vedic Tradition by re-establishing the authority of the *Śruti* (*Vedas* and *Upaniṣads*) which had become degraded by that time.

---

[1] Synthesis: in philosophy, the combination of parts, or elements, in order to form a more complete view or system. The coherent whole that results is considered to show the truth more completely than would a mere collection of parts. The term synthesis also refers, in the dialectical philosophy of the 19th-century German philosopher G.W.F. Hegel, to the higher stage of truth that combines the truth of a thesis and an antithesis. Encyclopedia Britannica.

[2] The purpose of the forward slash [/] in this text is to show the relationship of the two or more items either side of it. Thus it may indicate a single concept seen from two different perspectives or a concept of unity or wholeness. However, it is left to the intuition of the reader to appreciate the specific nuance imparted by the use of the slash each time it occurs.

To this end he compiled important commentaries (*bhāṣyas*) to the *Prasthānatraya* or 'Threefold Science'[1] of *Vedānta* (*Upaniṣads*, *Bhagavadgītā*, *Brahmasūtra*), as well as numerous other works, including the *Vivekacūḍāmaṇi*, the *Ātmabodha*, the *Aparokśānubhūti*, and the *Upadeśasāhasrī*, in which he summarises both the teaching and the discipline required to attain the realisation of *advaita*.

Śaṅkara placed the Vedic Scriptures on the highest philosophical plane by embracing, in his writings, the non-dual (*advaita*) aspect that was already present in them. With rigorous, profound investigations and the subtlest analyses, he established the Non-duality of ultimate Reality and proclaimed the grandeur of this vision not only in his 'commentaries' but also in the disputes and public debates which he held with the representatives of other schools and in which he refuted their theses.

Śaṅkara did not come to destroy, but to build up, and the philosophy which he taught must not be considered to be in opposition to other schools of thought or *darśanas*:

> '*Advaita* is a teaching which does not compete with the other orthodox schools ... but illumines them from within and demonstrates that a single Truth polarises the whole totality.'[2]

By codifying *Advaita*, Śaṅkara also supplied a solid ontological and metaphysical basis for all the types of worship of his time, purifying their rituals and guaranteeing

---

[1] Science: *Philos.* in the sense of 'knowledge' as opposed to 'belief' or 'opinion'. The Compact Edition of the Oxford English Dictionary.

The traditional concept of Science is that it includes an absolute guarantee of validity and therefore, like knowledge, the highest degree of certainty. In contrast to Science is *opinion*, which is characterised precisely by the lack of guarantee concerning its validity. The different conceptions of Science may be distinguished according to how much guarantee of validity is attributed to them. Dizionario di Filosofia di Nicola Abbagnano.

[2] P. Martin-Dubost, *Çankara et le Védanta*. Editions du Seuil, Paris 1973.

their survival, thus laying the foundations for a long-lasting and sound national unity.

Many see Śaṅkara as a philosopher, a mystic, an exegete of the *Śruti*, the founder of monastic orders and monasteries (*maṭhas*), a national hero, but, above all, we should see in him the supreme Teacher (*ācārya*) who is able to show us the true, supreme aim of human existence, an aim founded on knowledge and constituting the very purpose of the *Upaniṣads*, which is the acknowledgement of our real nature and liberation from the world of becoming/*saṁsāra*.

> 'The central focus, the incandescent nucleus of the vast edifice of Śaṅkara's thought, which has attracted and continues to attract great numbers of people, is liberation ... Focusing first and foremost on this fundamental interest in *mokṣa* is the safest way of ensuring that Śaṅkara is not betrayed ... Respect for liberating knowledge, which he accepts as a divine revelation (*Śruti*) given in past ages, lost in the mists of time, leads Śaṅkara to transmit it like a living flame rather than to mould it anew and thus impoverish it... Śaṅkara is happy to call himself, not a "supporter of *māyā*" – as many continue to describe him – but a "follower of the *Upaniṣads*" (*aupaniṣada*). In this designation, faithfulness to Brahmanical orthodoxy merges with the consciousness of being heir to mankind's most precious heritage: self-knowledge, which is the solution for the world and its painful contradictions, for this is the meaning which he assigns to the term "*Upaniṣad*".'[1]

In Śaṅkara we find an astonishing combination of knowledge (*jñāna*), devotion (*bhakti*), and action

[1] M. Piantelli, *Śaṅkara e il Kevalādvaitavāda*. Collezione Vidyā, Roma.

(*karma*). In him these three aspects come to complete and glorious maturity.

As a devotee (*bhakta*) Śaṅkara was filled with boundless compassion, faith, and devotion. His genius was able to produce the purest of abstract thoughts to proclaim the philosophical teaching of Non-duality as well as verse compositions (*stotras*) full of fervour, such as *Bhaja Govindam* and *Dakṣiṇāmūrtistotram*. Aware that not everyone is ready to set out on the metaphysical pathway leading to *Nirguṇa Brahman*, Śaṅkara composed numerous devotional texts in praise of various deities. Among these Hymns, the *Śivānandalaharī* occupies one of the highest positions on account of its fervour, poetical intensity, and aesthetic beauty.

The presence of knowledge and devotion side by side is a rare event by itself, but in Śaṅkara there also co-exists another aspect that is just as worthy of attention: indefatigable dynamic action (*karma*), which has given him such a special place in the galaxy of immortal Sages that he has become the symbol for 'triumphant action'. This prodigy of eternal wisdom was scarcely sixteen years old when he began his work, journeying across the length and breadth of the land. During the few years of his earthly life he established ten monastic orders (*daśanāmin*) to prevent the decline of spiritual practice, and he founded monasteries/ *maṭhas* – focal points for a very powerful Influence which can still be felt today – at the four cardinal points of India, by which he ensured the continuity of the Tradition.

> 'The Master (*ācārya*) who preached renunciation of the world and non-action did not withdraw into a Himalayan cave, but travelled unceasingly throughout the land, wrote continually, instructed his disciples, and spread the teaching of *Advaita*.'[1]

---

[1] P. Martin-Dubost, *Çankara et le Védanta*, op. cit.

These words of P. Martin-Dubost constitute the best answer to those who hold that Śaṅkara urged people to totally renounce the world.

The works composed by Śaṅkara may be classified into three principal groups:

1. *bhāṣyas* or commentaries on the fundamental texts constituting the 'Threefold Science' (*prasthānatraya*) of *Vedānta*: the *Upaniṣads*, the *Brahmasūtra*, and the *Bhagavadgītā*;
2. *stotras*, devotional songs or Hymns of praise;
3. *prakaraṇas*, specific works or treatises in prose and verse which expound some of the expressions found in the Scriptures.

Since the *Brahman*, in the course of the various works, will be presented with various descriptions and affirmations – let us remember that the *Brahman/Turīya* is indescribable, unthinkable, indefinable, and so on – and also with the aim of elucidating expressions in the *Upaniṣads* such as '*Brahman* is pure Consciousness', it is considered appropriate to quote a passage from Śaṅkara's commentary to the *Bṛhadāraṇyaka Upaniṣad* (II, III, 6):

> '[If one were to wonder] how, through these two expressions of "It is not this, it is not this", the "Truth of truths" is meant to be described, the answer is that through the elimination of all the qualifications arising from the limiting superimpositions [one reaches That, the *Brahman*] in which there is no longer any qualification, name, form, distinction, kind or attribute. Speech, in fact, can be employed solely on account of such means, whereas in the *Brahman* there is no qualification. This is why That cannot be defined as "It is this", in the way that current idiom may say "A cow with white horns is grazing there". The *Brahman* can

> be [indirectly] indicated only by means of the name, form, and activity which are superimposed on it and through expressions such as "*Brahman* is knowledge and bliss" (*Bṛhadāraṇyaka Upaniṣad*, III, IX, 28, 7), or [directly] by the use of terms such as *Brahman* or *ātman*. But if one wished to really describe its authentic nature, which transcends all the qualifications governed by the superimpositions, then one would find that there is no way in which this can be indicated. In this case there remains only this method: the designation given in the words "It is not this, it is not this" (*neti neti*, where *neti* consists of *na* and *iti*), whereby all the qualifications which could be attributed to it are eliminated one by one. And these two negative words (*na*) [in association with the word *iti*] are intended to suggest the repetition [of the negation] by extending it [to all qualifications] so as to eliminate every single thing [such as attribute and so on] that may be encountered ... There is no description better than this. Therefore this is the only [possible] description of the *Brahman*: *neti neti*.'

The writings gathered in this volume are just some of the many *prakaraṇas* (Treatises) and *stotras* (Hymns) composed by Śaṅkara or attributed to him. Not all are as well known as *Ātmabodha* or *Bhaja Govindam*, but there is no doubt that their contents share the same beauty and profundity.

In presenting them, we have done our utmost to allow Śaṅkara's words to speak for themselves; they are able to reach the consciousness of any reader who approaches them without prejudice.

Our notes, which are necessary, and at times indispensable, for a better understanding of the text, are kept short, and if at times we have had to lengthen them, this is in order to present aspects of the Teaching taken from the texts that may not be part of the heritage of those readers who are coming to Śaṅkara for the first time.

In presenting these works the criterion has been, as far as possible, to intersperse a longer Treatise (such as *Ātmabodha*) with a shorter work that typically describes a precise state of consciousness to be achieved (such as *Dhanyaṣṭakam*) or a Hymn (for example, *Dakṣiṇamūrtistotram*), thus allowing the note of knowledge and the note of love/devotion to sound alternately.

Nowadays Śaṅkara is beginning to be known in the West, too, even though there are times when his philosophical and operational vision may seem difficult and, for some, apparently arduous to implement. Śaṅkara is one of those great souls that appear from time to time on this planet to propound afresh Principles of a universal order in such a way as to constitute a precise and reliable reference point.

Our hope is that these writings will shed light on those consciousnesses that are sincerely seeking to find a direction and a pathway that will lead them beyond the world of becoming/*saṁsāra*, so that they may be 'what they are'.

We considered it our duty to begin this collection of Śaṅkara's writings by recalling his image, his works, and his function. We also thought it our duty to end this short Introduction by paying homage to the *Ācārya* with a verse from the *Mādhavīyaśaṅkaravijaya* (IV, 34), which declares:

> 'Knowledge embellishes those who cultivate it, but, in the case of Śaṅkara, it was he who embellished Knowledge.'

Associazione Ecoculturale Parmenides

HYMN FOR MORNING RECITATION

prātaḥsmaraṇastotra

The first thoughts that come to mind on awakening, the first words spoken, and the first action undertaken every day exert a powerful and beneficent influence on the rest of the day in particular and on the whole of life in general. If they are consecrated every day by being offered to the *ātman*, which 'shines by itself in the heart', a threefold result will ensue: they are purified, transformed, and resolved, and consequently so are the organs of mind, speech, and action.

Prayer recited in the morning has a profound significance, because dawn is seen as the outer symbol of inner awakening.

These verses, in addition to being recited with the voice or in thought, need to be contemplated with the heart, so that within it there may be fulfilled the ineffable occurrence of total comprehension and therefore of conscious realisation, like the dawn of knowledge which utterly dispels the darkness of *avidyā*.

1. At dawn I turn my awareness towards Reality: Reality is the ātman shining by itself in the heart. Being absolute Existence, Consciousness, and Fullness, the ātman constitutes the Fourth and is the final goal to which the sages aspire, the Witness that knows the states of waking, dream, and deep sleep. I am That, the eternal Brahman without parts, and not an aggregate of elements.

2. At dawn I bow before That which is unattainable by word or thought; That by whose grace words themselves shine; That which the sacred Scriptures designate with the expression 'It is not this, it is not this' and which, as they themselves declare, is the Deva of devas, the Supreme, having no birth and being beyond any kind of change.

3. At dawn I pay homage to That which, being beyond darkness, is the essence of supreme splendour; That which is fullness and everlasting Steadfastness and is known as the supreme Puruṣa; That which has an indivisible nature and in which this entire universe seems to manifest, like a snake appearing in the rope.

4. As embellishments to the threefold world, those who recite these three sacred verses everyday at sunrise will undoubtedly attain the goal supreme.

KNOWLEDGE OF THE ĀTMAN

ātmabodha

The *Ātmabodha* is a well-known *prakaraṇa*, the subject of many commentaries by scholars of *Advaita*. The explanation of the terms and expressions used in the Scriptures helps the student to understand the subtle subject-matter that is concealed in them, so that knowledge of this introductory text becomes an essential prerequisite for anyone who wishes to comprehend *Vedānta*.

Śaṅkara addresses those who have purified themselves through the practice of austerity (*tapas*), have acquired peace in their hearts, have freed themselves from all fear and sensory desire, and now yearn for one thing only: identity with the Being-without-a-second.

According to *Advaita Vedānta*, what imprisons us is *avidyā*, or metaphysical ignorance; and so it is only through a 'knowledge' of a metaphysical order that one can defeat ignorance that is concerned with the nature of Being. This knowledge involves a profound transformation, a realisative *sādhanā* whose stages are nothing other than moments of transformation/transfiguration of the being subsequent to acts of consciousness, or 'recognitions', since the being already has absolute knowledge within itself.

The required qualifications are: discrimination (*viveka*) between the Real and the unreal; detachment (*vairāgya*) from the unreal that is recognised as such; the six mental virtues (*śamādis*); and the yearning for Liberation, or *mumukṣutva*.

If this 'yearning',[1] or 'love for liberation', is missing, then the final goal cannot be attained, and Śaṅkara says with regard to this:

> 'The yearning for liberation is characterised by the intense inclination to dissolve the bonds of formal life through realising the identity of the *ātman* with the *Brahman*. Love of realisation is the basis of liberation; if this is missing, study and the assimilation of sacred works afford no fruit.'[2]

---

[1] See Śaṅkara, *Vivekacūḍāmaṇi*, 30 *et seqq*. Translation from the Sanskrit and commentary by Raphael. Aurea Vidyā, New York.

[2] Śaṅkara, *Sarvavedntasiddhntasrasaṅgraha* 226-227. The translation of the classical texts, both Eastern and Western, which appear in this work, unless differently indicated, are edited by Aurea Vidyā.

1. *This Ātmabodha (knowledge/realisation of the ātman) has been composed for the benefit of those who, yearning for Liberation, have totally purified themselves of error (pāpa) by means of constant austerities, and are mentally at peace and free from desire.*

From the very first *śloka*, Śaṅkara makes it clear that his intention is to write for those who are qualified. On the other hand, the *Ātmabodha*, being the quintessence of *Advaita Vedānta*, requires precise psychological and conscious prerequisites on the part of the neophyte.

In the course of the *sādhanā* there may be many failures brought about by the absence of those foundations or pre-existing causes which are indispensable in determining specific realisative effects.

It is not enough to be good, in a sentimental sense. It is not enough to have an emotional upsurge of transcendence. It is not enough to have an acute and penetrating mind. What is required is a *maturity* of consciousness as a result of deeply 'feeling' the way of Return.

Thus Śaṅkara is addressing those who have

– a yearning for liberation (*mumukṣutva*), the fruit of *maturity* and not a result of escapes or something else;

– purified – by means of austerity or *tapas* – their own heart of thoughts and actions that are not in conformity with universal *dharma*;

– attained calmness of mind because the duality of attraction/repulsion characteristic of egoic thinking, has been transcended;

– mastered desire/passion (*vītarāgiṇām*) for objects both external and internal, material and ideal, so as to find themselves in a state of 'dispassionateness'.

As may be noted, to realise the first verse requires considerable engagement, but we need to make a start, and those who are ready – despite all the circumstances of life, which may be very difficult – cannot help giving themselves to the work.

2. *Just as fire [is necessary]*[1] *for cooking, so, among all the various forms of discipline (vinā), only knowledge (bodha) is the direct means to liberation (sādhana mokṣa). Without knowledge there cannot be liberation.*

3. *Action (karma) cannot destroy ignorance, for action is not opposed to ignorance. Knowledge alone destroys ignorance, as bright light dispels darkness.*

Why is knowledge alone able to liberate? According to *Advaita Vedānta*, it is because what imprisons is *avidyā*, metaphysical ignorance, so that only *vidyā*, metaphysical knowledge, can overcome the ignorance that is concerned with the nature of Being. Darkness can be dissolved only by the splendour of light, and error can be resolved only by truth.

This, therefore, is a cathartic and transformative knowledge, having the power to dissolve the error of perspective made by the reflection of the embodied *jīva* when associated with the qualities (*guṇas*) of the vehicles/bodies.

There are *yoga* practices which can foster some forms of *samādhi* and lead the individual to hold a dialogue with the gods (if it is permissible to use such an expression);

[1] Square brackets are ours.

such practices can bestow psychic powers, and offer the realisation of the principial One, but they cannot give complete liberation.

It needs to be appreciated that Śaṅkara's *Advaitavāda*, like Gauḍapāda's *Asparśavāda*, aims exclusively at realising the metaphysical One, the *Nirguṇa Brahman* (without *guṇas*), the absolute Constant, beyond time, space, and causality. All human and superhuman states are nothing but *māyā*, 'movement which creates forms'.

Advaita is that pathway which transcends *saṁsāra* and *nirvāṇa*, the manifest and the unmanifest (*avyakta*), the world of men and the world of the gods (*devas*). This is why total liberation is attained through knowledge and not through particular psychological or physiological techniques, actions, rituals, or *mantras*.[1]

These means may lead to the world of *Hiraṇyagarbha* (the universal subtle state) or even to the world of *Īśvara* (the principial One), but, however elevated such states may be in comparison with the human condition, they are subject to the law of causality, and therefore to the law of *saṁsāra*. Thus it is necessary to distinguish complete liberation from a universal expansion of consciousness.

The *Advaitin*, like the *Asparśin*, does not seek the dualities of the world of becoming but, as a true metaphysician, seeks only the absolute Constant. However, the *Kaṭha Upaniṣad*[2] says that the *ātman* must first be realised as *jīva*, because this is favourable to the realisation of the *ātman*/*Brahman* itself. This can be compared to the One-Good of Plato and to the One of Plotinus.

---

[1] See 'Knowledge and Ritual Action' as 'Appendix' in *Aparokṣānubhūti* by Śaṅkara. Translation from the Sanskrit and commentary by Raphael. Aurea Vidyā, New York.

[2] See *Kaṭha Upaniṣad*, II, III, 13.

4. *It is, in fact, on account of ignorance that [the ātmā] seems to be in bondage; but when [ignorance] has been dissolved, the ātmā will shine forth, revealing itself as absolute and free, like the sun when no longer obscured by clouds.*

On the elimination of the projective mental veils that constitute the whole of our familiar, cultural, and social past, the *ātman* will reveal itself in its essential nature, just as the sun becomes free once more when the clouds have dispersed.

5. *Through the constant practice of knowledge/awareness, knowledge, having made perfectly pure the individual self that [was previously] obscured by ignorance, dissolves itself, like kataka powder when it has purified the water.*

What needs to be done in order to realise the eternal and imperishable *ātman/Brahman*? The obscuring mists that hide it must be dispersed.

The *ātman* is ever the same and assuredly cannot change its nature: it is merely veiled by the projecting power of *māyā*. Knowledge is the means of dispersing the mists; once they have been dispersed, the *ātman* reveals itself by itself. Knowledge does not work upon the *ātman* but upon *avidyā/māyā*. When the splendour of the *ātman* shines forth in its infinitude, both ignorance and knowledge disappear, just as the powder from the *kataka* nut disappears once it has purified the water.

We often see the snake instead of the rope, but knowledge (*vidyā*) lets us appreciate that the snake is a projection and, from certain perspectives, is none other than the rope itself. In other words, the rope appears as a snake. Similarly, *Brahman* appears as *jīva*, universe, and so on, but

Brahman is only *Brahman* and transcends these superimpositions, just as the rope transcends the superimposition of the snake.

6. *The world of becoming, characterised by attachment (rāga), aversion (dveṣa), and so on, is in effect similar to dreaming (svapna): it appears real while it lasts, but is seen to be unreal after waking up.*

7. *Just as mother-of-pearl [appears] silver, so the world appears real as long as the non-dual (advayam) Brahman, [which is] beyond everything, remains unknown.*

The world of becoming is nothing but an 'apparent movement', a changing phenomenon, an ephemeral appearing and disappearing, like a dream which seems real when one is enveloped in sleep, but not when one wakes up.

In a dream every event, every action, every coming and going, every exit and entrance, every image that comes into view, is within the consciousness/mind of the sleeper. In the same way, every action/event, every being at the macrocosmic level is within the cosmic mind (*Mahat*) of *Īśvara*.

From this perspective the world (*māyā*) is and is not. We cannot say that it is, because, in fact, everything appears and disappears. We cannot say that it is not, because something is perceived.[1]

The analogies of dream, mirage, magician's projection, mother-of-pearl shell mistaken for silver, ray of light reflected in water, and so on: these are quite enlightening, and they convey the idea of the world of becoming/*saṁsāra*.

---

[1] To go deeper into *māyā* as phenomenon/appearance, see Śaṅkara, *Vivekacūḍāmaṇi*, *śloka* 100 *et seqq.*, op. cit. See also '*Māyā*' in The *Pathway of Non-Duality*, by Raphael. Aurea Vidyā, New York.

It is good, however, to underline the fact that the universal phenomenon is not unreal or non-existent like the horns of a hare or the son of a barren woman (these are still examples given by Śaṅkara). In fact, for the dreamer the dream is true and real; it is only when he awakens that he will be able to say that he has experienced a merely 'apparent movement' devoid of absolute reality. In other words, a dream is a level of truth which can be contradicted by another level of truth and annulled by yet a third.

We could also speak of systems of co-ordinates which may have their reality/validity only in the context of their specific appearance. Thus, for us beings that live on earth, dawn and sunset are reality but have no reality for a hypothetical inhabitant of the sun for whom the problem never even arises.

When one awakens to the ultimate Reality as the permanent substratum and foundation, then every system of co-ordinates (the world of names and forms) is transcended, just as the dream disappears upon awakening. We may draw a parallel with Plato's 'Myth of the Cave'.

8. *It is from the substantial foundation, the supreme Lord and first cause, that the worlds arise, are preserved, and dissolve (laya), like bubbles of foam in water.*

'He is the supreme Lord … the Source of all; all things originate and dissolve in Him.'[1]

9. *It is within the all-pervading and eternal Viṣṇu, existence/consciousness/ātmā, that all the diverse and particular manifestations are represented [by*

[1] Gauḍapāda, *Māṇḍūkyakārikā*, Chapter I, 6. Translation from the Sanskrit and commentary by Raphael. Aurea Vidyā, New York.

those who perceive], like bracelets and other objects manifesting within gold.

All the countless forms in the microcosm and macrocosm come forth and are sustained by virtue of the *materia prima*, represented by the primordial *prakṛti* and therefore by the Principle of *Viṣṇu*, the custodian of forms, and into it they dissolve (the Principle of *Śiva* or the ontological state). In the same way, all ideas, all concepts, all forms/images arise from the mind and disappear into it.

10. Like ākāśa, the all-pervading Lord, when associated with the various limiting superimpositions (upādhis), appears manifold on account of their differentiation, but reveals Himself as absolute unity when the superimpositions are resolved.

Multiplicity is determined by names and forms (*nāma-rūpa*). The different forms of pots differentiate the unity of the clay (in the verse the example of ether/space/*ākāśa* is given); but in the final analysis their multiplicity of name and form is only apparent and not real in an absolute sense, because the pots – if we choose to look closely – are nothing but mere *modifications* of the clay, just as the gold forms (bracelets, pins, rings, and so on) are nothing but different expressions of gold.

From a mistaken view, there are some who see the multiplicity of form as separate from the substantial unity, and there are others who see multiplicity as an appearance of unity, or unity within multiplicity: the 'same within the different', as Plato puts it.

11. It is actually as a result of these multiple limitations that [ideas such as those of] social order, ancestry, stages of life, and so on, are superimposed on the ātman, just as different flavourings, colours, and so on [are perceived] in water.

Social differences, skin colour, and so on, like the disciple's stages of life and all other social conventions, are nothing but superimpositions on the *ātman*. There is nothing absolute about them: they belong to the world of *māyā*, being products of *nāma-rūpa*. The Awakened One transcends the various social orders (*varnās*), just as he transcends the stages of life (*āśramas*).[1] This implies that the Awakened One has resolved himself into Unity-without-a-second, without determination, qualification, or distinction.

We may say that it is one thing to see Essence/Quiddity/Unity as the foundation of things in the world of becoming, and it is another thing to see, in an exclusive way, the objectified forms.

12. *Consisting of the five quintuplicated*[2] *gross elements and determined by [one's own] past actions, the gross physical body (the waking state) is considered to be the seat of the experience of pleasure and pain (sukhaduḥkha).*

13. *Constituted by the five prāṇas (pañcaprāṇa), by the empirical mind and the intellect, as well as by ten organs [of perception and action], and thus originating from the five non-quintuplicated [subtle] elements, the subtle body is the instrument of experience (the dream state).*

---

[1] The traditional social orders are: *brāhmaṇa*, *kṣatriya*, *vaiśya*, and *śūdra*; the stages of life are: *brahmacarya*, *gṛhasthya*, *vānaprasthya*, *saṁnyāsa*.

[2] For the process of 'Quintuplication' see *Pañcīkaraṇa* and *Pañcīkaraṇavārttika* in this volume.

14. Avidyā, having no beginning (anādi) and being indefinable, is considered to be the causal body/ limitation. The ātman should be recognised as other than these three conditioned states.

That is to say, the *ātman* transcends the three states of Being, because it is *nirguṇa*.[1]

We now move to a consideration of what are known as superimpositions (*upādhis*): those limitations which cover the essence of the being or make the One appear multiple.

There are three bodies/vehicles which 'hide' the *ātman*: the gross (*viśva*), the subtle (*taijasa*), and the causal (*prājña*). These bodies are aggregates of energy at different levels of condensation, and they represent the supports, the instruments of relationship, or the windows that open onto the various levels of existence.

The gross or physical body (*viśva*, or the *annamaya* sheath, that is, the sheath made of food) is in relationship with the material physical plane as we know it, and through it one experiences physical and psychical duality. Those who are identified with this body interpret life in terms of materiality, physicality, mass, and the senses. Their consciousness is limited and confined exclusively to the plane of the 'crust' of life.

The subtle body (*taijasa*) has three levels of receptivity: prāṇic, manasic, and buddhic. That is to say, the entire sphere of the subtle body is composed of the sheaths, or bodies of relationship, that are known as *prāṇamaya*, *manomaya*, and *buddhimaya* or *vijñānamaya*. These are made of subtler energy, of hyper-physical substance that is not visible to the physical eye. They are sheaths located on other systems of co-ordinates.

---

[1] See *Kaṭha Upaniṣad*, II, III, 7-8.

The causal body (*prājña*, or *ānandamaya* sheath) represents the seed body, the body of first causes (*kāraṇopādhis*), by which the other sheaths/bodies are determined. It is called *ānandamaya*, the sheath/body of bliss, because within it everything resolves into the principial Unity and because the world of names and forms once more becomes latent there.

The being consists of these five bodies/sheaths, but most individuals who dwell at the physical level are so *polarised* towards the gross body/sheath that they see themselves only as physical entities. Hence the limitation, the prison, and the materialistic view of life.

The *ātman* is other than the three limitations (*viśva*, *taijasa*, *prājña*). To use an analogy from the physical world that is well known to us, the *ātman* is like the nucleus of the atom, while the sheaths are the various electronic elements. The nucleus, being different and equidistant from the electronic shells, gives life to the atom by its mere presence. Transferring this assuredly unsuitable analogy to the metaphysical sphere, we may recognise the *ātman* as a self-resplendent polar sun which, by its mere presence, gives life to the various sheaths/bodies of receptivity. Of the two – *ātman* and the vehicular complex – the former is eternal, permanent, omnipresent, and *akartṛ*; the latter, on the other hand, is transient, limited, and of the nature of phenomena (*nāma* and *rūpa*). From the relationship between *jīvātman* and the vehicles there emerges that compound and being known as the individual, with a precise qualitative configuration of its own.[1]

The 'death' of a sheath/vehicle does not diminish the *ātman*, which, being absolute, lives by its own life. The pain that the individual experiences through the loss, for

[1] See Gauḍapāda *Māṇḍūkyakārikā*, '*Āgama Prakaraṇa*'. Translation from the Sanskrit and commentary by Raphael, op. cit.

example, of the physical body comes from the fact that, as was previously suggested, he is identified with it and is polarised exclusively towards this vehicle by seeing himself solely as a body. The human being has yet to understand himself in his totality: he is immortal in essence, but through a process of identification with contingent and relative phenomena (name and form) he believes that he is mortal. Liberation actually consists in taking the reflection of the *jīva* back to its everlasting source, the *ātman*.

Let us consider anew the outline of the being's constitution, taken from the commentary to the *Māṇḍūkyakārikā* (II, 19).[1]

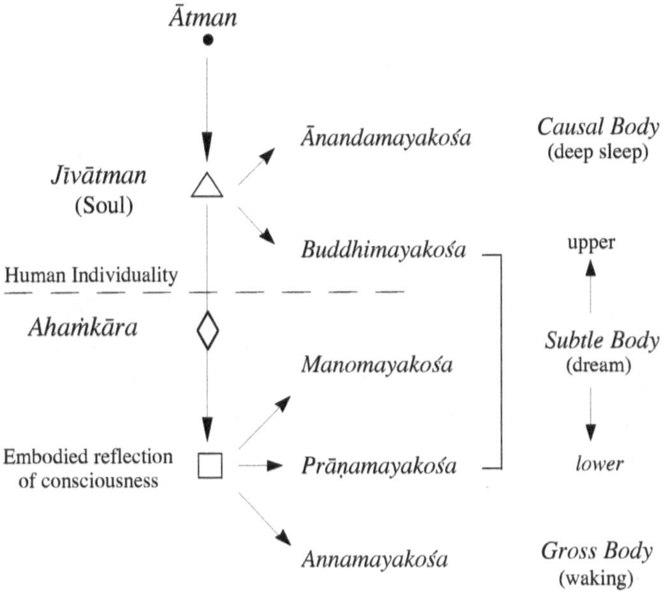

When the *śloka* says '*avidyā*, having no beginning...' it is indicating that the beginning of the first cause cannot be established because it itself is the effect of a preceding

[1] *Ibid.*

unresolved cause. Nor should we deduce that we have a process of infinite regression, because it can happen that a particular *manvantara* can resolve all the causes that have been set in motion. The analogy (understood within limits) is with the human being, who, although he may perpetuate himself in never-ending embodiments, is perfectly capable of resolving and exhausting the causes that he himself has set in motion.

> 15. *In its identification with the five sheaths and so on, the pure ātman seems to be of their very nature, like a crystal placed on a blue cloth, and so on.*

> 16. *Just as the grain of rice, which is initially enveloped in the husk, is totally separated from it, in the same way, through intelligent discrimination, one must separate the pure, innermost ātman from the sheaths with which it is identified.*

When the *jīvātman* is veiled by the *guṇas* (the qualities of *prakṛti*), then *ahaṁkāra* (the sense of the empirical ego), which operates at the level of subject/object, believes itself to be that object (physical body, mental body, and so on); the identification with the transitory object changes the perception of the subject, so that the *jīvātman* becomes 'hidden' or 'veiled'. A 'fall' into the world of shadows is also spoken of.

In other words, through a mistaken view the immortal becomes mortal, and we have all the consequences that this may entail.

It is inevitable that the subject *agendi*, upon recognising the mistake, resolves itself into the *jīva* and hence into the *ātman*, the sole immortal reality. This does not imply that the world of names and forms has disappeared, but the *jīva* simply recognises the world/object for what it is: movement/becoming/*saṁsāra*, which has neither aseity nor *esse*. But none of this is exclusive to the East, because every genuine philosophy and every system of metaphysics, which cannot occupy positions in space, lead to the same conclusions.[1]

> 17. *Although it is everlastingly all-pervading, the ātman does not reveal itself in all places. It manifests itself only in the pure Intellect, just as a reflected image is perceived only in clean mirrors.*

> 18. *The ātman must therefore be known – ever distinct from the body, senses, mind, intellect, and prakṛti itself – as the Witness, like a sovereign, of their modifications.*

The *jīvātman* is reflected principally in the sheaths that are closest to it: *ānandamaya* and *buddhimaya*, the 'windows' that open onto the universal states of consciousness.

With the sheath of *manomaya* the being becomes individualised, separate from the universal context. It becomes 'I am this' (*ahaṁkāra*). This attitude turns truth upside down: the egoic contingent and apparent complex becomes reality, and the *jīvātman* is veiled.

> 19. *Just as the moon seems to move when clouds cross the sky, so, for undiscriminating people, the ātman seems to be active on account of the functions of the sense organs (indriyas).*

When the physical/gross body or the mind is active, we attribute this activity/movement to the *ātman*, and herein

---

[1] See in this book quotations from Parmenides, pages 44-45, and 47; Plotinus, page 64; and the very clear indications from Plato on pages 44, 86, and 140. See also Plotinus, *Enneads*, I, 6, 8.

lies the 'error'. The *ātman* is the metaphysical foundation, the Unborn, which enables the vehicles to express themselves; but whereas the *ātman* can subsist even without the vehicles, they, on the other hand, cannot even have birth or manifestation without That.

It would be like attributing the scenes in a film to the white screen, which is *a priori* their foundation and support, ever identical to itself.

20. *Just as men can work by trusting in the light of the sun, so the body, senses, mind, and intellect, in fulfilling their respective functions, depend on the consciousness inherent in the ātman (ātma/caitanyam).*

21. *Through lack of discrimination the characteristics and activities of the body and senses are superimposed on the ātman, which is absolute Existence and Intelligence, just as the colour blue is attributed to the sky.*

22. *On account of the limitation imposed by the mind, functions such as activities are attributed to the ātman by means of ignorance (ajñānam), just as the movement of water [is attributed] to the moon that is reflected in it.*

Movement, conceived as a characteristic of the relative, becoming, and phenomenon, is attributed, for the reason given previously, to that which transcends movement and rest and every other kind of duality. Movement and inertia are always polar conditions belonging to the world of *māyā*/phenomenon. The individual, immersed in *saṁsāra*, attributes ideals, actions, passions, aspirations, thoughts, good and evil, to the *ātman*, which is without cause and effect, time and space, for it represents the foundation (*ādhāra*) which provides all that exists with the possibility of being.[1]

23. *In truth attachment, desire, pleasure, pain, and so on manifest in the presence of the intellect (buddhi). In deep sleep, when the intellect is inoperative, they do not exist. Thus they belong to the buddhi and not to the ātman.*

All the qualities of the *guṇas* belong to the vehicles constituted by substance/*prakṛti*, the substance from which all the forms of the microcosm and macrocosm are fashioned. *Prakṛti* is equivalent to Plato's χώρα.

24. *Just as luminosity is the nature of the sun, coldness of water, and heat of fire, so the nature of the ātman is pure (nirmala), eternal (nitya) Being in its fullness.*

As a reflection of the supreme *Brahman*, the *ātman* is positive Reality, not a void, not an absence of consciousness, for these qualifications are not applicable to the *ātman*, of which we can simply say *neti neti*, or state that it is, without further addition. The bliss that is being spoken of is clearly not sensory; it can be defined as 'fullness', because it contains all that can be contained.

25. *The notion 'I know' is produced by means of the dyad, which is due to the absence of discrimination, existence, and knowledge of the ātman, together with the modification of the intellect.*

---

[1] See *Bṛhadāraṇyaka Upaniṣad*, II, V, 15.

It was said earlier that the *ātman* is the foundation of all that exists, and therefore of the vehicles/bodies of manifestation and their modifications (*vṛttis*). These modifications are superimposed by *ahaṁkāra* upon the *ātman*, which is *nivṛtti* (beyond all modification), so that even the statement 'I know' can occur only because the light of the *ātman* exists. Movement exists only because it is determined by an unmoving centre. All polarities are interrelated and co-existent.

26. *In truth there is no modification on the part of the ātman, neither does knowledge originate from the intellect. The reflection of the embodied jīva, perceiving everything from a false perspective, falls into error and considers itself to be the one who knows and perceives [and acts].*

27. *[Mistakenly] considering the reflection of the jīva to be the ātman, one is seized by fear, as if confronted by a snake that is perceived in the place of the rope. If, on the other hand, one thinks, 'I am not an individualised being; I am the supreme ātman', one is freed from fear.*

The *ātman* is also mistaken for an individual soul, although the latter is merely a 'self-luminous ray' of the *ātman* itself[1], so that the awareness of 'I am' can cause disharmony and conflict. The *ātman* exists as the supreme Reality; all the other things, which are held to be agents or attributes, are superimpositions (*upādhis*) on the non-dual *ātman*.

---

[1] See *Bṛhadāraṇyaka Upaniṣad*, IV, III, 9; *Muṇḍaka Upaniṣad*, II, I, 1; *Śvetāśvatara Upaniṣad*, IV, 6.

From the interrelationship of the reflection of pure consciousness with the vehicle is born the awareness of 'I am', that is, of individuality with a name and a form.

Being a 'ray of light' of the *ātman*, the *jīva* is immortal, and the reflection of the embodied *jīva* in the threefold individual world is also immortal. *Ahaṁkāra* (the sense of 'I') is mortal, and so are the vehicles of expression pertaining to the *jīva* and the *ahaṁkāra*.

> 28. *It is only the ātmā that illumines the intellect and also the senses, just as a lamp illumines a jug, and so on. The ātman cannot be illuminated by such inert objects.*

> 29. *The ātman, whose nature is Knowledge, has no need of other means of knowledge in order to know itself, just as a lamp has no need of another lamp to illumine itself.*

The foregoing *śloka*s have given the teaching of *advaita*, which is summarised below:

a) The manifestation is a phenomenon/movement. It is *māyā* which produces the forms of becoming. From the perspective of the supreme Reality, it can be likened to a dream, which is not nothing, not nothingness; it may be defined as a contingent phenomenon, which appears on the horizon of awareness and disappears without leaving a trace; it is a mere 'appearance' (*ābhāsa*). This appearance is real for as long as the dreamer is identified with the dream, but reveals itself as unreal after the dreamer has awoken.

b) The *ātman* is the pure, transcendent Witness, which, with a ray of his consciousness, puts himself, by means of the *jīva*, into immanence.

c) The *jīvātman* is inside its sheaths/bodies of manifestation. When it operates with the sheaths of *manas*, *kāma*, and *deha* (the coarse physical body), then, by means of *ahaṁkāra*, it finds itself in the individualised state. When it operates with the sheaths of *buddhi* and *ānanda*, then it finds itself in the universal state, which is its natural abode.

d) What is it that causes the *jīvātman* to be covered over by the vehicles and their qualities/*guṇas*? It is *avidyā*, that ignorance which relates to the real nature of things. *Ahaṁkāra*, the empirical ego, the subject that operates by means of the five senses, sees the object and qualifies it for what it is: a mere object of form, with its qualitative characteristics. The error lies not in this, but in making this way of perceiving things something absolute and not going any further.

Identification with the qualities (*guṇas*) of the sheaths throws a covering over the true nature. This type of identification with that which is not represents *avidyā*. The reverse process is to *recall* what one really is (Platonic reminiscence), restoring one's wings and flying back to our true homeland.[1]

Thus the being may fall into the *error* of believing itself to be what it is not, but not in absolute terms, because it cannot change its immortal nature.

The Eleatics equate *dóxa* (δόξα) with *error*, but it is the whole of Greek philosophy that considers 'opinion' to be the source of error.

---

[1] Plotinus, *Enneads*, I, 6, 8.

'This is why I keep you far from this way of enquiry [that is, that *nothingness* can exist]
and also from the way where mortals who know nothing go wandering,
two-headed men; in fact,
indecisiveness in their hearts directs their senseless mind.'[1]

Contradiction (two-headed men) is typical of opinion, which is always dual and hence untrue.

According to Plato himself, δόξα is halfway between Being and nothingness, but is never positive. It is only by attaining science/knowledge that one can see opinion for what it is.[2]

The pre-eminence given to *epistéme*, to which alone truth is connected, is the thread that links Pythagoras, Parmenides, Plato, Plotinus, and others, and we may include Gauḍapāda and Śaṅkara, as is shown by the *Māṇḍūkyakārikā* and this short treatise.

If it is through an act of ignorance (*avidyā*) or non-knowledge that we have 'fallen' into the world of generation, then it is only through an act of knowledge (*gnosi*) that we can be freed from error.

Thus, through a process of negation (*neti neti*) which extends to all individual and universal conditionings (identification with *sattva*), one comes to realise the identity of the *jīva* with the *ātman* and of the *ātman* with the supreme attributeless (*nirguṇa*) *Brahman*.

30. Through a [conscious] process of negation extending to all conditionings by means of the axiom 'not this, not this' (neti neti), one must come – with the aid

---

1 Parmenides, *On the Order of Nature*, fragment 6, 3-6. Edited by Raphael. Aurea Vidyā, New York.

2 Plato, *Meno*, 96-99; *Politéia*, V, 477-480.

of the great statements[1] – *to the realisation of the identity of the soul (jīva) with the supreme ātman.*

Through intuitive discernment one recognises that every event/datum is relative and dependent, and we may therefore say that the limiting sheaths are not the *ātman* and that the soul itself (*jīvātman*) is none other than a ray of the light of the *ātman*.

At this point, if the previous *śloka*s have been assimilated, one may follow the *ācārya* Śaṅkara, who now begins a series of *śloka*s which directly stimulate the consciousness of the reader to recognise himself as the supreme Reality, transcending all phenomenal contingency.

'Since I am other than the body ... Since I am other than the mind ... I am without attributes ... ever existent ... I am that supreme *Brahman* which is eternal ... single ... non-dual' (*śloka*s 32-6).

31. Being brought forth by ignorance, all that is perceived (dṛśyam), such as the body and other material objects, is as transient as a bubble of foam. Therefore one must realise consciously 'I am Brahman' (ahaṁ brahma), pure and distinct from all this.

32. 'Since I am other than the body, for me there are no such things as birth, old age, decrepitude, death, and so on; nor is there any contact with the objects of the senses, such as sound and the others, since I do not possess sensory organs.'

33. 'Since I am other than the mind, there are in me no such things as suffering, attachment, aversion,

---

[1] For the 'great sentences' or *mahāvākyas*, see *Vākyavṛtti* and *Laghuvākyavṛtti* in this volume.

fear, and so on. [The ātman] does not have vital breath, is devoid of mind and therefore pure, and so on', as the Scriptures declare.

We need to avoid ascribing absoluteness to the relative. Being is not the physical body, not the conflictual mental body, and not anything else. It is pure, infinite Being, without any imprisoning attributes. We need to recognise, as was indicated earlier, that which is effect, that which is cause, and that which transcends the polarity of cause and effect.

Fear, anxiety, suffering, hope, desire, sensory happiness, and so on are attributes of the vehicular egoic compound, and not of the eternally equanimous non-dual *ātman.*

34. 'I am without attributes, non-acting (niṣkriya), eternal, undifferentiated, undefiled, immutable, and formless, ever free and without stains [such as avidyā, kleśa, and so on].'

35. 'Ever existing, I pervade all things from within and without, like space/ether. I am ever the same in all things and at all times, perfect, absolute, spotless, changeless.'

36. 'In truth I am that supreme Brahman that is eternal, pure, free, single, indivisible fullness, non-dual, infinite existence and knowledge.'

That Being is unborn, incorruptible;
indeed, it is whole in its entirety, motionless,
and endless. It never was and will never be,
because it is now all together one and continuous.
'What kind of birth for it will you actually be seeking?
How and in what way would it have grown?'[1]

[1] Parmenides, *On the Order of Nature*, fragment 8, 3-7, op. cit.

'This [*ātman*] is the eternal splendour of the knower of *Brahman*: it is not enlarged or diminished by any action.'[1]

'On a sudden he will glimpse a Beauty of astounding nature ... one that, first and foremost, is eternal, does not become or perish, increase or diminish.'[2]

In the same way, we may echo the words of Parmenides:

For It [Being], all of those things that the mortals decided, convinced
that they were true [that is absolute], will be names.[3]

37. Thus meditation on 'I myself am the Brahman', when practised without interruption, destroys the projecting movements of the mind which are generated by avidyā, just as medicine destroys diseases.

The *ātman* is one, bliss indivisible, eternal, ever identical to itself, whereas its *reflections* are interactive phenomena. Within the limits of conception, we may give this expressive sequence of the *ātman* (see the diagram below). *Ānandamaya* and *vijñānamaya* are the *jīvātman*'s instruments of relationship and contact.

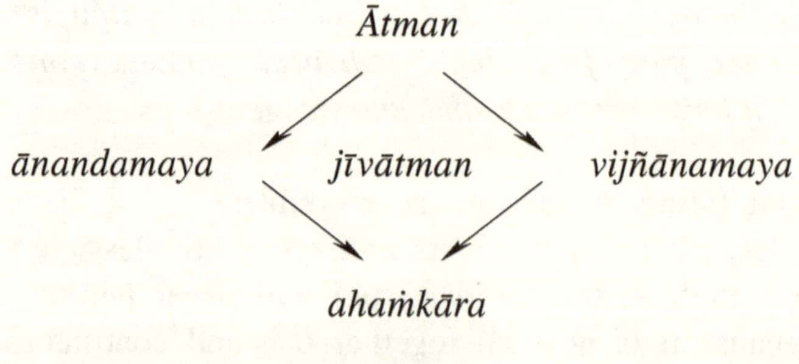

[1] *Bṛhadāraṇyaka Upaniṣad*, IV, IV, 23.

[2] Plato, *Symposium*, 210e, 211a.

[3] Parmenides, *On the Order of Nature*, fragment 8, 38-39, op. cit.

The relationship of the *jīvātman* with the vehicles occurs through a process of polarisation, while the return to the source occurs through a process of depolarisation.

Through its intrinsic nature of being, the *jīvātman* can express itself in three directions:

1. Towards the external objective object, through *ahaṁkāra*: this is the condition of most individualised beings.
2. Towards the subject of action, and this involves remaining detached from the world of sensible objects in general. This is the optimal state on the plane of *māyā*; in other words, the subject is conscious of his own noumenality, remaining free from the vicissitudes of the effects.
3. Finally, being liberated from the obscuring veils of the *guṇas*, he can re-orientate himself towards his own source, which is the *ātman*, resolving himself into the all-pervasive Silence.

In the same way, for further clarification of this matter of polarisation, the mind can: think (logical movement) and believe itself to be thoughts (I think, therefore I am); think and remain free from its projections of thought; and, finally, it can completely refrain from thinking by remaining in its transcendent state.[1]

38. Seated in a solitary place, free from attachment (virāga) and with the senses under control, [the disciple] should meditate on the ātman, the limitless One, without [allowing space for] any other thought.

39. When through meditation everything visible (dṛśyam) has been dissolved into the ātman, the sage [must

---

[1] See Raphael's commentary to *sūtra* VI, Gauḍapāda's *Māṇḍūkyakārikā*, op. cit.

regain] the true state of the one ātman, eternally unblemished like ākāśa.

40. *Having abandoned everything – form, social class, and so on – the knower of supreme Reality is [irreversibly] absorbed into his own essence (svarūpa), the boundless fullness of intelligence and bliss.*

41. *In the supreme ātman no distinction can be found between knower, knowing, and object known. Its nature (rūpa) is wisdom/fullness. It shines by itself.*

42. *Just as fuel is completely consumed by the flame issuing from the rubbing of the firestick, so ignorance is completely destroyed by constant meditation on the ātmā (ātmā dhyāna).*

Seated in a propitious place, with consciousness unencumbered by material and psychic attachments, the ascetic should meditate solely on the *ātman*, without allowing himself to be conditioned by conceptual movement.

By means of discernment (*viveka*) one should recognise phenomenon/*māyā*; then by an act of dis-identification (*vairāgya*) one should depolarise the mind itself. In this way, everything objective, phenomenal, conventional, and so on, depreciates until it is extinguished, just as fire burns up fuel.

In the supreme *ātman* every distinction vanishes, including that of knower, knowing, and object of knowing.

43. *[When] the darkness that was there is dispersed by the light of the sun, then the ātmā, like the sun, spontaneously appears.*

44. *Although in truth ever present, the ātmā nevertheless seems absent on account of ignorance (or the covering composed of the guṇas); when this is destroyed, the ātmā reveals itself in all its glory, like an ornament around one's neck.*

When, through knowledge, all the various interrelationships are burnt up or depolarised, then the *ātman* reveals itself by itself, just like the sun once the clouds vanish or one discovers that the ornament one thought was lost is around one's neck.

Knowledge serves to encompass the process of polarisation and depolarisation, thus removing that veil (*māyā*) which obscured the reality of the *ātman*, although the *ātman* has never been impoverished or diminished by the duality of *saṁsāra*. In the same way, although the sun is the giver of life and movement, it is never involved in the vicissitudes of the activities of its planets.

> 'You have reached the All and you no longer linger in one of its parts or say of yourself, "How great I am!", but you set this greatness aside in order to become "all". And yet, you were "all" before, too, but since you added something to yourself apart from the all, you – precisely on account of this addition – have become small, because the addition came not from the All – to which nothing can be added! – but from the not-all … You therefore augment yourself when you throw away the other things, and the All becomes present to you when you have eliminated them; but to one who stays with the other things It does not manifest itself. It has not come to be close to you, but you are the one who goes away when It is not present to you. And if you have gone away, you have not gone away from It – for It is ever present – and you have not even gone

elsewhere but, while staying present, you have faced in another direction."[1]

45. *Just as a tree can be taken for a man (puruṣa), so, through the same kind of error, the Brahman is conceived of as an individual soul; but this [illusion] disappears when the real nature of the jīva [as ātman] is recognised.*

46. *The knowledge arising from the direct experience (anubhava) of the nature (svarūpa) of Reality destroys at once the ignorance characterised by the notions of 'I' (aham) and 'mine' (mama), which is what happens to the erroneous cognition of orientation.*

47. *The yogi who has attained perfect knowledge sees with the eye of knowledge (jñānacakṣus) the entire universe contained within himself, and he considers everything as the single ātman.*

48. *This entire universe is really the ātman and does not exist outside the ātman. Just as every type of pot is nothing but clay, so [the knower] views everything [in its essence] as himself.*

The *Upaniṣads* tell us that we are drops of the same ocean, which means that we are ocean. The entire universe/ocean is contained in the drop, and the drop is contained in the universe/ocean. Behind the world of names and forms there is a single Essence which permeates the totality of life. Behind the multiplicity of forms (which are not absolute) there exists the Unity (which is). To see with the eye of Wisdom (*jñāna*) is to see Unity in multiplicity.

---

[1] Plotinus, *Enneads*, VI, 5, 12.

49. *The knower who has abandoned all previous limiting conditionings and their attributes, thus revealing the true nature of absolute Being/wisdom/fullness, becomes liberated in this life [jīvanmukta], like a chrysalis changing into a butterfly.*

This *śloka* expounds the ultimate end of *advaita* realisation. One who is liberated (*jīvanmukta*) is one who has integrated and transcended all previous limiting conditionings, that is, *avidyā* in its fullest expression.

Śaṅkara the Teacher has ended this exposition of the teaching of *Vedānta*, the 'vision' to which reference needs to be made. Now, in the verses that follow, he indicates the fruits that are obtained once the teaching has been assimilated and integrated.

50. *Having crossed the ocean of confusion (moha) and defeated the demons of pleasure (rāga) and rejection/suffering (dveṣa), and so on, the yogi, in perfect unity with peace, shines with the fullness of the ātman.*

51. *Surrendering with indifference the attachment to all transitory external pleasures, and being totally satisfied with the bliss that flows from the ātman, he shines inwardly, like a lamp placed inside a jug.*

52. *Although he lives immersed in limiting conditionings, the muni, like the ether, is not touched by their attributes; he who really knows everything lives [apparently] like a person deprived of intellect, and he moves with perfect detachment, like the wind.*

53. *On the dissolution of the conditioning sheaths (upādhis), the muni immerses himself in the all-per-*

vading Reality, being free of differentiation (nirviśeṣa), like water into water, space into space, light into light.

Thus, although the ascetic (*muni*) may live amid the limitations of the sheaths (*upādhis*), the being has regained its absoluteness by recognising itself as the undefiled *Brahman*, just as the ray of light recognises itself as light, and a clear drop of water as water.

54. *Realise the Brahman as that attainment beyond which there is nothing else to attain, beyond whose Fullness there is no further happiness, and beyond whose knowledge there is no higher knowledge.*

In this *śloka* and those that follow, Śaṅkara exhorts us directly to realise the *Brahman* as That, having 'seen' which there is nothing else to see and nothing else to know.

> 'My dear, it is in truth the *ātman* which should be realised; it is the *ātman* which should be heard of; it is the *ātman* on which one should reflect; it is the *ātman* on which one should meditate deeply. In truth, my dear Maitreī, when the *ātman* is known through hearing, reflection, and deep meditation, all this becomes known.'[1]

55. *Realise the Brahman as That which, once seen, there is nothing else to see; once realised, there is no further realisation; once known, there is nothing else to know.*

---

[1] *Bṛhadāraṇyaka Upaniṣad,* II, IV, 5.

56. *Realise the Brahman – which is bliss in the deep and in the intermediate space – as That which is Existence/Intelligence/Fullness, pure Non-duality, infinite, eternal, and One.*

57. *Realise that Brahman which is indicated by Vedānta as the unchanging essence revealing itself through the negation [of the superimpositions] as the non-dual Unity of indivisible bliss.*

The individual has just one *dharma*: to recompose himself, re-discover himself, find himself afresh. All his wanderings and *doings* are compensations; since he *is not*, he believes that by doing he *is*. But even if the incentive is right, the direction is mistaken. The being can find his true fulfilment only in Being.

One who has lost a treasure, the single source of life, will be able to have true peace only when he regains that treasure. Then alone will every enquiry, every movement, every anxiety, and every ambition come to an end. One who has realised *ātman* has nothing further to realise. One who has recognised himself as *ātman* has nothing further to know. One who is at peace does not move, does not act, and does not desire.

58. *Being dependent on a particle of the fullness of That, whose nature (rūpa) is absolute, indivisible fullness, all beings, from Brahmā downwards [to the human race and beyond], enjoy bliss to a greater or lesser degree [according to their relative proximity to the supreme Reality].*

59. *Every being [as Essence] is intimately united with That, and every manifestation is connected to That.*

Thus the Brahman pervades the entire totality, just as butter pervades milk.

Every Being, from *Brahmā* (as the causal Principle) to the individual, reveals bliss proportionate to the measure of its identity with the *Brahman.* All the beings which experience the numberless modalities of life perceive *ānanda* (bliss/fullness) in proportion to their closeness to the supreme Reality, the reality which is the substratum of every possible movement/*māyā.*

60. *Realise the Brahman, which is neither subtle nor gross, neither limited nor extensive, unborn and indestructible, without form or attributes, without qualifications or names.*

61. *Realise that Brahman whose splendour illumines the sun and the other stars, though it itself is not illumined by their light, [that Brahman] thanks to which this whole [universe] is manifested.*

62. *Comprehending within itself everything inner and outer, the Brahman bestows splendour on the entire phenomenal universe, thereby making itself manifest, just as fire, with its heat, makes a metal ball incandescent.*

The *ātman/Brahman* cannot be conceived by the mental categories, because they are always characterised by subject/object, whereas the *ātman* is beyond all possible polarity and duality.

The *ātman* is not the eye, but that which allows the eye to see. The *ātman* is not the mind, but that which allows the mind to exist and think.

The *ātman* is not happiness or even bliss, but that which allows happiness/bliss to manifest and be. The *ātman* is not the sun, but that which allows the sun to rise and set.[1]

> 'Realise that *Brahman* … thanks to which this whole [universe] is manifested' (*śloka* 61).

> 63. *The Brahman, in truth, is other than the [sensible/intelligible] universe, [although] nothing else exists outside the Brahman. Where something other than the Brahman seems to manifest, this is a fallacy, just like the appearance of a mirage in the desert.*

> 64. *All that can be seen or heard is none other than the Brahman. But it is [only] through the knowledge of the supreme Reality that [one comprehends and realises that] That is the non-dual Brahman, Existence/Consciousness/Bliss.*

Although the *Brahman* is not the eye, the mind, or the whole universe of names and forms – and this is how all pantheistic conceptions are excluded – nevertheless, this entire phenomenon/mirage cannot appear without *That*, because *That* constitutes the foundation which enables everything to be and exist (*śloka* 61).

> 65. *It is [only] through the eye of knowledge (jñānacakṣur) that one can contemplate the ātman, all-pervading existence, and knowledge; but if the inner view is darkened by ignorance, this eye will never be able to know, just as a blind man is unable to see the blazing sun.*

---

[1] See *Bṛhadāraṇyaka Upaniṣad*, III, VII, 3-23. See also *Muṇḍaka Upaniṣad*, I, I, 3.

66. The soul in manifestation (the jīva), consumed by the fire of knowledge (jñānāgni) kindled by hearing (śravana) [reflection and meditation], and being freed [muktaḥ] from all impurities, shines by itself like bright gold.

67. In truth, the ātman, sun of wisdom centred in the space of the heart (hṛdākāśa) is what dispels the darkness. Being the all-pervading substratum of everything, it shines without limits and makes everything shine.

Only knowledge (*jñāna*) liberates, because it is metaphysical ignorance (*avidyā* or *ajñāna*) that covers or darkens the consciousness. There is no other means of liberation except that which can break the chains of the bondage of *saṁsāra*. Nothing but the blazing sun can disperse the constricting darkness.

68. One who renounces all activities and, being free from the limitations of space, place, time, and so on, pays devout homage to the tabernacle of the all-pervading and undefiled [ātman], which is free from cold [and heat and all the other dualities] and is eternal fullness, he becomes omniscient, all-pervading, and immortal.

He who transcends time, space, and causality (movement/the apparent) re-discovers the hidden treasure and (it is merely an image) enters the beatific sanctuary of the non-dual *ātman*.

Here ends
'The knowledge of the Ātman'

HYMN OF PRAISE IN TEN VERSES

daśaślokīstuti

This work is a Hymn of praise addressed to the ultimate Reality, the *Brahman*, which the *Upaniṣads* denote with the term 'That'.

We, in essence, are *That*, but we live as if drowsing within ourselves, projecting individualised ideals and identifying ourselves with them. We must therefore rouse ourselves from the dreams of the mind and penetrate the darkness of the sleep of *māyā* in order to awaken to our authentic reality and consciously recognise ourselves as *Brahman*. Everything else is a question of being lived by a world of appearances.

> 'One must continually take the mind back to the heart, until one has reached [its] solution: this is knowledge, this is liberation. Everything else is but academic prolixity.'[1]

One who knows how to penetrate the essence of these verses, by realising it in his own consciousness, in his own heart, gathering the mind together and becoming absorbed in the unlimited nature of pure consciousness, resolves himself into the *Brahman*.

---

[1] *Maitry Upaniṣad*, VI, 34, 8.

1. *That Reality which reveals itself when one has become totally indifferent to all conditions – having recognised their emptiness – apart from that of the Lord himself, and when one has renounced everything, with a mind purified by offerings, sacrifice (yajña, ritual sacrifice), discipline, and so on: That same [Reality] am I, the supreme eternal Brahman.*

2. *That Reality which the sage, having enquired intensely into his own essence, attains – after continually meditating on it – through the grace bestowed on him by a benevolent guru established in Brahman and totally at peace: That same [Reality] am I, the supreme eternal Brahman.*

Only a *guru* who is realised and firmly established in the non-dual Reality can impart knowledge of *Brahman*. The qualified disciple, for his part, opening himself to this spiritual influence, 'with a mind purified by offerings, sacrifice, discipline, and so on' (verse 1), can, by turning his awareness inwards, reveal Reality/*Brahman*.

3. *That whose nature is bliss and whose essence is pure splendour, That which transcends the phenomenal world and is devoid of all limitation, the Fourth, which is realised only through the awareness of one's own identity with Brahman: That same am I, the supreme eternal Brahman.*

4. *That which through ignorance (ajñāna) manifests itself as the universal world that disappears the*

moment one realises the knowledge of the ātman, That which transcends speech and thought and which is ever pure and absolutely free, That same am I, the supreme eternal Brahman.

5. *That which, through the total negation accomplished by statements such as 'It is not this, it is not this', reveals itself as perfect Fullness to those who are absorbed in profound contemplation, that One which is beyond the three states, the Fourth, That same am I, the supreme eternal Brahman.*

The total negation/transcendence (*neti neti*) of the mental states, conditions, and modifications leads to the establishment of oneself in pure a-dimensionality, the metaphysical Absolute.

Beyond the three relative states of consciousness – waking, dream and deep sleep – there is the Fourth (*Turīya*), absolute Reality, which is their unchanging and ever-present foundation, and in relation to which they are merely accidental and superimposed modifications.

Turīya corresponds to the metaphysical One of Plotinus:

'If you seek this Principle, seek nothing outside It, but seek the things that come after It; yet let It be!'

'It occupies the highest place or, rather, does not occupy it but is it. It is the Highest and has all things at its service, but not by accident: it is they that yield to It or, rather, stand around It, for It does not look towards them, but it is they that look at It.'[1]

6. *That from the drops of whose bliss everything reaches its own innermost joy, That through whose light everything shines, That in whose conscious-*

[1] Plotinus, *Enneads*, VI, 8, 18; VI, 8, 16.

ness all takes form: That same am I, the supreme eternal Brahman.

7. *Infinite, omnipresent, the principle of all things, unchanging, beneficent, That which is without supports and is realisable through the syllable Om, That which is pure, self-luminous consciousness, having no form and transcending death: That same am I, the supreme eternal Brahman.*

8. *When the being consciously merges itself into That One's ocean of bliss, then the whole universe, which is the expression of ignorance, by a great marvel ceases to manifest: That One am I, the supreme eternal Brahman.*

9. *Moved by deep devotion, the being that zealously recites this hymn of praise, which is a true celebration of its own authentic nature, or hears it again and again with full concentration, will become the All-pervading, even here, for this is what the Veda declares.*

10. *Anyone who has taken hold of the raft of discriminating knowledge will cross the ocean of [transmigratory] existence, which is founded on ignorance (ajñānamaya). Being established in knowledge and having thus extinguished all desire, he will attain the supreme state of Viṣṇu: he himself is the Blessed One.*

Desire – the first of all desires is to exist and express oneself as 'I' – constitutes the cause of transmigration and is in turn the effect of that hidden cause which is ignorance (*avidyā*)[1]. Once knowledge has extinguished desire, no further obstacle will be able to hinder the realisation of the fullness of *Brahman*, even in this very life.

One who is realised is steadfastly established in the knowledge which is self-supporting and which he naturally and spontaneously radiates, just as a star radiates its own light and a flower diffuses its own fragrance.

He is beyond giving and receiving, *dharma* and *adharma*, the stages of life, the social orders, religious creeds and philosophical opinions, and so he has transcended not only *avidyā* but even *vidyā* itself. In other words, as *ātman*, he is beyond all duality.

> 'I am not the body. How can birth and death belong to me? I am not *prāṇa*. How can hunger and thirst belong to me? I am not perceptive consciousness. How can sorrow (*śoka*) and mental turmoil (*moha*) belong to me? I am not the agent of action. How can freedom and bondage belong to me?'[2]

---

[1] See Chapter II, 3-9, *The Regal Way to Realisation* (*Yogadarśana*) by Patañjali, edited by Raphael. Aurea Vidyā, New York.

[2] *Sarvasāra Upaniṣad* in *Five Upaniṣads*, edited by Raphael. Aurea Vidyā, New York.

THE OCEAN OF BLISS OF ONE LIBERATED IN LIFE

jīvanmuktānandalaharī

This work describes the state of the *jīvanmukta*, one who – through the blessing of the teaching and initiation imparted directly by the Teacher (*guru*) and his supporting grace (*prasāda*) – has reached the point of revealing within himself the full consciousness of the non-dual Reality.

For one who has 'recalled' his essence, the presence or absence of form, and particularly of bodily form, is consequently not a determining factor. If awakening (*bodhi*) occurs at the moment of physical death, when the spirit, now instructed and ready, frees itself from body and mind, this is called 'liberation without form' or 'liberation when the body is absent' (*videhamukti*). But if it occurs when the body is still alive, it is called 'liberation with form' or 'liberation in life' (*jīvanmukti*). However, considering that Reality transcends form, one must acknowledge that liberation is unique and that this distinction is purely of the mind, valid for those who are not liberated. For one who is liberated (*mukta*), the one who knows, there is only the constant and infinite[1] awareness of Reality.

[1] 'We need to look carefully at these two terms: "infinite" and "indefinite". "Infinite", in its purest meaning, is "beyond all limit, series, beginning, and end; beyond all conditioning, number, point, line, and constraint". The "indefinite" is a *series* of data which, although they may extend indefinitely, are nevertheless finite and under the law of necessity. Thus a series of numbers, which can be combined indefinitely with each other, is still *finite*.' See *Tat Tvam Asi*, page 63, Aurea Vidyā, New York.

Though living in a body/form, he is bodiless and formless. Though able to express himself through thought and word, he is beyond both. Though present at the fulfilment of karmic fruits, he forges no further bond with beings, objects, states, or conditions.

Though acting, he acts not, for he has no 'ego' and is therefore not conditioned by any finality/causality. Though apparently occupying a given space and time, he dwells beyond space and time, having embraced them in a synthesis. Though immersed in *māyā*, he is not conditioned by it and contemplates its wondrous sport (*līlā*) with detachment, or rests within himself in his own infinite awareness that is devoid of modification (*nirvikalpacaitanya*).

One who is liberated in life, having recognised himself as *ātman*/*Brahman*, 'is no longer subject to confusion', no longer falls into ignorance, turmoil, or error (*tamas*), but is constantly immersed in an ocean of bliss (*ānandalaharī*).

1. Observing the inhabitants of the city as if in a representation, a host of men and women – the men well dressed, the women adorned with jewels of gold – and noting that in this view he clearly perceives himself, too, as he partakes of their company, the sage (muni), whose ignorance has been dissolved by the grace of the Teacher (guru), is no longer subject to confusion (vyāmohaṁ).

To realise this ineffable state there is no need to abandon the aspect of form/body, but, rather, to remove the identification with the psychosomatic vehicle and its objects. Thus the *sādhaka*, having reached maturity, must have the firm resolution to leave the *jīvātman* free to express its authentic nature, which is to *be*.

The one who is liberated in life (*jīvanmukta*) abides constantly in *Brahman*, and wherever his eyes fall he sees nothing but *Brahman*. He faces the world like a spectator who is watching a show. He is therefore never disturbed or distracted by what he happens to encounter or perceive in different places and circumstances, viewing it all with equanimity, that is, keeping himself at the same remove from all things.

For this state to be reached, two factors have to operate: the first is that innermost prompting which is determined by a deep maturing of consciousness and a specific qualification, which manifests in the devotion of the disciple (*śiṣya*), in perfect spiritual attunement, and through the vision expressed by the Teacher; the second is the influence (*prasāda*) of the Teacher that flows into true and rightful initiation (*dīkṣā*), which is not only potential but also actual if the disciple is prepared and ready.

2. *Seeing the trees in the forest that bow their lovely heads under the weight of foliage and fruit, cast a deep shade, and provide shelter on their branches for a choir of melodious birds, the sage, whose ignorance has been dissolved by the grace of the Teacher, sits at their feet by day [for prayer or meditation] and at night lies on the ground for a bed, no longer subject to confusion.*

3. *Whether he lives in a temple or a rich man's sumptuous palace, whether he dwells at times on the mountain-top or on the river bank or, again, in the simple abodes of the best of the ascetics who are dedicated to silence and have extinguished their own minds, the sage, whose ignorance has been dissolved by the grace of the Teacher, is no longer subject to confusion.*

4. *Whether he takes occasional delight in carefree children who clap their hands in play, whether he is in the presence of young and attractive women, or whether he grieves with old people whose hearts are troubled by worries, the sage, whose ignorance has been dissolved by the grace of the Teacher, is no longer subject to confusion.*

The *jīvanmukta* is never conditioned by relationships with human beings or others. For him, every being is an aspect of Being, and he recognises himself in each.

He is free in thought, word, and deed; each of his actions no longer has an individualistic character but is spontaneous, non-repetitive, and therefore absolutely pure and impersonal.

In his limitless awareness he reveals the innocence of divine childhood (*bālya*), all-embracing silence (*mauna*), and the expression of the highest wisdom (*pāṇḍitya*).

5. *Whether he occasionally finds himself engaged in deep discussions with learned people athirst for knowledge, whether he is discussing at other times with eminent bards conversant with the human heart and expert in lyrical composition, or whether he is debating with distinguished sophists intent on abstruse ratiocinations and the subtlest of deductions, the sage, whose ignorance has been dissolved by the grace of the Teacher, is no longer subject to confusion.*

Not being conditioned by the flow of thought, the sage is able to create a mind that is adapted to all circumstances without being imprisoned by it. He sees the mind as a mere *instrument*. Having transcended the individual condition, he expresses himself through a universal mind that is able to embrace the totality and to grasp the real essence of every subject.

6. *Whether he is immersed in practices of continual deep meditation or occupied with acts of devotion with regard to the deities, undertaken in total, humble submission and with a heart overflowing with joy as he brings bunches of flowers that are fully open and fragrant or simple offerings of petals and leaves, the sage, whose ignorance has been dissolved by the grace of the Teacher, is no longer subject to confusion.*

The sage has comprehended. He knows that every form of expression, every kind of vibration, is valid within its own context, where it occurs with perfect harmony and balance.

7. *Whether there are times when, his eyes full of joyous tears, he invokes the name of Śiva's consort (Śakti) or the name of Śambhu (Śiva), and other times when he calls upon Viṣṇu or Gaṇapati or the dazzling Sun, the sage, whose ignorance has been dissolved by the grace of the Teacher, is no longer subject to confusion.*

8. *When purifying himself in the waters of the Ganges, when immersing himself in the waters gushing from a spring or the waters of a pool, which are sometimes hot and sometimes cold, or when sprinkling himself with white ashes, such as the essence of camphor, the sage, whose ignorance has been dissolved by the grace of the Teacher, is no longer subject to confusion.*

The different waters are equal in their effects. Purifying oneself in either kind, or sprinkling ash on the body represents, apart from the simple act of ritual, a symbolic and conscious value that is lived in its entirety: the purification of the body denotes that of spirit.

9. *Whether he is in the waking state, experiencing sensible objects, whether he is having an experience of objects that are present only in the dream state, or whether he is experiencing the uninterrupted bliss of the state of deep sleep, the sage, whose ignorance has been dissolved by the grace of the Teacher, is no longer subject to confusion.*

The *jīvanmukta* has transcended the three relative states of waking, dream, and deep sleep, which correspond to precise conditions of consciousness, and he has taken himself into the Fourth (*Turīya*), which is the foundation of all that exists.

10. Sometimes space is his garment (āśavāsas), sometimes he is clothed in a magnificent coat, and sometimes his loins are girt with a simple lion-skin, [but always] his awareness is alert and awake, he is in a state of complete absoluteness and radiant with the bliss pouring from the heart of one Perfected: the sage, whose ignorance has been dissolved by the grace of the Teacher, is no longer subject to confusion.

Whatever his clothing – physical, mental, and so on – the sage ever dwells in his own nature, which is without supports (*niḥsaṅga*). Whatever the outer condition, Fullness expands naturally.

11. Sometimes established in sattva, sometimes impelled by rajas, at other times under the influence of tamas, and, lastly quite independent of these three [guṇas], in the guise of a transmigrating being or of one following the path indicated by the Scriptures, the sage, whose ignorance has been dissolved by the grace of the Teacher, is no longer subject to confusion.

The *guṇas* are the attributes of substance/*prakṛti* by means of which the manifestation unfolds. *Sattva* expresses qualities of luminosity/balance/purity. *Rajas* pertains to dynamism/activity. *Tamas* governs static, inertial, and passive conditions. They exit solely in reciprocal relationships and mixtures, and they correspond to the three planes of existence (causal, subtle, gross); by analogy they are therefore also in relationships with the different states of consciousness.

We would say that one who is liberated may occasionally express himself through the *guṇas*, but their properties do not concern him because his consciousness always transcends qualifications and is totally independent.

> 12. *Whether he is immersed in total silence, actively engaged in lengthy discussions, suddenly deprived of speech, and absorbed in the bliss of the ātman, or subsequently intent on observing with detachment the manifold activities of the world, the sage, whose ignorance has been dissolved by the grace of the Teacher, is no longer subject to confusion.*

Though in the world, the sage does not belong to the world, with the result that he is never engaged in intentional activities or ones motivated by desire. His conduct is always appropriate to the circumstances or is totally isolated from them.

> 13. *Whether he takes rice from his mouth and places it as an offering in the open, lotus-like mouths of the deities, or takes such offerings from their mouths and puts them into his own, or whether he celebrates Non-duality, in which all distinction between his own being and that of others disappears, the sage, whose ignorance has been dissolved by the grace of the Teacher, is no longer subject to confusion.*

> 14. *Whether he finds himself in the company of the Śaivas or the Śāktas, whether he occasionally dwells*

with the devotees of Viṣṇu or with those of the Sun, or at times with the worshippers of Gaṇapati, all distinction having been resolved by the awareness of Non-duality, the sage, whose ignorance has been resolved by the grace of the Teacher, is no longer subject to confusion.

Having embraced the specific nature and function of the different deities, he participates in every form of worship, and so he is equally at home with the devotees of any aspect of the Divine because he himself has realised the *Formless.*

15. *While remaining ever conscious of his own pure nature that is identical to Śiva as 'formless', he may at times, thanks to permeation of the different guṇas, perceive that which has form, or, again, he may perceive the miracle [of the cosmos] or be fully satisfied in himself; but the sage, whose ignorance has been dissolved by the grace of the Teacher, is no longer subject to confusion.*

16. *Having acknowledged the totality as pure Non-duality, ever existent and essentially benign, on account of the effective comprehension of the true significance of the great statements, supported by the continual practice of meditation, since [for him] all appearance of duality has disappeared and he himself murmurs nothing but 'Śiva! Śiva! Śiva!', the sage, whose ignorance has been dissolved by the grace of the Teacher, is no longer subject to confusion.*

Thanks to the conscious appreciation of the Vedic statements, and by means of the constant practice of meditation, the sage has realised identity with the supreme and unchanging Reality, the foundation of the visible and the invisible, the sensible and the intelligible.

> 17. *One who, being exceptional among men thanks to the merits he has acquired, day by day immerses himself repeatedly and directly in this expanse of innate bliss and dwells for a long period in this state of liberation, based on the supreme Śiva, that is realisable only by means of the grace bestowed by the Teacher through his sublime glance, he is known by the sages as a yogi, one who has realised total detachment, a perfect knower [of the mind].*

If it is true that only the grace bestowed by the Teacher, his acceptance, his conscious *radiance*, can dispel the disciple's ignorance, it is also true that only one who ventures to reach total emancipation can attain it, can free himself from the conditionings of *avidyā*, or realise himself; in brief, he is the one who, having regained balance, will be able to remain 'without supports'. Reality reveals itself in supreme detachment (*paravairāgya*), even in facing the actual state of realisation.

FIVE VERSES ON THE ASCETIC

yātipañcakam

The *yāti*, or renunciate, is one who recollects himself, merges him anew into himself, and ceases to turn towards worldly experiences.

In this position of consciousness, when the 'garment of individuality' has been cast off, there is a move to a state of steadfast *attention* directed to surpassing the limits imposed by 'appearances'; in other words, there is a withdrawal from the individual condition and a disposition to contemplate and *comprehend*.

Asceticism is not an arbitrary life-choice motivated by desire or a need to escape or a sort of psychological compensation expressing itself in the assumption of an artificial attitude. On the contrary, it corresponds to an unbreakable requirement which is placed on those who, having acknowledged the absolute Reality within the *ātman*, have fostered the firmest conviction of the need to enquire into it and make it known.

The ascetic garb (*kaupīna*) is a symbol, and for someone who has donned it, being convinced of its symbolism, it denotes the spiritual attitude, although the spiritual attitude is quite independent of the symbol. 'Those who wear the ascetic garb' (*kaupīnavantaḥ*), those who gird their loins with the least clothing required for covering themselves, but also those who have embraced the life of the monk, are totally immersed in asceticism and are indeed detached, wholly or partly, from their own psychosomatic individuality.

The renunciate (*yāti*) does not 'don' a particular garment, but takes care of his body in an impersonal way, being free from all identification with it. To free oneself in this way from one's own bodily and mental form, and yet be connected to it, means raising oneself above the level of form, penetrating the world of substance, and resolving oneself, sooner or later, into pure Essence, the substratum or witness of both.

1. *Continually experiencing the statements of Vedānta and ever fully satisfied with food received as alms, enjoying the total absence of suffering in their own hearts, those who wear the renunciate's garb are undoubtedly bearers of perfect bliss.*

2. *Taking shelter at the foot of a tree, simply joining the two hands in order to eat, and experiencing what represents [for others] the highest happiness as if it were just a patched-up piece of cloth, those who wear the renunciate's garb are undoubtedly bearers of perfect bliss.*

3. *Having completely removed all identification with the body, always holding within themselves perfect awareness of the ātman, and experiencing nothing inside or outside or in between, those who wear the renunciate's garb are undoubtedly bearers of perfect bliss.*

4. *Absorbed in the ātman and totally content with their own fullness, having brought all the senses to complete peace, and being ever immersed, day and night, in direct awareness of the Brahman, those who wear the renunciate's garb are undoubtedly bearers of perfect bliss.*

5. *Uttering the sacred fivefold invocation (pañcākṣara), meditating in their hearts on the Lord of all beings, sustaining themselves only with the offerings they receive, and being free to go in any direction, those who wear the renunciate's garb are undoubtedly bearers of perfect bliss.*

EIGHT VERSES ON THE BLESSED

dhanyāṣṭakam

In the *Dhanyāṣṭakam* Śaṅkara honours the state of the *dhanyas*, those who have attained realisation and have dedicated their lives to the investigation of the *ātman*, putting all else on one side.

Realisation – as we often try to show – is not an act, not a condition, not a change, and not even a process or result of something. It is the re-gaining or uncovering of Reality, and therefore the restoration of one's own authentic nature. However, it is not concerned with the psychic or energy spheres of the individual, but transcends individuality and even universality, and it entails the total solution of all uncertainty.

Realisation, therefore, is not a fortuitous eccentricity, but the fruit of iron will, maturity of consciousness, genuine aspiration, and unconditional surrender. It does not smile on all and sundry, but yields to the few who know how to offer themselves to Truth totally and disinterestedly. These are the Accomplished, the Liberated, the Blessed, those that radiate limitless awareness; those that, by their spiritual presence alone, can dispel doubts and drive away fears; those that, being 'the very few chosen from among the great many who are called', reveal themselves as beings that benefit the whole of humanity.

1. *True knowledge is that which brings the senses to total peace. It is that which, according to the authentic meaning ascertained in the Upaniṣads, has to be realised. Blessed are those who, in this world, are fully absorbed in the supreme Reality; all others, by contrast, stray in the state (nilaya) of error (paribhrama, the absolute condition of error).*

2. *Those who, having first gained mastery over the objects [of the senses and the mind], have routed that host of enemies consisting of pride, imagination, attachment, repulsion, and so on, thus attaining the realm of yoga; those who, having taken cognisance of [their own] immortality [as the ātman] and being ever conscious of the bliss issuing from the knowledge of the supreme ātman, which is the object of the highest aspiration, have withdrawn to live in the forest: those are the blessed.*

3. *Those who, having renounced the pleasures of family life, which constitute the cause of the fall [into the world of becoming], quench their thirst with the juice of the true meaning of the Upaniṣads; those whose will is directed exclusively to the realisation of the ātman; those who, having calmed the passions, have become indifferent to the enjoyment of objects; those who are wont to frequent solitary places, being perfectly free from all attachment: those are the blessed.*

Realisation of the *ātman* constitutes the highest ideal conceivable. Experience in the world binds us to the world itself according to the degree of our identification with the acting subject and our involvement in action with attachment to its fruit. Renunciation of family life – as of all other forms of individualised experience – entails emancipation from the bonds that it inevitably brings with it, but only if this detachment happens as a result of the twofold acknowledgement of the nature of worldly experience and of ourselves as independent Consciousness. Otherwise, even detachment would come to be seen as nothing but a self-imposed psychological attitude, bringing in its wake further suffering, nurturing unresolved egoity, and extending the sense of duality. Therefore 'detachment must not occur through reaction, inhibition, or irrational enforcement, but must show itself as the simple result of a profound, logical, and intuitive recognition.'[1]

4. *Those who, having cast aside the notions of 'I' and 'mine', the cause of bondage, give equal reckoning to good fortune and bad and consider [all things] with equanimity; those who, having understood that the subject [witness] of the action [of knowledge, experience, and so on] is distinct [from the ego] and act by offering the fruits of their actions to That: those are the blessed.*

The *ātman* does not act and is ever free. To identify oneself with the acting subject entails accumulating the related *karma*. We have to reach the point of acknowledging that, with regard to acting, it is not *us* but *our qualities* (*guṇas*) which, as they unfold, manifest themselves through vehicles and situations. Nor, on the other

[1] Śaṅkara, *Vivekacūḍāmaṇi*, commentary to *śloka* 69 by Raphael, op. cit.

hand, is one that 'I' that believes it possesses or acquires 'mine' and so on. These are notions, and a notion is an object, but we clearly cannot be the object, for an object appears, changes, and becomes, which means that *it is not.* Who are we, then, if we are not the object and not even the subject represented by the 'sense of I'? We are that Consciousness which is the substratum/witness of both and which represents the one and only means of being able to integrate and synthesise the 'I' and the 'my', as well as their apparent relationship.[1]

> 5. *Those who, having transcended the three principal desires, contemplate nothing but the way to liberation; those who provide for the maintenance of the body with the nectar of what is received as alms; those who, in the depths of their heart, perceive that Light which is higher than even the highest Being, recognising it as the supreme ātman: those, the twice-born, are the blessed.*

The illusion of self-perpetuation through progeny, of self-assertion through the accumulation of goods of all kinds, and, finally, of wishing to experience sensory enjoyment in realms beyond the earth: these three fuel the threefold desire which chains the being to the world of becoming. Only one who has taken his living attention away from the object – however sublime it may be, or however alluring it may appear – can reveal within himself that Consciousness which is free from all limits and transcends everything, but at the same time enfolds every entity, totality, and all possible universal limitlessness.

---

[1] See 'Transcending the mind' in *Beyond the illusion of the ego*, by Raphael. Aurea Vidyā, New York.

The 'twice-born' are indeed those who, being dead to the three desires and to the ego that feeds them, are born anew to the universal.

6. *Those who, having attained the unity of consciousness, have realised the Brahman as the single seed [of all], which is not being or non-being, not being and non-being together, not large or small, not masculine or feminine or sexless; those who are ever detached: those are the blessed. All others are constrained in the conflict of existence.*

The supreme *Brahman* is not Being, because It is more than Being. It is not non-being, because the relative sensible cannot be its own foundation but needs to find its *raison d'être* in something else.

It is not Being and non-being together, because That is not of a pantheistic order, which resolves itself exclusively into the intelligible and sensible world. It is not large or small, because It is beyond all possible qualities of number and size. Nor is It polar, because, being absolute Unity, It transcends all polarity.

> 'It is not only all the things that come to be known one by one that are granted by the Good the very possibility of being known, but Being and esseity themselves also come forth from It. And yet, even so, the Good is not Being. Oh! The Good completely transcends Being in majesty and power.' At this Glaucon exclaimed, 'By Apollo! What astonishing transcendence.'[1]

7. *Those who have recognised as absolutely valueless all that is immersed in the swamp of ignorance*

[1] Plato, *Politéia*, 509 b-c.

(ajñāna), for, consisting, as it does, of birth, illness, and death, it is endless suffering; those who, acknowledging it to be non-eternal, have severed the bond with existential becoming by wielding the sword of knowledge (jñāna) and are aware of the Truth: those are the blessed.

8. *Those who live with others who have attained total peacefulness and no longer entertain any thought, with those of beneficent nature who have revealed the awareness of Unity and have freed themselves from illusion; those who, having withdrawn into the forest, continually contemplate That, the authentic essence known by the Scriptures as the ātman: those are the blessed.*

Being pure aseity, the realised one, in identity with the *Brahman*, creates neither *karma* nor *dharma*, nor any action produced by a relation with the object (*asparśa*).

HYMN TO DAKṢIṆĀMŪRTI

dakṣiṇāmūrtistotram

Dakṣiṇāmūrti ('the Form facing south') represents the beneficent image of Śiva in his function of *guru*, conferring instruction (*upadeśa*) and initiation (*dikṣa*) by means of Silence (*mauna*).

In this Hymn (*stotra*) of great beauty of form, Śaṅkara addresses *Śrī Dakṣiṇāmūrti* as the personification of the knowledge attained through renunciation. *Śrī Dakṣiṇāmūrti*, in the likeness of a young ascetic seated in meditation in the shade of a *banyan* tree, imparts to a group of elderly sages the teaching concerning the Reality of the non-dual *Brahman*. The young ascetic faces south, the home of Death, which has been overcome by Śiva.

In *dakṣiṇāmūrtistotra* Śaṅkara uses terms that are peculiar to the *trika* Shaivism of Kashmir[1], which supports the teaching of 'spontaneous freedom' (*svātantrya*) as the nature of the *ātman* that is identical to the *Brahman*.

Sureśvara, one of the first disciples of *Śaṅkarācārya*, will take up and develop, in his work *Mānasollāsa*, some of the poetical images and metaphysical concepts that are present in his Teacher's poem.

---

1 *Śivasūtra* by Vasugupta and *Paramārthasāra* by Abhinavagupta.

1. *I bow before Śrī Dakṣiṇāmūrti, whom I acknowledge as the embodiment of my guru, through whose mercy the universe is seen within [the mind], like the image of a city reflected in a mirror, even though – as in a dream and through the work of māyā – it appears outside. Illuminated by his grace, the universe is perceived as the ever-existing and non-dual ātman.*

2. *I bow before Śrī Dakṣiṇāmūrti, whom I acknowledge as the embodiment of my guru, who, through the mere power of his will – like a magician or a yogi – projects this unqualified universe in the beginning, like a shoot in the seed, but after [manifestation] there appears [qualified] multiplicity through the powers of māyā.*

3. *I bow down before Śrī Dakṣiṇāmūrti, whom I acknowledge as the embodiment of my guru, whose expression, in the form of manifestation, is an apparent phenomenon but is perceived as real. With the mighty Vedic declaration 'tat tvaṁ asi' (You are That), he enlightens his disciples concerning the reality of the Brahman, by realising which one puts an end to the cycle of re-births (saṁsāra).*

4. *I bow down before Śrī Dakṣiṇāmūrti, whom I acknowledge as the embodiment of my guru, whose knowledge – filtered through the senses, such as the eye, and so on, like light coming forth through the apertures of a pot – is revealed in the form of*

the experience 'I know', and whose light causes all the beings in the universe to shine.

5. *I bow down before Śrī Dakṣiṇāmūrti, whom I acknowledge as the embodiment of my guru, who destroys the error and illusion brought about by māyā, although there are ill-equipped, childish, and blind philosophers who consider the ātman to be the body, prāṇa, cognition, the senses of perception, and the organs of action, all of which are, on the contrary, fleeting and unreal.*

6. *I bow down before Śrī Dakṣiṇāmūrti, whom I acknowledge as the embodiment of my guru, and who exists in deep sleep as pure Being, although hidden by māyā, just as the sun and the moon still exist when hidden by Rāhu, and who, on awakening, recollects having slept well.*

7. *I bow down before Śrī Dakṣiṇāmūrti, whom I acknowledge as the embodiment of my guru, who reveals to his disciples the ātman which, throughout the changes of waking, dream, and deep sleep, throughout infancy, youth, maturity, and old age, shines unceasingly and reveals itself – by means of the auspicious jñānamudrā – as the eternal ātman.*

8. *I bow down before Śrī Dakṣiṇāmūrti, whom I acknowledge as the embodiment of my guru, who, being associated with māyā, in the states of waking, dream, and deep sleep, perceives the manifold world as having the relationship of cause and effect, possessor and possessed, teacher and disciple, father and son.*

9. *I bow down before Śrī Dakṣiṇāmūrti, whom I acknowledge as the embodiment of my guru, beyond whom – for those with discrimination – no higher being exists, for he embraces the moving and the unmoving, which has manifested in the eightfold form of earth, water, fire, air, and ether, as sun, moon, and jīvātman.*

10. *This hymn to Śrī Dakṣiṇāmūrti clearly reveals the all-pervading nature of the ātman. Therefore, by hearing it, meditating upon it, contemplating it, and reciting it, one attains the all-pervasiveness of the ātman, with its divine splendour, lordship over the universe, and the essence of the eightfold manifestation [of the powers].*

THE EXPOSITION OF THE SENTENCE

vākyavṛtti

Introduction

One of the sentences or great statements (*mahāvākyas*) of *Vedānta* is tat tvam asi (You are That), taken from the *Chāndogya Upaniṣad* (VI, VIII, 7). Since this sentence, more than any other, constitutes the very essence of Śaṅkara's *Advaita Vedānta*, it was considered appropriate to give some notes which may help the reader to appreciate the underlying problems, from the viewpoint of philosophical/metaphysical knowledge and from the perspective of its actualisation.

1. Taking an *Upaniṣad*ic context which declares 'You are That', Śaṅkara re-presents, in this short treatise, a philosophical question of vast import. This sentence that is pregnant with metaphysical significance implies the identity of the Existent with that which may be defined as the metaphysical and transcendent Root of the Existent.

2. Being, in the sense of noumenal Existence, is of the same nature as *That* to which it actually owes its existence. Being is on a plane of objectification, determination, and the cause of movement, and it can be so by virtue of an uncaused cause or *causa sui*.

3. The principal/universal Existent, with its categories of Being/Intelligence/Fullness, represents all things, whereas

That represents the foundation of the entire Existent and of all that lives.

4. Whatever lives has its foundation in the Existent, which in turn takes its *raison d'être* from *That*, which is Unity-without-a-second or metaphysical Being, from which empirical thought recoils, being unable to grasp it.

5. The Existent, in which causality subsists, may be thought of as a reflection, an image, an ontological representation of *That*, which is beginningless and therefore outside time and space.

6. Thus we need to distinguish Being – inasmuch as it is and does not become, and is the single, unqualified support of the Existent and of all that lives – from Being/ Existent, which, being determined and qualified, generates all that lives, meaning the world of names and forms.

7. Whatever lives is mere appearance, phenomenon, movement, producing planes, volumes, or forms in a continuous process of birth and death. Whatever lives is multiplicity pure and simple, a 'medium' of the will of the Existent. Of itself it would not be unless it had the Existent behind it to give it life or movement. The Existent is therefore the giver of life to the phenomenal.

8. The individual Existent is a reflection/image of the principal/universal Existent, which apparently represents the One/Many. We say 'apparently' because ontological Unity cannot be broken or changed.

The individual Existent, while being of the same nature as the universal Existent and thus of the same nature as non-dual Being, can be obscured, covered, by the qualities/ *guṇas* (*sattva*, *rajas*, *tamas*) to the point of being alienated.

9. Whatever lives is substance/χώρα. The Existent is Essence/οὐσία. Substance, in its turn, is a polar aspect or a projection of Essence/οὐσία.

10. The 'You' of the *mahāvākya* refers to the Existent/ Essence/οὐσία, while the 'That' refers to non-dual Being, which – it is good to repeat – designates the metaphysical foundation of the Existent and whatever lives and is the only authentic Reality.

11. Our deduction is that the Existent is not the effect or the product of the scissure of non-dual Being, but represents – as we have already seen – a mere *image*/otherness of it. It needs to be agreed that the Absolute cannot divide itself, split itself, reduplicate itself, or make itself dual. An already existing datum cannot be re-born. That which is beyond birth and death, that which is immortal, eternal, and infinite cannot suddenly find itself born, mortal, and finite. The absolute Real cannot therefore generate a real datum, because it cannot infringe its own nature of Reality/Unity, or an unreal datum, because an unreal effect cannot be born from a real cause. Beyond the metaphysical *That*, there can be only a phenomenal representation which appears and disappears, a representation which covers the being, just as the sun disappears behind the clouds (*guṇas*).

12. Knowledge of the Existent as identified with whatever lives is indirect knowledge, because it is known by means of that which lives. This acts like a mirror, so that the Existent knows itself by reflection. It is, therefore, a knowledge that is reflected and distorted, a knowledge of shadow, image, impermanent representation.

To truly know itself, the Existent must look away from what lives, that is, from the mirror, and by an act of what we may call self-contemplation it must know itself for what it really is. Only in this way can it discover itself to be not only independent of what lives, not only capable of recognising itself as the giver of life to whatever lives, but also able to comprehend that it is of the same nature as *That*, non-dual and unqualified Being. This is how the 'You' realises itself in 'That'.

13. The *That* cannot be known through reflected/mirror-like knowledge (that is, knowledge which is dianoetic/object knowledge), simply because the contemplated image (the sensible and intelligible world) hides, covers, camouflages the Essence/οὐσία and, more importantly, the very root of the Existent. We may say that that image superimposes itself on the pure Being, just as a cloud superimposes itself on the splendour of the sun, covering it and concealing it. Those who contemplate the cloud or the reflected image obviously acknowledge nothing but these data; but those who are able to discern and to remove the distorting and darkening cover can reveal the dazzling radiance of the sun to which the Existent, as such, belongs.

14. We therefore have: 'That', as Reality-without-a-second; the Existent (the 'You' of the *mahāvākya*), as the Image/Reflection of 'That'; lastly, the world of names and forms, or whatever lives, which represents the image of the Image and which – according to Parmenides, Plato, Plotinus, and others – actually expresses non-being.[1]

[1] For a deeper understanding of *That*, 'the Being', and 'whatever lives', see by Raphael 'The One-Good as metaphysical reality' in *Initiation into the Philosophy of Plato*, and 'Being' in *On the Order of Nature*, edited by Raphael. Aurea Vidyā, New York.

Homage to Śrī Gaṇeśa

1. *I bow down before that absolute unity of pure knowledge which is Śrī Vallabha, who, being endowed with inscrutable power, is the cause of the manifestation, the preservation, and the dissolution [of everything]. He is the Lord of the universe, who objectifies a countless variety of forms, to whom everything is known, and who is always absolutely free from all limitation whatsoever and is a measureless ocean of infinite fullness.*

2. *I offer eternal homage to the lotus feet of him by whose grace I can realise the nature of the true ātman, recognise that I myself am the All-pervading, and appreciate that the whole phenomenal universe is projected by me.*

3. *Burnt by the fire of the threefold suffering and tested by deep inner travail, a certain [disciple], already endowed with peace of mind and the other virtues which are the necessary prerequisites [for liberation], asked a true Teacher:*

4. *'O Lord, through your benevolence, reveal to me concisely that by means of which I may at once free myself from the bondage of existence.'*

The yearning for liberation does not arise from promptings of an individual character and does not reflect an egoistic desire. It mirrors the innermost maturity of consciousness of someone who, sated with identification with the world of becoming/the relative world, is fully inclined towards the absolute *Brahman* and ready to realise the *Brahman*.

The Teacher said:

5. *'The prompting which you have just expressed is obviously sublime. Listen to me with all your attention as I prepare to expound this to you as clearly as possible.*

6. *'The knowledge which pours out of such statements as "You are That" and others concerning the identity of the jīva with the supreme ātman, constitutes the [only] means of liberation.'*

The disciple said:

7. *'What is the nature of the jīva (soul) and what is the nature of the supreme ātman? How can there be identity between them? How can a statement such as "You are That" prove this identity?'*

The Teacher replied:

8. *'I shall answer your question in the following way. Who else is the jīva? Only you yourself. And if you ask me, "Who am I?", you are indeed, and beyond all doubt, the very Brahman."*[1]

The disciple said:

9. *'My Lord, I do not yet know clearly the meaning of the [separate] words. How, then, can I grasp the*

---

[1] See *Bṛhadāraṇyaka Upaniṣad*, III, IV, 1 – IV, III, 9; *Muṇḍaka Upaniṣad*, III, 1-2; *Śvetāśvatara Upaniṣad*, IV, 6.

meaning of the sentence "I am Brahman"? Kindly explain it to me!'

The Teacher replied:

10. 'What you say is right! In truth, no uncertainty on this topic should arise. The exact interpretation of the individual terms is indeed of the utmost importance in reaching an understanding of the sentence.'

The correct intellectual interpretation is a valid support for the act of consciousness. The sentence 'I am *Brahman*'[1] expresses an absolute identity, and to be understood it requires an effective realisation of consciousness, as is the case with all the great Vedic statements.

The *jīva* is 'darkened' by the *guṇas* and their qualities, with the result that it becomes passive or potential. The 'I' (*aham*) is born from contact with the properties/qualities of the *guṇas*, so that it declares, 'I am this, I am that; I am happy, I am unhappy; I have to do that or that', and so on. Until these superimpositions (*adhyāropas*) are resolved, they hold the *jīva* prisoner in the formal state.

11. 'Why do you not recognise the ātman, which is pure Being and has the nature of pure fullness, as the intelligent unity which is the witness of the inner organ (antaḥkaraṇa) and its modifications?

12. 'Having removed the [false] notion by which [the ātman] is identified with the body and so on, realise – by means of the awareness of being ever the ātman – the unity of Consciousness/Knowledge,

---

1 *Bṛhadāraṇyaka Upaniṣad*, I, IV, 10.

which has the nature of absolute existence and bliss and is the witness of the intellect.

13. 'The gross body cannot, in fact, be the ātman because it is endowed with form and so on, just like pots, for example, and other objects [that have been produced], and also because it consists of a transformation of space/ether (ākāśa) and the other gross elements, like a jug [with respect to clay].'

The disciple said:

14. 'So if this gross body were truly recognised as something totally different from the ātman, then, on the basis of what has been said, please show me the ātman directly, like a myrobalan fruit held in the palm of the hand.'

The Teacher said:

15. 'You must carefully consider the following. Just as someone perceiving a jug is distinct from the jug itself and is in no way identified with it, in the same way I, the perceiver of the gross body, am not the body itself.

16. 'Similarly, recognise that the following conclusion is reached: I, who am the witness of the sensory organs [and so on], am not those organs themselves. Therefore meditate thus: I am not the mind, the intellect, or even the vital force,

17. 'and I am not any combination [of them]. Discern clearly and intelligently that the Witness/Seer is distinct from whatever is the object of perception.'

Just as sight is distinct from the object perceived, so the *ātman* is different from the object of knowledge, with which it is 'confused' through error and from which it must be distinguished.

> *18. 'Meditate thus: I am That in whose presence alone all those [inert] beings such as the body, the senses, and so on, become capable of producing activities in a dependent way, and so on.*

> *19. 'Meditate thus: I am he who, being by nature without any change and being within [all], impels to movement the intellect and the other functions, exactly as a magnet acts upon iron filings.'*

Just as the mere presence of the magnet, through the field it produces, is enough to generate a certain dynamism in the surrounding space, so the *ātman* activates its sheaths/ vehicles without even coming into contact with them, while remaining a witness of their functions.

On the other hand, just as empirical dynamism presupposes a central static condition of balance and reference point, so phenomenal relativity, at both the universal and individual levels, presupposes and requires a metaphysical *absolute*, that is, *Brahman*.

> *20. 'Meditate thus: I am he thanks to whose proximity the body, the senses, the mind, and the vital forces – though inert of themselves – appear endowed with consciousness like the ātman.'*

The body, the senses, the *prāṇa* or vital 'breath', the mind, and the intellect do not shine with their own light but reflect the pure splendour of the *ātman*, from which they receive their being. They constitute successive condensations of substance/*prakṛti* which only the fire of Awareness is able to purify, re-integrate, transform, and resolve.

> 21. *'Meditate thus: I am he who is witness of the working of the intellect [and may be expressed] as, "Now my function of mind is absent, now it is present."'*

The intellect (*buddhi*) and the other sheaths are mere 'functions' by which the reflection of consciousness (*jīva*) is able to express itself without thereby changing its own nature.

> 22. *'Meditate thus: I am he who, being free of all transforming activity and being immediately present, is witness of the waking state, the dream state, and the state of deep sleep, and, at the same time, witness of the presence or absence of the working of the intellect.'*

The supreme Being is the absolute witness of the relative and conditioning states, which are superimposed modifications. There is a precise correspondence between the levels of Being and the states of consciousness, and hence an analogy with the individual conditions of waking, dream, and sleep. To realise *Turīya* (the Fourth) it is necessary to comprehend, transcend, and consciously resolve the various superimposed states of consciousness/existence.

> 23. *'Just as a lamp which illuminates a jug is other than the jug itself, so am I that absolute unity of consciousness which, as the jīva, illuminates the body [and so on].*

24. *'Meditate thus: I am the witness which is dear to the hearts of all and by virtue of which all the things that exist, such as offspring and wealth, are loved.*[1]

25. *'I am the witness, the object of supreme love, on account of which [it is said], "I have never ceased to love; and on account of this may I always exist."*

26. *'It is held that the meaning of the term "You" [in the sentence "You are That"] consists of the same knowledge/awareness as is signified by the witness. The function of knower is therefore not other than that of witness, exercised by the unchanging ātman.*

27. *'Thus that which is indicated by the term "You" is totally distinct from the body, senses, mind, vital force, and even the feeling of I, and is completely untouched by the six typical transformations characteristic of inert objects.'*

The term 'You' refers to the *jīvātman* as the unitary principle of consciousness (the first reflection of the *ātman*), which is amenable to countless possibilities and, as such, has an immortal nature. The sentence 'You are That' establishes the essential identity between *jīvātman* and *Brahman*, an identity that is realised with spontaneous self-knowledge when the conditioning and differentiating superimpositions are resolved, as if the mind, being transformed and no longer considering itself to be a human being, suddenly recognises what it really is.

The six transformations are birth, growth, maturity, illness, decrepitude, and death.

---

[1] See *Bṛhadāraṇyaka Upaniṣad*, I, IV, 8.

28. *'Having thus come to understand perfectly the true meaning of the term "You", one should meditate unceasingly on the essential meaning of the term "That", both by negating the superimpositions and by affirming "That" directly.'*

Negation by *neti neti* leads to the removal and solution of the superimpositions. Affirmation by *iti iti* takes multiplicity into the principial Unity.

29. *'One who completely transcends every limiting condition of the world of becoming and is defined as not gross, and so on; one who by nature cannot become an object of perception/knowledge and transcends even the impurity/superimposition which is ignorance,*

30. *'one beyond whom there is no further bliss; who is the absolute singularity of existence and knowledge; who is defined as the self-existent Being, and who is absolute Fullness: that is known as the supreme ātman.*

31. *'Now acknowledge the Brahman as That whose omniscience, supreme lordship, perfection/completeness, and boundless power are celebrated in the Vedas.*

32. *'Acknowledge the Brahman, as declared by the Scriptures through the numerous examples of clay and so on, to be That which, by being known/realised, there is consciousness of all things.'*

By knowing substance/clay, one also knows all the objects made of clay, their differences being merely the effects of name and form. In the same way, by realising the pure *Brahman*, one realises the foundation of all knowledge and existence, beyond the multiplicity of name, form (*nāma-rūpa*), cause, beginning and end.

> 'O venerable one, how then is this teaching imparted?' 'My dear, from just a piece of clay all that is made of clay becomes known, while all its modifications are nothing but the mere designation of name, so that the sole reality is the clay.'[1]
>
> 'Once indeed Śaunaka, the head of a large dynasty, having approached Aṅgiras in the prescribed manner, asked him, "O blessed One, what is it then that, once it is known, all that exists becomes known?"'[2]

33. 'Acknowledge the Brahman as That whose limitlessness the Śruti seeks to demonstrate by defining the universe as one of its appearances.'

The whole of the universe is merely a phenomenon which appears and disappears at the touch of the unity of the *Brahman*. Just as the rope is the substratum of the image of the snake, so is *Brahman* the substratum of *māyā*. *Brahman* does not transform itself into the phenomenal universe, for the universe is a mere condition/phenomenon that appears and disappears on the principial screen.

34. 'Acknowledge the Brahman as That which is defined very carefully in the Upaniṣads as what is to be sought by those who yearn for liberation.

35. 'Acknowledge the Brahman as That spoken of in the Vedas with regard to its permeating the jīvāt-

---

1 *Chāndogya Upaniṣad*, VI, I, 3-4.

2 *Muṇḍaka Upaniṣad*, I, I, 3.

mans and the function of maintenance which [although not acting] it exercises in relation to them.'

'This Divinity [the original Being] considered, "Then I, as *ātman*, can manifest name and form by penetrating into these three divinities as their *jīva*!"'[1]

'He deliberated: "Let me become many by manifesting myself through coming into being!" He practised spiritual discipline. Having completed the meditation, he created all this and everything that is. Having created it, he penetrated into it.'[2]

36. 'Acknowledge the Brahman as That which is said in the Śruti to confer the fruits of actions and impel the jīvas to accomplish them.

37. 'Once the real meaning of the terms "You" and "That" have been ascertained, we now move to examine the meaning of the whole sentence. In this context, the sentence expresses the true and rightful identity between the meanings of the two terms.

38. 'The sentence, therefore, must not be interpreted to mean a reciprocal connection or a mutual qualification [of the two terms]. According to the wise, the meaning of the sentence consists in an absolute identity.

39. 'He who manifests himself as the innermost consciousness/knowledge [jīva] is none other than non-dual bliss; and that essence which consists in

---

[1] *Chāndogya Upaniṣad*, VI, III, 2.

[2] *Taittirīya Upaniṣad*, II, VI, 1.

non-dual bliss is none other than the same innermost consciousness.'

'The Self-existent made the outer gateways incapable [of grasping Him]. This is why [the individualised being] sees [only] external things and not the innermost *ātman*. Sometimes a wise man, yearning for immortality, having become one, and turning his [outward] gaze inwards, sees the innermost *ātman*.'[1]

40. *'Thus when there is a conscious realisation of [their] reciprocal identity, then the [assumed and superimposed] difference from the Brahman of what is indicated by the term "You" vanishes on the instant,*

41. *'and the same happens through the indirect knowledge of that which is indicated by the term "That". What, then, happens if this occurs? Listen. [When this identity is appreciated] the innermost consciousness [which is the jīva] resolves into its own essence, which is absolute Unity and the fullness of bliss.*

42. *'The sentence "You are That" and the other sentences are meant to establish the identity of that which is indirectly expressed through the two words "You" and "That".*

43. *'We have thus explained how the sentence itself, once the direct meanings of the two terms have been set aside, reveals its true significance [of unity/identity].'*

---

1 *Kaṭha Upaniṣad*, II, I, 1.

Between the 'you'/*jīva* and the 'That'/*Brahman* there is a perfect identity.

44. *'The awareness which is associated with the inner organ and which constitutes the essential content of the word and notion "I" expresses the indirect [or figurative] meaning of the term "You".*

45. *'On the other hand, the direct meaning of the term "That" represents the one on whom māyā is superimposed, the one that is the foundation of the cause/origin of the world. He is defined as omniscient, and so on, having the nature of true Being, and so on, and signifiable only indirectly.*

46. *'Now, for the same single being to have the properties of being known directly and indirectly and of having a second, and simultaneously to be an absolute unity is a manifest contradiction, and so [in the sentence "You are That"] an implicit interpretation must be deduced.*

47. *'In a case where the admission of a term's directly expressed meaning gives rise to an inconsistency with another mode of knowledge, that meaning which is clearly self-evident and yet is connected to what is directly expressed is called the implicit meaning.*

48. *'In sentences such as "You are That", the indirect interpretation consists in a partial inference [that is, an inference which removes only the contradictory part of the direct meanings by making it self-evident], as in the case of the two terms, or in*

a sentence such as "This is that"and so on. There is no other kind of [partial] inference.

49. *'One should practise hearing [as well as reflection and meditation] of the Scriptures together with control of the mind and the other inner disciplines until an understanding of the true significance of the sentence "I am Brahman" has become fully effective.*

50. *'When, through the grace of the Teacher and the Scriptures, this knowledge is firmly established, then the being has eradicated for ever the entire cause of transmigratory existence.*

51. *'Since such a being, at the dissolution of the gross body and the subtle body, is quite independent of the subtle elements and is freed from the imprisoning effects of [goal-oriented] action, it is instantly liberated.'*

The body and its binding activity are the result of the movement of the mind, and the mind itself is the result of those latent causes (*saṁskāras*) which impel the *jīva* to objectivise itself. When one recognises the insubstantiality of all these contents – thoughts, tendencies, impressions, seeds – they disappear on the instant.

52. *'Thus, on the cessation of the bondage caused by past actions which have not yet come to fruition – whenever that occurs – by witnessing with detachment the fruition of past actions, one becomes liberated in this life,*

53. *'and one realises the supreme absolute nature, which is the highest bliss, that is, one attains the supreme abode of Viṣṇu, from which there is no return.'*

'In truth, the man who has discrimination as his charioteer and has firm control over the reins of the mind reaches the end of the journey: the supreme state of Viṣṇu.'[1]

One who is liberated in life (*jīvanmukta*) is the one who, having realised his own identity with *Brahman*, has resolved himself into the supreme abode of the *Brahman*.

Here ends the 'Exposition of the Sentence' composed by the venerable Śaṅkarācārya, supreme Instructor among the itinerant paramahaṁsa ascetics

[1] *Kaṭha Upaniṣad*, I, III, 9.

THE FIVE-FACETED JEWEL OF INSTRUCTION

upadeśapañcaratnam

In this very short work Śaṅkara condenses the essence of the Teaching and the discipline given to the disciple. These verses could constitute the rule of conduct for someone aspiring to the realisation of the *Brahman*, his way of life both inside and outside an *āśram* or spiritual com*muni*ty and so on, and his intellectual attitude towards the empirical plane. The five verses present every aspect of the realisative *sādhanā*, and the seeker will need to be sufficiently astute to bear this tiny collection in mind and comply with its meaning whenever there is a doubt or uncertainty in carrying out a given procedure or experiencing a particular stage of development.

This composition, which contains Śaṅkara's final teachings, imparted at the request of his disciples prior to his departure from the physical realm, is also known by other names: *Sopānapañcakam* ('The five means [for realising the *ātman*]') and *Sādhanapañcakam* ('The fivefold discipline').

1. *Study the Veda constantly. Fulfil properly the [ritual] activities prescribed in the Veda. By these activities cultivate devotion to the Lord. Abandon the thought of desire [for the object related to the fruit of action]. Free yourself from the assemblage of vices. Bear in mind that [continually going in search of] pleasure in existence constitutes an obstacle. Strive tenaciously to establish the will [to realise the ātman]. Abandon with all dispatch [attachment to] your old dwelling-place.*

The *Smṛti* underlines the necessity of carrying out one's daily duties in the case of someone aspiring to knowledge, although realisation is independent of all activity whatsoever. However, Śaṅkara the Teacher points out that the fulfilment of the duties prescribed both by the *Śruti* and by the *Smṛti* is a great help in awakening to the reality of oneself as the ultimate Subject.

The 'old dwelling-place' denotes more than anything else – and in addition to the physical abode – the reinforced psychic attitude or the assemblage of the conscious and subconscious entities – such as the character, personality, experience, and convictions – that form the psychological burden of the individual and the habitual expressive vehicle of the ego. The pleasure/pain provided by experience is not one of its qualities but denotes one of our attitudes; its persistence is a sign of spiritual immaturity.

2. *Seek the company of the wise. Acquire steadfast faith in the Lord. Practise the mental virtues, such as peacefulness. Refrain at once from the most*

compulsive activities. Betake yourself to a sage who has realised Being; show your devotion at his feet every day. Have as your goal nothing but the realisation of the knowledge of the one unchanging Brahman. Hear with full attention the great sayings of the Upaniṣads.

The mental virtues are peacefulness, self-control, the attitude of withdrawing, enduring patience, faith in the teaching and the Teacher, and the ability to focus on the truth that has been intuited.[1] To cultivate these virtues until they are part of one's being is the first step on the Path of metaphysical knowledge.

Compulsive activities are those that are undertaken as a result of the impulse given to our ego by the image relating to the enjoyment of their fruits. The individual, identified with his own psychosomatic vehicle, acts only with a view to obtaining the fruits of the action and certainly not because the action needs to be carried out regardless of any result.

3. *Therefore enquire into the meaning of those sentences. Participate fully in the principal and unparalleled vision of the Śruti. Abandon decisively all vain sophistry, but support with your intellect only that line of reasoning that is in harmony with what the Śruti declares. Realise consciously [the sentence] 'I am Brahman'. Day by day relinquish pride. Dispense with the [false] conviction 'I am the body'. Avoid all dispute with the wise.*

Having acquired the cognition of what is expressed in the *Upaniṣads*, one must practise what has been learnt.

[1] See Śaṅkara, *Vivekacūḍāmaṇi*, 18-30, op. cit.

If the mind is steady, attentive, and without ideations, the hearing becomes cathartic because it allows the vibration of sound to penetrate directly into the awareness of the embodied reflection of the *jīva*.

4. *Apply a cure to that disturbance known as hunger. Every day accept the medicine which takes the form of alms. On the other hand, do not nurture any desire to receive food that tastes pleasant. Be content simply with what is obtained as a gift. Patiently bear heat and cold and the other pairs [of opposites], but do not utter vain words. Be totally indifferent [towards whatever comes from the empirical plane]. Have nothing to do with the attitude of behaving gently towards some people and severely towards others.*

5. *Sit comfortably in an isolated place; focus your awareness on the Supreme; seek to perceive within yourself the ātman, which is the fullness of bliss; see how this universe resolves into That. Destroy the karma which has been accumulated [but not yet activated]. Availing yourself of the strength issuing from consciousness, seek not to cling to that [which may yet take form as the] future, but experience here and now [and with utter detachment] that which comes into being. In this way resolve yourself into the ātman, which is [identical to] the supreme Brahman.*

Verse 5 makes a reference to *karma*. This term denotes the connection between cause and effect. The individual has a *karma* in the sense that he is obliged to undergo the effect of that cause which resides in his unresolved past and has its origin in *avidyā* itself. If this effect has already occurred – and appears as a specific body, mind, and so on – it is known as *karma* that is already activated and not subject to resolution (*prārabdha*). On the other hand, if it has not yet occurred (*saṁcit*), then it can be completely resolved by means of knowledge, so that it can no longer condition the actual being.

Then, with regard to the future (*āgāmin*), it is simply a matter of observing that, in the absence of the cause, the effect will also be absent. However, *karma* is not absolute, which means that we can check it, rectify it, or annul it.

THE SACRED REPROACH FOR THE NON-SELF

anātmaśrīvigarhaṇa

In this *prakaraṇa* (composition) in verses Śaṅkara, with a style that is simple in form but sublime in content, urges us to consider the futility and worthlessness of all acquisition.

Through the mouth of Socrates, Plato declares, 'There is only one Good, called knowledge.' According to *advaita*, the only end to pursue is the knowledge/realisation of the *ātman*, which is the supreme goal of the being.

Once the *ātman* is known – which is equivalent to being finally resolved into one's own authentic nature – one is freed from any kind of false superimposition and has accomplished all that really needs to be accomplished.

When even the greatest experience has been achieved, the questions that have to be asked are: What is its purpose? What does it mean? What is its effect upon us? What is left of it when time passes and circumstances change? The repetition of *tataḥ kim* 'Then what?' or 'What good is that?', occurring after every possibility under consideration, lays its validity open for discussion and raises a doubt about the basis of the experience, its object, and our yearning for it which impels the ego to manifest, to come into being, and to entangle itself ever more obstinately in its own projections. This kind of enquiry is a powerful stimulus for transcending the experience, detaching oneself from the plane of the relative and apparent, and revealing within ourselves – directly and immediately – the real Absolute, the *ātman*.

Of what benefit is experience and the dualism that underlies and strengthens it, when our nature is unchangeable and totally without relationships? To what end do we immerse ourselves, consciously or unconsciously, in the incessant whirlpool of a universe populated by changing, evanescent forms, when our own being is Steadfastness, Completeness, Fullness?

The question 'Then what?' is what every consciousness on the return journey should always bear in mind, both when facing everyday experience and when passing once more through the span of life: it is that which frees us from the bonds of the past and destroys the uncertainty of the future. For the *sādhaka* the earthly condition is merely a school to help us appreciate the value and utility of our various experiences. Thus we need to reflect, meditate, and intuit the source of the impulse to experience; and we need to reflect upon what experience itself stands for and who it is that garners the fruits of experience. One who *is* is sufficient unto himself.

1. *If you acquire the most brilliant wisdom of erudition: then what? If you become rich and powerful: then what? If you enjoy the company of ladies of exquisite form, then what? It is certainly not on account of all this that the ātman can be realised.*

2. *Adorn yourself with bracelets and other jewels: then what? Dress yourself in the finest silk garments: then what? Feast on all sorts of food and drink: then what? It is certainly not on account of all this that the ātman can be realised.*

3. *Visit enchanting places: then what? Provide good care for relatives and friends: then what? Keep yourself ever away from the distress of poverty: then what? It is certainly not on account of all this that the ātman can be realised.*

4. *Bathe in the waters of the Ganges or other sacred rivers: then what? Undertake the sixteen types of sacrifice: then what? Recite the mantras, too, repeating them thousands of times: then what? It is certainly not on account of all this that the ātman can be realised.*

5. *Maintain your own family in comfort: then what? Sprinkle sacred ashes on your body: then what? Gird yourself with a rosary of the 'eyes of Śiva': then what? It is certainly not on account of all this that the ātman can be realised.*

6. *Honour the wise with offerings of food: then what? Win the favour of the gods with sacrificial oblations: then what? Let your own fame spread through all the worlds: then what? It is certainly not on account of all this that the ātman can be realised.*

7. *Purify your body through fasting: then what? Produce sons from your own wife: then what? Acquire full control of the vital energy: then what? It is certainly not on account of all this that the ātman can be realised.*

True fasting is of the mind. True lineage is not of flesh or thought but of the pure Spirit, which radiates and reveals itself by awakening in each one and remaining ever identical to itself.

8. *Defeat your enemy in battle: then what? Feel pleased with newly acquired friendships: then what? Acquire all powers by means of yoga: then what? It is certainly not on account of all this that the ātman can be realised.*

9. *Walk across the ocean: then what? Assimilate the vital energy through the retention of the breath: then what? Raise the mighty Mount Meru aloft on the palm of one hand: then what? It is certainly not on account of all this that the ātman can be realised.*

10. *Even when you can drink poison as if it were milk: then what? Or when you can eat fire as if it were rice: then what? Or you can fly into the sky like*

a bird: then what? It is certainly not on account of all this that the ātman can be realised.

11. Gain full control over fire and the other elements: then what? Penetrate effortlessly even metals such as iron: then what? Bring hidden treasures from the earth simply by using magic unguents: then what? It is certainly not on account of all this that the ātman can be realised.

We must be on our guard against the easy achievements and the unusual experiences which can be produced by the powers that have been acquired through spiritual discipline. These powers are merely *qualities* which, by distinguishing the ego, strengthen its image and its state of inertia.

Whatever their nature, acquisitions entail – sooner or later – a relapse into need and constraint (*saṁsāra*). They are of no value to someone for whom the *ātman* has not yet become perfectly evident, and they are of no help in achieving this aim.

12. Gain dominion over the whole earth: then what? Reign over all the gods: then what? Have authority over those whose heads are shaven: then what? It is certainly not on account of all this that the ātman can be realised.

13. Lord it over any entity whatever by means of mantras: then what? Be pierced by arrows without suffering any harm: then what? Even if the knowledge of time were acquired: then what? It is certainly not on account of all this that the ātman can be realised.

14. Even if the scourge of desire were extirpated: then what? If the consequences of anger were totally obliterated: then what? And even if all the evil accruing from attachment were finally removed: then what? It is certainly not on account of all this that the ātman can be realised.

15. Even if the darkness of illusion were dispelled: then what? Even if every form of pride were taken from you in this life: then what? And lastly, if the anguish caused by jealousy were also erased: then what? It is certainly not on account of all this that the ātman can be realised.

16. Win the world of Brahmā: then what? Contemplate the world of Viṣṇu: then what? Or attain dominion even over the world of Śiva: then what? It is certainly not on account of all this that the ātman can be realised.

To attain the world of causes may be a stimulus to transcend the world of effects, but this does not constitute the ultimate goal. The *ātman* is the uncaused Cause, beyond the creation, preservation, and destruction of every universal and individual aspect.

17. One in whose heart there springs spontaneously this sacred reproach for the anātman, such a one becomes the tabernacle in which the direct realisation of the ātman may be fulfilled.

18. But many are those who have fallen into the grip of the veiling power (māyā), which arises from the error accompanying identification with the world of appearances. Never in this life-time is the immediate realisation of the ātman granted to such as these.

We may *know* everything and we may experience everything, which means that we are *other* than all that constitutes the object of knowledge. To feel attraction or repulsion towards anything whatever is to confuse one's own nature with this vast, superimposed projection. To remain equidistant from it all by employing the sacred reproach for the *anātman* (the non-Self) means to swiftly reveal perfect awareness of the *ātman*.

WORSHIP GOVINDA

bhaja govindam

Bhaja Govindam or *Mohamudgara* ('he who destroys ignorance') – one of the most popular lyrical poems of the Teacher of Kālaṭi – is a devotional hymn dedicated to Govinda (one of Kṛśṇa's names). These verses are sung everyday in India by millions of young Hindus, in homes, in temples, and in places of pilgrimage or retreat (*satsaṅgha*).

According to tradition, during Śaṅkara's sojourn at Vārāṇasī (Benares) he was walking with his disciples when he met an elderly scholar on the road who was reciting grammatical rules and instructing some students.

At this sight Śaṅkara came to a standstill and, feeling compassion for the scholar, addressed him with a Hymn of twelve verses which became known as the *Dvādaśasamañjarikāstotra* (the 'Hymn of Twelve Flowers in Verse').

It is thought that the fourteen disciples who were accompanying the *Ācārya* each added one verse, and these verses were called the *Caturdaśamañjarikāstotra* (the 'Hymn of Fourteen Flowers in Verse').

The Hymn aims to show that all the branches of knowledge may be mastered, but if the knowledge of the *ātman* has not been attained, then whatever knowledge we may have is unable to assist us in freeing ourselves from the cycles of re-birth (*saṁsāra*), the cause of suffering and conflict.

Hymn of Twelve Flowers in Verse

dvādaśasamañjarikāstotra

Worship Govinda, worship Govinda, worship Govinda, you thick-headed one.

When the hour [of death] draws near, you will find no salvation in grammatical rules.

1. *Free yourself, you dunderhead, from the thirst to pile up wealth and be content with the simple fruits of your karma. Achieve non-attachment and consecrate your mind to Reality.*

2. *Sensuality in seeing a female [or male] form is born from ignorance. Be ever mindful that bodies are nothing but flesh, blood, and fat.*

3. *Life is as transitory as drops of water on a lotus leaf. All individuals are marred by suffering, egotism, and disease.*

4. *While you remain vigorous, self-seekers will stay close to you; but when your body becomes infirm, no one will wish to speak to you any more.*

5. *As long as you breathe, the family members will take care of you; but once the vital breath has left your body, they will flee in fear.*

6. *Remind yourself that riches bring conflict; it is truly the case that they do not confer happiness. The rich may fear even their own children: this is the truth.*

7. *In childhood we are attached to games; in youth, to pleasures of the senses; in old age, to preoccupations; but no one, alas, is attached to the supreme Truth (Brahman).*

8. *Who is your consort? Who is your child? This empirical world is truly strange! Whose are you? Who are you? Where do you come from? My brother, reflect on these questions.*

9. *The company of the holy stimulates non-attachment. Non-attachment frees us from illusion. Without illusion we discern Reality/the Constant. And when we are established in Reality/the Constant, we attain liberation in this life.*

10. *When youth is finished, what possible passion can there be? When water evaporates, how can there ever be a lake? When wealth is spent, which friends can we have? When the Truth is realised, what kind of empirical world will be able to persist?*

11. *Do not feel proud of your wealth, youth, or parentage. Time sweeps these things away before you can blink. Remove your attention from the empirical world, which is made of māyā. Know the Brahman and resolve yourself into the Brahman.*

12. *Day and night, dawn and sunset, spring and winter alternate unceasingly. Time is a game, and life*

a lightning flash. And yet the individual seeks to prolong his desires.

Through these twelve verses the grammarian received the teaching of the greatest of the sages, Śrī Śaṅkarabhagavatpāda.

Here ends the 'Hymn of Twelve Flowers in Verse', in which Śrī Śaṅkarācārya, exalted paramahaṁsa among the wandering ascetics, provides Instruction during his meeting with the grammarian, as related by the tradition.

Hymn of Fourteen Flowers in Verse

caturdaśamañjarikāstotra

1. *Why do you concern yourself with your consort, with wealth, and so on? Why are you as restless as the wind? May there not be one who watches over you? Know, my friend, that in the three worlds the company of the just (the realised) alone is the boat that will ferry you across the ocean of saṁsāra.*

This verse is attributed to Padmapāda.

2. *The ascetic with matted locks, the one with a shaven head, the one whose hair is drawn back, the one who wears ochre robes: they are all fools; though seeing, they see not. These disguises are often adopted from love of the stomach.*

This verse – so incisive and biting – is attributed to Toṭaka.

3. *One who has grown old has a frail body, a toothless mouth, and grey hair, and he walks with the support of a stick, but [even in this state] he does not relinquish his desires.*

This verse is attributed to Hastāmalaka.

4. *[The ascetic sits] before the fire or in the sun, with his knees drawn up under his chin at night. With his hands he eats the results of begging and resides beneath a tree. Even so, the bondage of desires does not leave him.*

This verse is attributed to Subodha.

5. *You can make a pilgrimage to Gaṅgāsāgara, keep your vows and offer gifts, but if you lack knowledge, you will not attain liberation even in a hundred lives.*

This verse is attributed to Sureśvara.

6. *Living in a temple or at the foot of a tree, sleeping on the ground, wearing deerskin, renouncing one's goods and all that comes from them: who would not derive bliss from this [total] detachment?*

This verse is attributed to Nityānanda.

7. *Whether absorbed in yoga or in enjoyment, whether in a crowd or in profound solitude, one whose mind is absorbed in the Brahman is blessed, blessed, truly blessed.*

This verse is attributed to Ānandagiri.

8. *One who has meditated on the Bhagavadgītā, even for a short time, who has drunk a single drop of the Ganges, or has, even if only once, worshiped the slayer (Kṛṣṇa) of the demon Mura, such a one fears not Yama [the god of death].*

This verse is attributed to Dṛḍhabhakti.

9. *Endless births and deaths, repeated journeys through a mother's womb: how arduous it is to cross this ocean of saṁsāra! Save me by your grace, O slayer of Mura (Kṛṣṇa).*

This verse is attributed to Nityanātha.

10. *The yogi who wears clothes made of rags found on the road, who is free from merit and demerit, whose mind is concentrated on yoga, he, like a child or an enthusiast, finds delight [in the Brahman alone].*

This verse is attributed to Yogānanda.

11. *Who am I? Who are you? Where do I come from? Who is my mother and who is my father? Meditate on this and detach yourself from the entire universe by considering that, like a dream, it has no reality.*

This verse is attributed to Surendra.

12. *In you, in me, and in each thing there is only the One/Viṣṇu; so, as far as I am concerned, your anger and your impatience are non-existent. See the ātman in everything, and in all places remove ignorance, the cause of differentiation.*

13. *Be not identified with friend or foe, son or parent, peace or war. If you yearn for the state of Viṣṇu, view everything with equanimity.*[1]

[1] In some editions the first part of verse 12, together with the second half of verse 13, is attributed to Medhātithi. The remaining two parts together form what is called *mohamudgaraśeṣa*, that is, a 'further' verse of the *Mohamudgara*.

14. *Abandoning desire, anger, deceit, and yearning, ask yourself, Who am I? Those who do not seek the ātman are foolish. Prisoners of error, they are tortured by suffering.*

This verse is attributed to Bharatīvaṁśa.

15. *Recite the Gītā and the Sahasranāma. Meditate on the names of Viṣṇu. Find delight in the company of saints, and give any surplus to the needy.*

This verse is attributed to Sumati and is the final verse of the *Caturdaśamañjarikāstotra*, verses 12 and 13 being considered as a unit.

The foolish grammarian, taken by the study of grammatical rules, has been freed from his restricted vision and enlightened by Śaṅkara's disciples.

Here ends the 'Hymn of the Fourteen Flowers in Verse' added by the enlightened disciples of Śrī Śaṅkarācārya, exalted paramahaṁsa among the wandering ascetics, on the occasion of his meeting with the grammarian, as related by the tradition.

16. *We often indulge in sensory pleasure and let our bodies be prey to disease. Although death is the final outcome, none of us turns away from this error.*

17. *Control the prāṇa, remove the senses [from their respective objects], discriminate the true from the untrue, calm the mind, and repeat the japa. Aim to do this carefully.*

18. Surrendering yourself at the lotus feet of your guru, you will release yourself from saṁsāra. Master the senses and the mind and contemplate the ātman in your heart.[1]

[1] Verses 16 to 18 are additions.

THE WAY OF BEING

sadācāra

The word *sadācāra* is composed of *sat* (Being) and *ācāra* (way, spiritual journey, conduct), and Śaṅkara here shows us exactly the way we need to travel in order to realise Being. It consists of a sequence of spiritual steps which, when taken as a whole, constitute the foundations of the conduct that the wise should always observe, conduct which, starting from the empirical plane of behaviour, action, and so on, gradually comes to include higher planes, first of all changing the psychological attitude, then the spiritual condition and hence the state of consciousness free of all identification/limitation. Here, then, we do not find an exposition of meditation techniques or *mantras* or philosophical reasonings of various kinds, but a way of realisation pertaining to consciousness by which one reaches, in actual fact, a full and effective apprehension of Reality.

Each being's expression of life is commensurate with its degree of conscious/spiritual maturity. The level of the appreciation of Reality is reflected by the state of existence/experience. For each one, according to its existential position, there is a clear moment when two mutually incompatible paths are presented to the consciousness/life: one is the path of experience, fruition, accumulation, and therefore of dispersion into the limitlessness of existence and form (*bhoga*), while the other is the way of reintegration, return, total reunification (*yoga*) and the expansion of consciousness. The first is a way of exclusion and separation, while the second is a true and proper way to total comprehension.

In the *Bṛhadāraṇyaka Upaniṣad* we read:

'Do you perhaps know how to reach the path which is the way of the gods or that which is the way of the ancestors, having recourse to which [the beings which depart] gain access to the way of the gods or the way of the ancestors? In truth, we heard the words of the *Ṛṣi*: "I have heard of the two paths for mortal beings. One for the ancestors and the other for the gods."'[1]

Plato describes these two paths through the words of Er, son of Armenius:

'He said that when the soul had departed from him it had gone on a journey with many others, until they reached a wondrous place in which there opened, quite close to each other, two chasms into the earth and, in perfect correspondence, two more up into the sky. Between them sat judges, who, with every verdict they gave, ordered the just to go up on the right, towards the sky ... and the unjust to go down on the left.'[2]

Parmenides bases his Teaching on these two ways (ὁδός): the way of truth which liberates and the way of error (δόξα) which imprisons.[3]

---

[1] *Bṛhadāraṇyaka Upaniṣad*, VI, II, 2. See also *Bhagavadgītā*, VIII, 23-28. Translation from the Sanskrit and commentary by Raphael. Aurea Vidyā, New York.

[2] Plato, *Politéia*, X, 614 c-d.

[3] See 'Parmenides and his Vision' in The *Pathway of Non-Duality* by Raphael, op. cit. See also Parmenides, *On the Order of Nature*, op. cit.

1. *To the one who is absolute existence, consciousness, and bliss, and the cause of the flowering of the universe, the one who is eternal Presence and total Fullness, the one who, being Viṣṇu, is the all-pervasive infinite: to this one let homage be made.*

2. *I am preparing myself to expound the discipline that leads to Reality, which is the pure and beneficial essence of the realisative teaching expressed by the whole of Vedānta, so that those who are committed to yoga may realise the knowledge (jñāna).*

3. *That which is the light of the ātman and which I contemplate at dawn as the dazzling sun; That which is in truth always propitious: may That illumine our intellects, pervading them with the bliss of consciousness.*

In this *śloka* – which re-presents, with some modifications, the well-known Vedic *Gāyatrī* - Śaṅkara offers us an image which is singularly significant and rich with symbolic value: just as the sun, blazing from the sky above, illumines and empowers every form of earthly life and activity, so the *ātman*, though motionless in its own nature, pervades and substantiates the intellects of all beings and everything that exists.

4. *That which is single and which – in the states of waking, dream, and deep sleep – is [recognised as] absolute knowledge through the criterion of affirming and negating: That same am I, the supreme Support.*

5. *This [universe] is but a game produced by [relative] knowledge and ignorance (ajñāna), and as much knowledge as ignorance can be perceived in it. But once ignorance and [relative] knowledge have been transcended, then that which remains is absolute knowledge alone.*

The knowledge that we obtain from the senses and from reasoning, and so on, is undoubtedly of a relative order, inasmuch as it posits a subject (I) relative to an object (this) and it is dependent on the characteristics of these two elements and on the particular contingent situation and the dimensions of time, space, and causality in which it arises. Such knowledge, therefore, cannot lead to the foundation of Reality. We would say, then, that every form of knowledge has its own location and that nothing should be rejected *a priori*.

On the other hand, we cannot attribute to the relative/becoming that which pertains to the Absolute/Being, or project reality onto that which is fundamentally unreal.

Plato writes in the *Politéia*:

'It would indeed be a sufficient defence to maintain that one who loves knowledge must naturally reach out towards Being, not losing himself in the multiplicity of details which is an object of opinion, but going away straight along his path, unhesitatingly and without deviating from his love, until he has grasped the essential being of each particular object with that faculty of the soul which is intended to comprehend this reality; and it is intended for this purpose because that is its very nature.'[1]

[1] Plato, *Politéia*, VI, 490 b. Italics are ours.

6. *Whereas the body is extremely impure, the jīvātman is infinitely pure. [True] purification occurs when one has fully acknowledged, 'I am devoid of all relationship.'*

7. *The sage, having become [identical to] the pure ātman, plays, like a fish, for ever immersed in the ocean of bliss, because he has totally purified himself by bathing in the waters of immediate knowledge.*

Absolute knowledge requires no means because, we repeat, pure consciousness is self-present in every state, condition, modality, and entity. It is therefore *immediate*, all-inclusive, limitless, constant, and changeless. Absolute or metaphysical reality can be attained through knowledge of identity that is immediate, not mediated through the senses. Plato would say that the One-Good is reached through *nóesis* (νόησις), pure and immediate knowledge.

Vedānta embraces three levels of reality/truth (*satya*):

- *pāramārthika*: supra-sensible reality;
- *vyāvahārika*: empirical or phenomenal reality;
- *prātibhāsika*: purely imaginary reality.

8. *It is precisely in this way that the true act of purification is to be accomplished, by withdrawing from the rising and falling flow of the breath. This is how, when one allows the mind to be absorbed in the plenitude [of that which is, one becomes] like a jug [of water] immersed in the ocean.*

9. *When one successfully merges absorption with the projecting movement, then the mind becomes devoid*

of desires. One who has attained this state of unity is liberated. Of this there is no doubt.

10. *Everywhere, in the bodies of all living beings, the japa 'haṁsa' is repeated. Becoming conscious of this, one is freed from all bonds.*

Haṁsa, the sacred Swan which symbolises the Reality of the *ātman*, is present, by means of the *jīva*, in every living form of expression. The cycle of breath, in which are harmonised the rising currents (exhalation/withdrawal, *sa*) and the falling currents (inhalation/identification, *ham*) of the vital energy and the projecting tendency of the mind, is a silent way of uttering the *mantra* 'haṁ *sah*, which means 'I (the *jīva*) am That'.

11. *Just as the satisfaction of each of the senses can be achieved only through acquiring the respective object of satisfaction, so the ātman reveals itself only when the mind examines itself by means of itself.*

While the senses find satisfaction in their respective objects, the mind finds final appeasement only if it is resolved into its conscious substantiality. For this to happen, it is necessary to stop directing it towards objects, both outer and inner, and bring it back to itself. When the *manas* (the empirical mind) is resolved into the *buddhi* (the noetic mind), and the *buddhi* into pure reality, the *ātman* reveals itself.[1]

12. *Only someone who offers his whole mind as a sacrifice into the bright fire that is the ātman can be considered to be like the one who truly ac-*

---

[1] See Śaṅkara, *Vivekacūḍāmaṇi*, verse 369, op. cit.

complishes the Agnihotra[1], *whereas all others bear merely the name.*

The ritual act inherent in accomplishing a sacrifice is an outward symbol of an inner operation that is conscious and truly transforming. A sacrifice is not a sacrifice – that is, it does not make what is done sacred – unless the consciousness is transformed or the being's awareness goes beyond merely verbal expression.

13. *The body is said to be the temple of divinity, where the embodied soul is the divine Being devoid of stain. Worshipped fervently in all that exists, through the innermost experience [of the ātman], it shines by itself.*

14. *The study of the Scriptures [must lead], through the act of consciousness, to silence, while meditation must resolve itself into the object of meditation, that is, into the contemplation of Brahman. From these two factors there arises at once the conscious experience of total extinction.*

Silence is the synthesis of knowledge, the revelation of integrated totality, the essence of self-fulfilment, the expression of the Inexpressible. Conscious silence guides us to the *ātman*.

15. *'Of the past I have no memory; of the future I have no concern. Having become free from attachment and repulsion, I can experience here whatever befalls, good or bad.'*

[1] Vedic ritual sacrifice in homage to Agni.

16. *The sages call knowledge the absence of fear with regard to all forms of being. It is their conviction that absorption into inherent plenitude is the height of detachment.*

17. *One should assiduously practise hearing the Upaniṣads, reflection that is supported by logical examination, and continual exertion in yogic discipline: from all these there arises the conscious vision of the ātman.*

18. *The power of speech (śabda) is unimaginable. The immediate awareness [of the ātman] arises from speech alone, just as a man sunk in deep sleep is awakened just by [the utterance of] speech.*

The hearing of the Teaching, the consequent reflection upon the Teaching, and the continual practice of any yogic disciplines imparted by the Teacher to suit the nature of the neophyte, these constitute the working basis that will cause the conscious vision of the *ātman* to appear. The power of speech (*śabda*) – such as the *mantra so'ham*, or *'haṁ saḥ* (I am That), spoken by the reflection (*jīva*) of embodied consciousness and not by its mind – awakens the consciousness and thus leads to the revelation of the *ātman*, just as a man is awakened from a deep sleep when his name is uttered.

In *sūtra* 70 of his *Vivekacūḍāmaṇi* Śaṅkara asserts:

'Then comes the "hearing" of the teaching, reflection (*mananam*) on what has been heard, and a long period of meditation on Truth. After this practice, the aspirant becomes a *muni*.'

19. *Pure knowledge is revealed through discrimination between ātman and anātman. The disciple, awakened by the teacher, transcends the mere word 'Brahman'.*

20. *You are not the body, you are not the senses, you are not the vital energy, you are not the mind, and you are not the intellect, just as you are not [something external like] a pot, given that this is subject to change and destruction and is an object of perception.*

21. *That which is unique and perfectly pure, That which is absolute knowledge, devoid of qualifications and shadows, That which is the highest bliss and the supreme state, That which is without a second: 'That you are' (tat tvam asi).*

22. *Established before the beginning and after the end of speech, but eternally present even in the middle, being the witness, That itself you are. Therefore dispel the error [of the mind] by the mind itself!*

Identity with the *ātman* is always real and present: it is only a question of being conscious of it. The direction 'You are That' – which comprises the whole teaching of *advaita* – does not concern the empirical ego, corporeity, and so on, but is addressed to the reflection of embodied consciousness, to the *heart* of the being, that it may awaken to its own true nature.

If the erroneous interpretation of our existence is the result of superimposition by the mind (*manas*), all that needs to be done is to remove this image by means of the mind itself (*buddhi*).

23. *There is identity between the individual gross body and the universe as a whole, between the individual mind and the universal mind. There is identity between individual ignorance (ajñāna) and universal māyā, and between the innermost self-awareness [of the jīva] and the fullness [of consciousness of the ātman].*

24. *Just as the appearance of a snake is imagined in the rope, so the illusion of the birth of the world [is projected] upon Viṣṇu, who is essentially pure consciousness and whose intrinsic nature is identical to the ātman/Brahman.*

25. *The sages know both the jīva and the Lord [Brahmā] in their literal meaning, on account of logic, and in their implicit meaning on account of Sāṁkhya and Yoga. But it is exclusively on account of Vedānta that they can recognise their perfect identity.*

26. *Those two parts [in the statement 'You are That'] which indicate the causal connection in the relationship between the jīva and the Lord have to be set aside. On the other hand, the implicit meanings of the two terms ['You' and 'That'] – that is, those two parts which indicate the jīva and the ātman/Brahman, which are of the same nature – must not be set aside.*

27. *How is it possible for the knowledge to be expressed in the Scriptures pertaining to ritual action? With logic, indeed, no conclusion is reached. Sāṁkhya and Yoga do not go beyond duality, while*

the grammarians are intent solely on establishing the literal meanings of the words.

28. *All the others, then, who are far from having knowledge as their objective, are weak-minded. The knowledge which is expressed by Vedānta and is unique shines by itself on account of the direct experience born from intuiting the ātman.*

The *ātman* shines by itself in every being. Everyone is conscious of being, even if there is identification with that which is not; yet the *ātman* remains ever identical to itself and undergoes no decline, no change, no destruction.

29. *'I' and 'mine' constitute [the cause] of bondage. 'I [am] not' and '[it is] not mine', [on the other hand, are the cause of] liberation. However, both bondage and liberation exist in relation to attributes, and attributes exist only in relation to the forms of nature (prakṛti).*

30. *A single Intelligence shines forever, without any impurity, in all the states. Those whose intellect is darkened do not know their own authentic nature, which is that of absolute Support/Foundation.*

31. *One who acknowledges that 'I am that knowledge which is the witness of all the contents of thought and is the source of existence in all the worlds' is liberated. Of this there is no doubt.*

This *śloka* alone – if contemplated and comprehended by the consciousness – is capable of giving wings to someone who, duly qualified, yearns to take flight towards unchanging truth. The knowledge that is spoken of represents the principial archetype from which are derived all the thoughts, concepts, and so on that the mind is able to contrive.

The verses that follow explain how the supreme knowledge reveals itself in different ways and how, by means of these ways, it is always possible to return to the supreme knowledge.

> 32. *The knower, the means of knowledge, the known, as well as the knowledge of the object: all these shine by the light of That [alone]. But what is the means for realising the direct knowledge of That?*

> 33. *The object is made manifest when, through the effect [of conscious perception], the modification [of the mind] assumes the form of the object itself. But one who knows the knowledge [of the object], he alone possesses, of himself, the awareness of the supreme object (the ātman).*

> 34. *How could one verify [for oneself] a [conscious] permeation of the effect [of perception], when pervasiveness in relation to modifications can exist solely on account of the ātman, which is pure [noetic] knowledge? By its own nature this knowledge is self-luminous and is constantly present, for it is ever complete.*

The object of knowledge is such if there is a principial knowledge which permeates the perceived image of the object, the act of perceiving, and the perceiving subject. These three, we would say, are not self-luminous or self-existent, but they constitute accidental factors with respect to principial knowledge, like superimpositions with respect to their foundation.

35. *While the modifications change from one object to the next, that which has no support and assumes no form is known as the condition which transcends the mind.*

36. *When the mind (citta) is freed from the syllable 'ta', it will be immediately recognised as nothing but pure knowledge/cit. The syllable 'ta' thus represents the superimposition of objects, just like the colour of the hibiscus on transparent glass.*

If a hibiscus flower is placed near a glass tumbler, the tumbler's transparency seems to be modified and assume the flower's red colour. However, the purity of the glass has not been modified and the presence of the colour is due solely to the object which has been placed near it. In other words, something that is colourless, pure, and transparent can take on any colouring while remaining ever identical to itself or, equally, the transparency of the glass is a property which cannot undergo change because it is the *nature* of the glass. The same may be said of the *ātman*: although ever pure, limitless, devoid of all objectivity, and without a second, the *ātman* seems to manifest qualities and conditions which do not reflect its nature but which are superimposed upon it, by *māyā*, according to circumstances.

37. *Transcending all that has the nature of object, knowledge perdures. Having resolved the [distinction which forms the] triad [of the subject, means, and object of knowledge], one attains the Brahman.*

38. *All this [universe] has the nature [of an ideation] of the [universal] mind, and mind has the nature of knowledge, that is, of pure Essence. It has been*

revealed that ajñāna is the erroneous condition, while authentic knowledge is the true state of supreme Reality.

39. Both ignorance and false knowledge answer to the name of māyā. Acknowledge that the Lord (Īśvara) is he who exercises dominion over māyā and that That which transcends māyā is the attributeless [Brahman].

Īśvara represents the first qualification – in relation to the present manifestation – of the infinite possibilities in the heart of the *Brahman* and, in relation to the *Brahman*, stands as the One in relation to the metaphysical Zero. This is why the Reality which we must reach is represented by the *Brahman*, which alone is absolutely real.

'Here in the beginning there was absolutely nothing. This was enveloped only by Death, by Hunger. Hunger is indeed death. Death then conceived the mind by thinking, "May I have a mind". Praying thus, it began to move'[1], and this is how the manifestation began.

40. In the sky of absolute intelligence, permeated by the fullness of pure Being, māyā is like a cloud, mind is the lightning flash, and the notion of being an 'ego' is the rumble of thunder, while the overshadowing that comes from it is the torrential rain.

41. In this darkness caused by confusion (moha), the divinity pours down the rain [of karma/dharma] as in a game. Knowledge alone can be the wind that disperses the rain clouds.

---

[1] *Bṛhadāraṇyaka Upaniṣad*, I, II, 1.

42. *The appearance of the seer and the seen constitutes [ordinary or relative] knowledge, while the total emptiness of the knowable corresponds to authentic knowledge. Brahman is One alone, without a second. Indeed, no multiplicity exists in the One.*

43. *This [form of] knowledge which is reduced to cognition of the field and the knower of the field is also called knowledge, but perfect knowledge is, in truth, that which sanctions the identity of the two, that is, of the knower of the field with the supreme ātman.*

44. *The knowledge which is born from the Scriptures is indirect, while authentic knowledge comes only from direct awareness of the ātman, knowledge which is absolutely devoid of the twofold superimposition inherent in the ātman [as jīva] and in the Brahman [as Īśvara].*

45. *Individual knowledge has the term 'You' as its object. Universal knowledge is concerned with 'That'. But true knowledge, which resolves both individual knowledge and universal knowledge, is that which reveals the identity of the two terms.*

46. *The wise, in truth, consider knowledge to be discrimination between ātman and anātman, and ignorance to be that which generally is a different [knowledge]. [On the other hand, the knowledge which reveals that] the world is [dependent on] That is called authentic knowledge.*

47. *That [knowledge] which, by the criterion of concordance and discordance, reveals the unity of*

everything is called the knowledge that arises from modifications. But, in truth, that which has the nature of pure consciousness, that alone is authentic knowledge.

48. *The lower knowledge dispels ignorance, while authentic knowledge substantiates both [knowledge and ignorance]. That which is the Knowledge of knowledge is founded on That, the pure Being which is Brahman, whose very nature it is.*

49. *It is said that one who is the subject of experience corresponds to the guṇa of sattva, which is pure. The experience, which represents the means, is said to correspond to rajas. The object of experience corresponds, for its part, to tamas. The ātman is that which illumines these three.*

50. *He who is engaged in the study [of the texts that treat] of the Brahman, who always displays conduct conformable to the Brahman, and who recognises that everything is Brahman, he is said to be a [true] brahmacārin.*

The first stage of life – that of the student (*brahmacārin*) is not limited to learning the Scriptures but is fulfilled by their effective implementation. To observe a way of behaviour that is inherent in the *Brahman* means not just respecting obligations and prohibitions but also acting, thinking, feeling, living – in a word, *being* – in a way conformable to the awareness of one's own nature as *Brahman*.

51. *He who dwells at the centre of the qualities is said to be a gṛhastha, inasmuch as his body alone*

constitutes his dwelling. As a true sage, he acknowledges, 'I am not the agent. Actions are performed by the qualities [in me].'[1]

This verse defines the stage of life that corresponds to the condition of the householder. A *gṛhastha* may be said to be one who, considering his own body as a temporary garment and a mere dwelling-place, has freed himself from it and has become aware of the fact that the subject of his own actions is not he himself but the unresolved *guṇas* which are finding expression through his psychosomatic vehicle. In this act of consciousness he has placed himself, as the verse says, 'at the centre of the qualities/*guṇas*', that is, at that point of equidistance and equilibrium from which alone he can recognise their true nature in such a way that he is not overwhelmed by them.

52. *What further austerity can ever be prescribed for one whose discipline is substantiated by knowledge? In truth one who has made himself indifferent to pleasure and pain is called a vānaprastha.*

The third stage – that of withdrawal from the world (*vānaprastha*) – entails not only a physical withdrawal (although this is certainly useful and sometimes even necessary) but also, and most importantly, an inner recollection of a purely conscious nature. The true *vānaprastha* is not someone who merely mortifies his own body and subjects himself to austerities of various kinds by retiring to live at the margins of the world, but someone who, through conscious discrimination, has effected total detachment from the worldly life.

---

[1] See *Bhagavadgītā*, III, 28, op. cit.

53. *[Authentic] renunciation is, in truth, detachment from one's own body and not the action of donning the ochre robe. He is truly a great soul (that is, a saṁnyāsin) who acknowledges, 'I am not the body.' This is the unequivocal sign of knowledge.*

When all the stages of life have been experienced, the mature being devotes himself spontaneously to renunciation, because from that time onwards renunciation becomes his natural condition. Renunciation, when lived consciously, is no longer a deliberate act with an individual nature, but a state of impersonal consciousness, the fruit of *awakening* to one's own Being, a state in which all possibility of identification has vanished. Furthermore, renunciation concerns the psychological sphere, so that one obtains what the *Bhagavadgītā* describes as action that is free from the conditioning of the ego (*ahaṁkāra*) and therefore free from the fruits.

54. *The sages who have the constancy to traverse this path that leads to the uncovering of Being will be liberated at once. Of this there is no doubt.*

The message of *advaita* has immediacy as its essence: You *are* the *ātman*. You are already that single Consciousness which is of itself and knows the Essence of everything, and you yourself are therefore the Infinite, *That* beyond which no real being exists. Nothing else is necessary, except to reveal this present and ever-existent Reality. The whole path can be summarised in a few essential steps. Remember your own Essence and rediscover yourself in *Brahman*, the foundation of all that exists.

THE SONG OF THE KNOWLEDGE OF BRAHMAN

brahmajñānavalī

In this Hymn, Śaṅkara offers the reader's consciousness some *notes* or *seeds* of meditation to absorb, contemplate, and put into practice in his daily life. When the current of perception, the typical flow of thought, and even the potentiality inherent in the subconscious items have been put under conscious control – in other words, when one has attained within oneself a stable condition of silent recollection – then it is appropriate to focus the concentration upon oneself as the self-existent *jīva*, thereby revealing one's identity with *Brahman*. To meditate on a *sūtra*, a word, or a symbol entails not only a steady focus of the attention upon it but also the need to resonate at the level of consciousness the note that is represented, even to the point of *assimilating* it in one's consciousness.

Let us remember that if the practice of repetition is adopted with clarity of mind, and if one avoids falling into a *routine*, it is capable of impressing upon the structure of the mind a *rhythm* that is steadying, penetrating, transforming, and resolving. Thus the declaration which ends each verse – 'I, I myself, am the Immutable' – when contemplated by the consciousness, leads to the instant transcendence of all difference in time, space, and causality, and of all formal distinction created by the mind.

1. *No ties have I (asaṅgo 'ham), no ties have I, no ties have I – over and over again. I am That, whose nature is being/intelligence/bliss (sat/cit/ānanda). I, I myself am the Immutable (avyaya).*

Ultimate Truth has no relationship with anything (*aja*), whereas everything must be referred to it. Even *māyā* draws from the *ātman* its own *raison d'être*, for the *ātman* is its foundation.

2. *I am eternal, pure, totally free, and without attributes. I am Imperishable. I am infinite Being permeated by fullness. I, I myself, am the Immutable.*

3. *I am beyond time and impurity, beyond contingency and destruction. My nature is fullness supreme. I, I myself, am the Immutable.*

According to Plato, time is born 'together with the sky' (*Timaeus*, 38a), which means that time is not prior, but subsequent, to the generation/manifestation of the cosmos. Time is nothing but the 'moving image of the Unmoving' (*Timaeus*, 37e).

Generation is contingency and, because it is not a self-sufficient reality, it must have something else as *its raison d'être*.

4. *My essence is pure intelligence, and I am fully content to be the ātman. I am all-pervading fullness, beyond all distinctions. I, I myself, am the Immutable.*

5. *I am the innermost intelligence. I am the Supreme, at peace and beyond the universal form. My nature is constant fullness. I, I myself, am the Immutable.*

Even when we think that we are unconscious, we are still conscious. In fact, on awakening we say that we have been unconscious. We are conscious of the waking state and the dream state, and we are also conscious of not having dreamt. We are indebted to *Vedānta* for highlighting the factor of consciousness as 'presence' and as the metaphysical foundation of the being and of Being.

6. *I am the supreme ātman, which transcends all [relative] truths. I am the supreme Śiva, which is beyond the centre. I am the Light which is beyond māyā. I, I myself, am the Immutable.*

The Reality that is without a second cannot be an object of proof or knowledge, because this would presuppose a subject/object relationship, and because Reality has the nature of the absolute witness.

This is what Plotinus says:

> 'You must also think of it [the One] as infinite, not because it is unending in size or number, but because its power is unlimited. Indeed, if you think of it as Intelligence or God, it is more than that. If you embrace it in unity with your thought, It exceeds all that your thought can conceive, because It is within itself and of itself, devoid of all accidents.'[1]

7. *Independent of everything, I transcend the nature of multiplicity. I am formless, indissoluble intelli-*

[1] Plotinus, *Enneads*, VI, 9, 6.

gence. My nature is the essence of pure fullness. I, I myself, am the Immutable.

The *ātman*/unity is infinite, not because it expresses quantity or size, but because it has no limit, no quality, and no form. Moreover, the One has no need of a 'second' because, according to Plotinus, 'the Principle has no need of the things which come after It, for the principle of everything has no need of this everything.'[1]

This is also made clear in the following *śloka*.

8. *In truth, I am not in the least concerned with māyā or with any of its effects, such as the body. My true essence is that of self-splendour. I, I myself, am the Immutable.*

9. *I am fully independent of the three guṇas. I am the witness even of Brahmā and the other [gods]. My nature is infinite Fullness/Bliss. I, I myself, am the Immutable.*

The *guṇas* are expressions of *qualities*, and so the *ātman* is beyond all the possible qualities which form can express (that is, the *ātman* is *nirguṇa*). Thus the metaphysical One is beyond all number, size, and quality that can be manifested by these factors. According to Plato, too, the One-One, or the One-Good, is beyond Being, beyond the World of Ideas, and therefore beyond quality/quantity, even of a principial order.

10. *I am the true inner Ordainer, for I am constantly present and all-pervading. I am the witness of all things. I, I myself, am the Immutable.*

---

[1] *Ibid.*

'This is the Lord of All (*sarveśvara*), the Omniscient, the inner Ordainer ... the Source of everything, from which all that exists arises and into which it is re-absorbed.'[1]

11. *am the witness of [the experience that is expressed by means of] the pairs of opposites. I am unmoving and everlasting. I am the witness of the whole. I, I myself, am the Immutable.*

12. *I am the distinctionless unity of pure knowledge (prajñāna), and I am also the homogeneous unity (ghana) of distinctive knowledge (vijñāna). I am not a doer (akartāham) or an enjoyer. I, I myself, am the Immutable.*

13. *My nature is the absence of supports, while I myself am the support of all. In my being every desire is extinguished. I, I myself, am the Immutable.*

14. *I am completely devoid of the threefold affliction and utterly distinct from the three bodies. I am the witness of the three states. I, I myself, am the Immutable.*

The threefold affliction is that which comes from the presence of the three *guṇas*/qualities. The three levels of being – causal, subtle, and gross – form part of the manifestation, the first one without form and the other two with form, and therefore come forth from qualification/*prakṛti*; the *ātman* is beyond the three states of Being/*Īśvara*, because it is *nirguṇa* and *akartṛ*.

---

[1] *Māṇḍūkya Upaniṣad*, VI.

15. There are only two entities: the Seer (dṛg) and the seen, and these are mutually opposed by their nature. The Seer is Brahman, whereas the seen is māyā. This is what all the Upaniṣads declare.

16. 'I am the Seer.' One who has recognised this and has repeatedly discriminated in this way is undoubtedly a sage and will attain liberation. This is the affirmation of Vedānta.

17. Pots, cups, and other objects: all these are but clay alone. The whole world, likewise, has nothing [to support it] but Brahmā (Īśvara). This is the affirmation of Vedānta.

The multiplicity of forms in the manifestation has a single matrix as its immediate cause: *prakṛti* (the Platonic χώρα), which is an aspect of the polarity of *puruṣa/prakṛti* (essence and substance), and this primordial polarity has its foundation in the *nirguṇa Brahman* (the metaphysical One-One of Plato). The vision of *Vedānta* is not pantheistic, idealistic, or nihilist, and nor is that of Parmenides, Plato, or Plotinus, for they are all moulded in the pure Tradition.

18. Brahman is reality; the world is appearance/phenomenon (mithyā). The jīva is none other than Brahman itself. That by which this can be learnt is [to be considered as] the true Scripture. This is the affirmation of Vedānta.

This single verse synthesises the entire teaching of *Vedānta* and the *sādhanā* that can lead to its effective realisation. It should be deeply contemplated and kept in mind in all circumstances. If That is real, and this, the second, is mere appearance/phenomenon, being contingent, then the act of becoming aware of one's own identity with That is a simple but astonishing proof.

> *19. I am the light within. I am the light without. I am light in the deepest essence and beyond the supreme [saguṇa Brahmā]. I am the Light of lights, self-shining light. I am the light of the ātman. I myself am Śiva!*

Referring to the 'Light of lights', Śaṅkara says in another of his works:

> 'What is the light for you? For me it is the sun during the day, and it is the light of a lamp and similar objects during the night.
> Yes, but tell me, then, what is that light by means of which you can see the sun and the lamp? It is the eye. And when the eye is closed or unable to see, what is it then? It is the mind. And what is the light by means of which you can see the mind? In this case it is my self-consciousness (*tatra aham*)! Then you yourself are the supreme Light (*paramakaṁ jyotis*)! Yes, Lord, I am That (*tad asmi prabho*)!'[1]

When every possibility has been pervaded by knowledge, then the Infinite is re-discovered. There is a single Consciousness that shines in every condition and within every being. By traversing this pathway of knowledge, one is resolved once and for all into that unlimited and unmodified consciousness which is the source and basis of all knowledge and existence, that Essence without a second which is the very nature of self-existent eternity, free from all attributes whatsoever.

---

[1] *Śataślokī* ('A hundred verses'), 95.

I AM ŚIVA, I AM ŚIVA

Śivo 'ham Śivo 'ham

In relation to form/entity, Śiva represents the principle which destroys, that is, 'transforms', in the sense of that which resolves the formal condition and leads beyond the limitations of form. Śiva is therefore the 'Terrifying one' (*bhairava*) for the being that is bound to its own particular expression; but Śiva is also the Resolver inasmuch as he frees the spiritually mature consciousness from the bondage of *saṁsāra* and for the same reason he is the Benevolent (*śambhu*) or the Propitious (*śaṅkara*) because he bestows on the individualised being (*kāma/manas/ahaṁkāra*) emancipation from the world of becoming and forms.

> 'By realising Śiva, like the cream [which surfaces] on top of the clarified butter [when it is melted], extremely subtle and deeply hidden in all beings; by realising the single *Deva* which embraces totality, one is freed from all bonds.'[1]

This short composition is also known by the name of *Nirvaṇaṣaṭkam* ('Six verses on *nirvaṇa*') because, once the witness has been discriminated from the superimpositions and one's own nature as Śiva has been realised, one sinks into the bliss of *nirvāṇa*, in which the insubstantial phenomenon of *saṁsāra* has disappeared into the clarity of non-dual Reality.

---

[1] *Śvetāśvatara Upaniṣad*, IV, 16.

The affirmation of 'I am Śiva' (*śivo 'ham*), which is presented by consciousness, does not apply, however, to the empirical ego, which is a product of the mind, but to the *jīva*. It is a potent *mantra*/seed that is capable of awakening in us the awareness of our real immortal essence.

1. *I am not the mind, not the intellect, not the sense of 'I', not the citta, not the sense of hearing, tasting, smelling, seeing. I am not space, earth, fire, air. I am consciousness/intelligence and the essence of fullness. I am Śiva, I am Śiva!*

2. *Again, I am not the prāṇa, and I do not know myself as the five vital breaths or the seven constituent elements or the five sheaths. I am not the organ of speech or the hands or feet. I am not the organ of generation or the organ of excretion. I am consciousness/intelligence and the essence of fullness. I am Śiva, I am Śiva!*

3. *In me there is no place for aversion, pleasure, greed, delusion; no place for pride or envy; no place for duties, desires, or aims to pursue; no place even for liberation. I am consciousness/intelligence and the essence of bliss. I am Śiva, I am Śiva!*

4. *I am not virtue, not vice, not pleasure, not pain, not mantra, not pilgrimage. I am not the Vedas, not the sacrificial rite, not the object of enjoyment, and not, in truth, the enjoyer or the act of enjoying. I am consciousness/intelligence and the essence of fullness. I am Śiva, I am Śiva!*

5. *In me there is no place for fear, death, or caste-distinction. Thus I have no father, no mother, and no birth. I have no family, no friends, no teacher, and*

no disciple. I am consciousness/intelligence and the essence of fullness. I am Śiva, I am Śiva!

6. *I am without modifications, without name, without form. I am the expression of omnipotence and all-pervasiveness. Being beyond the senses, I am not identified even with liberation. I am consciousness/ intelligence and the essence of fullness. I am Śiva, I am Śiva!*

QUINTUPLICATION

pañcīkaraṇa

The *Pañcīkaraṇa* is a synthetic composition which examines the states of Being spoken of in the *Māṇḍūkya Upaniṣad*, in relation to which it may be considered to be a valid help and complement.[1]

It consists of only seven verses or *śloka*s, in which are condensed both the expositional aspect or philosophical/teaching aspect – that is, the correspondence between the letters which constitute the syllable *Om* and the states of consciousness or planes of existence – and the eminently realisative aspect, by which is meant the realisation of the non-dual *Brahman* by means of meditating on the syllable *Om*.

The work is furnished with a full commentary (*vārttika*) in verses (*śloka*s), which is a work in its own right, composed by Śrī Sureśvara, one of Śaṅkara's immediate disciples. This commentary amplifies the exposition given in the *Pañcīkaraṇa* and also highlights the threefold aspect which Reality seems to assume when it is darkened by the veil of *māyā* by means of the distinction between the universal sphere (the sphere of principles), the intermediate sphere that is elemental/objective, and the strictly individual sphere.

The two works, taken together, form a *prakaraṇa* or 'specific treatise' that is appended to the traditional liter-

[1] See Gauḍapāda, *Māṇḍūkyakārikā*, I-XII. Translation from the Sanskrit and commentary by Raphael. Aurea Vidyā, New York.

ature. The theme is the fundamental topic of *Advaita*: the supreme Reality is Non-duality, but the being is conditioned by duality because it does not know its true nature; since ignorance (*avidyā*) is the cause of bondage, liberation can be attained only through knowledge.

It is therefore knowledge (*jñāna*) that represents the means but also – and most importantly – the end, for, as the *Upaniṣad* puts it, '*satyaṁ jñānamanantaṁ brahma*: *Brahman* is truth, knowledge, infiniteness.'[1]

The term *pañcīkaraṇa* (literally, 'quintuplication') refers generally to the process by which the single, unmanifest, and transcendent Reality appears qualified and manifest in the empirical universe, which is made up of five gross elements. To become conscious of this Reality, therefore, the reverse process has to be implemented – *reintegration* (*yoga*), *extinction* or solution (*nirvāṇa*) – taking indefinite multiplicity back to the principial and undivided whole and then resolving this whole into the non-dual Infinite.

In the *Pañcīkaraṇavārttika* of Sureśvara we can find phases or stages of a realisative path: first and foremost, an interpretative analysis of the manifestation in elemental terms; then the acknowledgement of the projecting activity of the mind in relation to its scissure into the subject/object of individual experience; the threefold manifestation of *Brahman* in the universal/principial sphere, the elemental/intermediate sphere and the individual sphere; the transcending of the gross, subtle, and causal planes, which gives rise to the identification of the microcosmic aspect (*jīva*) with the macrocosmic aspect (*Īśvara*); and finally the total solution of the qualified principial unity into the non-dual and unqualified Absolute (*Brahman*), effecting the supreme *Identity here and now*.

---

[1] *Taittirīya Upaniṣad*, II, I, 3.

1. *Om. The whole composition constituted by the five gross elements – that is, the quintuplicated elements – and their derivatives is defined as Virāṭ. It forms the gross body of the ātman (jīvātman). The waking state is that in which – by means of the organs of perception, that is, the senses – one experiences gross objects. When the ātmā is identified with these two [the gross body and the waking state] it is called viśva. These three [the gross body, the waking state, and viśva], when taken together, constitute that which is expressed by the letter 'A' [of the syllable Aum or Om].*

This verse defines the significance of the first measure (*mātrā*) of the syllable *Om*. The individual gross body (*viśva*) is contained in the universal body (*Virāṭ*). The waking state (*jāgrat*) corresponds to empirical or sensory knowledge; *viśva* thus points to knowledge which is reflected, indirect, and mediated by the senses of perception and which characterises the ordinary state of awareness. *Viśva* therefore indicates the out-turning of consciousness into objective duality or into the unlimited possibility of expression of a dual relationship between an empirical subject/ego and the totality of gross objects.

With regard to 'quintuplication', see verses 7-11 in the *Pañcīkaraṇavārttika*.

2. *Prior to the process of quintuplication, the five gross elements, together with their derived combinations, the gross physical body, and the subtle body – which is composed of seventeen parts, namely, the*

five vital breaths, the ten sensory organs (five of perception and five of action), the empirical mind, and the pure intellect – all these are defined as Hiraṇyagarbha, which constitutes the subtle body of the ātmā.

3. *When the sensory functions are quiescent, the modifications of the mind, which are caused by the impressions of objects perceived in the waking state, form what is called the dream state. When the ātmā is associated with these two [the subtle body and the dream state], it is known as taijasa. These three [the subtle body, the dream state, and taijasa], considered together, constitute what is expressed by the letter 'U'.*

4. *Connected with the reflection [of consciousness, that is, the jīva], ignorance, being associated with the ātmā and being the cause of the two bodies [gross and subtle], is known as the Undifferentiated. It constitutes the causal body of the ātmā. This ignorance is neither real nor unreal, and is not simultaneously real and unreal. It is neither different nor same, and it is not different and same together with respect to something (the ātman). Again, it is neither simple nor composite, but is something that can be removed only on the conscious realisation of the identity between ātman and Brahman.*

5. *When all the contents of the mind [in the waking and dream states] are dissolved and the intellect has sunk into its causal condition, there is the state of deep sleep. When the ātmā is associated with these two [the causal body and deep sleep], it is called prājña. These three [the causal body, deep*

sleep, and prājña], considered together, constitute what is expressed by the letter 'M'.

Although the *jīva* originates from the causal plane, it manifests only at the level of intellect (*buddhi*), because undifferentiated unity cannot contain emerging modifications except potentially or virtually.

While the subtle and gross levels, or the states corresponding to dream and waking, are in relationship with causes and effects, and are themselves effects that have occurred, the Undifferentiated (*avyākṛta*), which corresponds to the causal plane (*Īśvara*) or deep sleep, represents the sole cause.

6. *The letter 'A' must be resolved into the letter 'U', the letter 'U' into the letter 'M', and the letter 'M' into the whole syllable 'Om'; finally the syllable 'Om' must be resolved into the state of 'I'. 'I am the ātman, the Absolute, the witness whose nature is pure consciousness. I am not avidyā and I am not identified with its effects, but I am Brahman, eternal, pure, awake, free, the self-existent Reality. I am supreme fullness, the One without a second, the innermost, ever-present wisdom.' Thus, to remain in this state [of identity] without any trace of differentiation constitutes samādhi.*

This verse summarises the resolutive process of the consciousness, a process which is directed to the realisation of the Non-duality of the *ātman* and also offers important meditation seeds which may give a stimulus, at the right time, for conscious self-identification.

The term 'I' (*aham*), which we meet in the verse, does not refer, of course, to common empirical subjectivity or to that ego (*ahaṁkāra*) which, in normal conditions, manifests in the waking or dream states, and to which are ascribed the manifold activities and experiences. The empirical ego is the product of a *karma* or past action and in its turn creates new *karma*, being the subject and enjoyer of the action.

7. *'You are That', 'I am Brahman', 'Brahman is pure knowledge', 'This ātman is Brahman', and similar statements are found in the Śruti [and they declare one's own identity with Brahman]. This is what constitutes the short work entitled 'Quintuplication'.*

Here ends 'Quintuplication',
a composition by Śrī Śaṅkarācārya

COMMENTARY TO 'QUINTUPLICATION'

pañcīkaraṇavārttika of Sureśvara

1. *The syllable 'Om' is the essence of all the Vedas. It reveals the supreme Reality. For those who yearn for liberation, a method is now being expounded for the solution of the mind [into Reality] by means of this syllable.*

2. *The supreme Brahman, eternally free and immutable, is absolute, self-existent unity. In relation to māyā, which is superimposed upon it, the Brahman constitutes the unqualified substratum [of all].*

Māyā expresses its twofold power of veiling and projecting (*āvaraṇaśakti* and *vikṣepaśakti*) through universal mind (*Mahat*), in whose heart the image of the world is manifested, and through individualised egoic mind (*manas*), which is an 'inert mass'. Thus it is necessary to resolve the mind into the *buddhi*, which is the direct vehicle of the *jīva*.

3. *From That [the principial cause, by means of māyā] arises space/ākāśa, which is characterised by the quality of sound. From space arises the element of air, which has the quality of touch. From air comes the element of light/fire, which has the quality of colour.*

4. *From fire issues the element of water, endowed with the quality of taste; and, finally, from water comes the element of earth, which has the quality of fragrance. This is how space is characterised by the single quality of sound; air by the qualities of sound and touch;*

5-6. *light/fire, by the three qualities of sound, touch, and form/colour; water by the four qualities of sound, touch, colour and taste; lastly, the earth, by the five qualities sound, touch, colour, taste, and fragrance. From these [subtle elements] is constituted that limitless and all-pervading entity known as Sūtra (Hiraṇyagarbha).*

According to *Vedānta*, from the qualified *Brahman* there manifests, by means of polarisation, substance/*prakṛti*, with its three principal attributes (*guṇas*) which correspond to the generic qualities of balance, activity, and inertia (*sattva*, *rajas*, *tamas*); then from these, through a process of combination, emerge the subtle elements.

For greater clarity, see the diagram on page 177.

7. *Then from the subtle elements come the five gross elements, which in turn form what is called Virāj (the empirical universe). These are the elements which – after the process of quintuplication – are known by the sages as the gross elements.*

8. *[The process of quintuplication may be described as follows:] each subtle element, starting from the element of earth, is divided into two equal parts. Then, for each element, one of these two parts is taken and is further subdivided into four equal parts.*

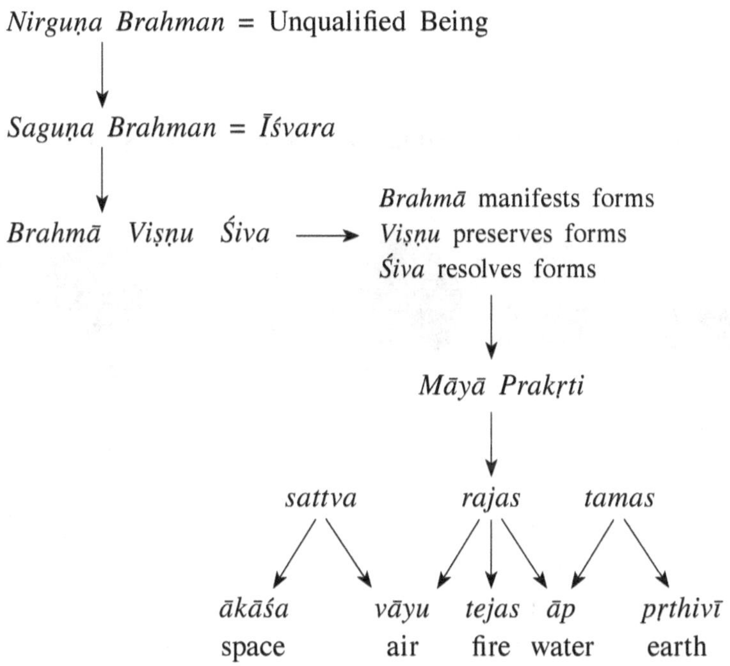

9. *Then, following the right sequence [of the formation of the elements], each of these four parts is taken [and combined with one part taken from each of the other elements]. This is how, in every element, for example, space, there are five parts:*

10. *[apart from the half that is constituted by space itself] there are the four parts coming from the other elements, such as air. This is the process of quintuplication, which the knowers of Reality have taught us.*

11. *The gross elements, therefore, are those that have been quintuplicated. The result of their commingling constitutes the empirical universe, which*

represents the gross vehicle for the ātman, which of itself is formless.

Here is a visual representation of the process of quintuplication:

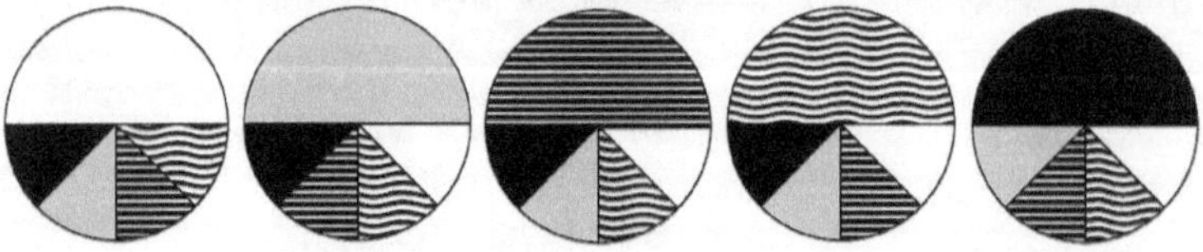

Space (*ākāśa*) Air (*vāyu*) Fire (*tejas*) Water (*āp*) Earth (*pṛthivī*)

With the formation of the gross elements we have the constitution, or condensation, of the coarse/physical plane, and hence the sphere of 'nature' in its entirety.

While *Hiraṇyagarbha*, or *Sūtra*, represents the totality of the manifestation at the subtle plane, *Virāj* is the totality of the manifestation at the gross/physical plane.

Just as the unique substance of water – which is clearly ever identical to itself – may appear in different states, so the principial causal body appears in many ways (*nāma-rūpa*) to the eye of the individualised being. Ice, steam, and so on are nothing but the qualities manifested by water, and it is through these qualities that water expresses its specific possibilities within relative phenomena. In the same way, the various planes of existence are nothing but vehicles or bodies for the *jīvātman*.

The gross elements are the result of the combination/precipitation of the subtle elements, with respect to which they exhibit a lower degree of freedom. The threefold variety of the principial attributes, or *guṇas*, can also be understood as a 'vertical' sequence, whereby the causal plane corresponds to *sattva* (unity), the subtle plane to *rajas*, and the physical plane to the quality of *tamas*.

12. The sphere of principles/divinities, the individual sphere, and the sphere of the elements: it is in this triple way that the unity of Īśvara appears, being differentiated by the power of illusion (māyā), but not so in reality.

On account of *māyā* a triple distinction seems to traverse the planes of being.

The attributes of universal Being give way to the principles that constitute the divine sphere (*adhidaivata*). Their objectifications are the elements/forms of the objective sphere (*adhibhūta*), and these, finally, are the objects of knowledge for the individual subjective sphere (*adhyātma*).

13. Empirical knowledge (vijñānam) arises from the sensory organs, which are supported, in their function of perception, by their respective principles. Thus the knowledge that it is inherent in objects such as sound is defined as the waking state.

14. In this case (the waking state) the faculty of hearing is said to belong to the individual sphere, the object of hearing – which consists of sound – to the elemental sphere, and the element of space to the sphere of principles.

15. The faculty of touch is said to belong to the individual sphere, the object of touch – which is characterised by tangibility – to the elemental sphere, and the element of air to the sphere of principles.

16. The faculty of sight is said to belong to the individual sphere, the object of sight – which is characterised by form – to the elemental sphere, and the sun – the source of light – to the sphere of principles.

17. *The faculty of taste belongs to the individual sphere, the object of taste – which is substantiated by the quality of the taste – to the elemental sphere, and the god Varuṇa – who presides over the function of taste – to the sphere of principles.*

18. *The faculty of smell is said to belong to the individual sphere, the object of smell – endowed with the quality of fragrance – to the elemental sphere, while the goddess Earth is said, in this context, to represent the sphere of principles.*

19. *The organ of speech is said to belong to the individual sphere, the object of utterance – which is substantiated by sound – to the elemental sphere, while the god Agni [who presides over this function] belongs to the sphere of principles.*

20. *The hands [as the organs of grasping] are said to belong to the individual sphere, the object of grasping to the elemental sphere, while Indra [who presides over this function] represents the sphere of principles.*

21. *The organ of movement is said to belong to the individual sphere, the object of movement to the elemental sphere, while Viṣṇu [who presides over this function] represents here the sphere of principles.*

22. *The organ of excretion belongs to the individual sphere, the substances that are excreted belong to the elemental sphere, while the god Mṛtyu [who*

presides over this function] represents the sphere of principles.

23. *The organ of reproduction belongs to the individual sphere, the inducements to pleasure in the corresponding function – for example, women – belong to the elemental sphere, while the god Prajāpati [who presides over this function] represents the sphere of principles.*

24. *The empirical mind (manas) is said to belong to the individual sphere, the object of mental representation to the elemental sphere, while the god Candra [who presides over this function] represents the sphere of principles.*

25. *The intellect (buddhi) is said to belong to the individual sphere, that which is clearly known by its means to the elemental sphere, while the god Bṛhaspati [who presides over this function] represents the sphere of principles.*

26. *In the same way, the sense of 'I' (ahaṁkāra) belongs to the individual sphere, whatever becomes an object for the ego belongs to the elemental sphere, while the god Rudra [who presides over this function] represents the sphere of principles.*

27. *The mental substance (citta) is said to belong to the individual sphere, whatever becomes an object of imaginative projection belongs to the elemental sphere, while the one who is called 'the knower of the field' (the witness consciousness) belongs to the sphere of principles.*

In the four functions of the *antaḥkaraṇa*, too, (see verses 33 and 34), there is the threefold distinction that is inherent in the individual/subjective aspect, the elemental/ intermediate aspect, and the principial, universal aspect.

On the other hand, we have to acknowledge that every item of knowledge, every experience, and so on, implies the triad consisting of subject, object, and the mean which links them to each other and maintains their relationship, and that this triad itself constitutes an object of knowledge for the *jīva*.

28. *Darkness (ignorance, tamas) is said to belong to the individual sphere, all that is subject to the transforming power of the world of becoming belongs to the elemental sphere, while Īśvara (principial Being) represents the sphere of principles.*

29. *In this way – both through the internal sensory functions (the organs of perception) and through the external active functions (the organs of action) all of which are supported by the corresponding deities/principles – there is, for each of these, the knowledge/experience of the respective object. This is what is defined as the waking state.*

30. *The term 'viśva' means [the reflection of the embodied jīva] when it is veiled by these two: the waking state and the gross body as the seat of the above-mentioned functions.*

31. *Now viśva must be recognised as identical to Virāj, so that whatever difference may be imagined to exist between them is brought to a solution and thus totally obliterated. There are five organs of*

perception/knowledge (jñānendriya) and five organs of action (karmendriya).

32. *The five organs of perception are: the ear, the skin, the eye, the tongue, and the nose. The five organs of action are: the organ of speech, the hands, the feet, the reproductive organ, and the organ of excretion.*

33. *Then there are the four aspects [of the inner organ, the antaḥkaraṇa], which are: the empirical mind, the intellect, the sense of 'I', and the imaginative memory. The function of the empirical mind is to analyse conceptually the data/objects that are represented, while the function of the intellect consists in grasping [succinctly] the exact nature of things.*

34. *In the same way, the sense of 'I' is defined as having the nature of self-awareness that is susceptible to [indefinite] identification, whereas the projective memory is described as that aspect of the mind whereby reflection takes place.*

In relation to the senses as the external organs, the mind is defined as the 'inner organ' (*antaḥkaraṇa*). The mind, therefore, is not an autonomous entity but a vehicle for the *jīva*.

The structure of the mind has four aspects, each of which is connected to a specific function.

The empirical or sensory mind (*manas*) is the aspect of the inner organ that is directly related to the senses, from which it draws the data for processing.

The projective memory (*citta*) – the seat of the faculty of imagination – constitutes the receptacle for all representations, the totality of what we call the 'content' of the mind, at both the conscious and the subconscious levels; it also defines the 'mental substance' in general terms, as mentioned in verse 27.

The sense of 'I' (*ahaṁkāra*) is that tendency of the individualised mind to express itself autonomously through a fictitious subject (*aham* = I) in which are focused the activity of perception, the activity of projecting/representing, and the activity of expressing. Strictly speaking, *ahaṁkāra* is not the ego but that 'which produces the [contingent] ego'. Therefore the ego is not the *jīva*, but represents its contingent or instantaneous expression as the result of the identification of the reflection of consciousness with the bodily vehicle; at the level of *manas* it expresses itself as the seat of the analytical reasoning.[1]

The pure intellect, on the other hand – that is, the *buddhi* or pure reason, the direct organ of the *jīva* – possesses the faculty of unitive intuition and therefore displays a quality of a universal nature.[2]

35. Prāṇa, apāna, vyāna, udāna, and samāna: these five are the modifications of the vital breath.

Prāṇa, or the 'vital breath', which includes its primary and secondary modifications, constitutes the link between the mind and the bodily senses and is thus the vehicle for relating mind and body.

36. The subtle elements also number five: space, air, fire, water, and earth. Together with avidyā, desire, and the action performed, they make up the 'eight

[1] See Śaṅkara, *Vivekacūḍāmaṇi*, 298-308, especially Raphael's commentary to verse 308, op. cit.

[2] *Ibid.*, commentary to verse 184.

cities', which are known as the constituents of the subtle body.

37-8. This subtle body, which is a product of māyā, represents the subtle vehicle of the innermost jīvātman. When all these sensory faculties [of perception and action] are suspended, that [dream] projection – which arises from the seeds/impressions received in the waking state and which, being self-luminous awareness, takes on the forms of the subject and object of the experience – characterises the condition that is known as the dream state. When the ātmā is hidden by these [the subtle body and the dream state], it is known as taijasa or luminous.

39. The sage must recognise this taijasa as essentially identical to Hiraṇyagarbha. Connected to the buddhi, it constitutes the cause of the two bodies [subtle and gross].

40. [The cause] is described as the Unmanifest or the Undifferentiated (avyakta). It is neither real or unreal, so that it is neither different from the ātman nor the same as it.

41. Moreover, it is not simple, not composite, and not simultaneously simple and composite. Ignorance, having the nature of falsity (mithyātva), can be destroyed only by the knowledge of one's own identity with Brahman.

By means of the *guṇas*/qualities, the world of names and forms veils the *jīva*, whose vehicles of expression are the *buddhi* and plenitude at the principial level. In addition, its embodied reflection is veiled by the vehicles of *kāma-manas* and *ahaṁkāra*. This veiling, or darkening, leads to *avidyā*, that is, to the failure to recognise what one is, and therefore to the denial of the *ātman/Brahman*.

The ancients used to say that 'nature (*prakṛti*/the *guṇas*) loves to hide herself'.

42. *When all cognitions [related to the waking and dream states] are dissolved – that is, when the intellect is re-absorbed into itself and lies within its own cause, like the banyan tree within its own seed – this condition is known as the state of deep sleep.*

When the flow of thought stops, the mind – being without content or projective movement – ceases to manifest, so that subject and object disappear.

43. *When [the ātmā] is identified with these two [the causal body and deep sleep], it is known as prājña or the unity of knowledge devoid of differentiation. In the state of prājña, therefore, one must recognise the ātmā – that is, the unitary awareness – as identical to the universal cause (Īśvara).*

Prājña is also a *state* of consciousness and represents the qualifying aspect of the causal principle.

Prājña, then, being aware of existential unity, is identical to *Īśvara*, the principial One (the ontological state) as the source of indefinite multiplicity.

44. *Therefore, the single Reality, whose nature is pure Intelligence, appears, through the power of clouding (moha), as multiple, that is, as viśva, taijasa, and prājña [at the individual level] and as Virāṭ, Sūtra, and Akśara [at the universal level].*

Viśva, *taijasa*, and *prājña* represent the states of consciousness with reference to the individual order, while *Virāṭ*, *Sūtra/Hiraṇyagarbha*, and *Akśara/Īśvara* indicate the planes of existence with reference to the universal order.

As we have seen already (in verses 28, 31, and 39), since their substratum or foundation is single, the two orders are equivalent and, at the level of consciousness, are absolutely identical. The following verse clarifies what has been said so far.

45. *Now the tripartite individual sphere, consisting of viśva and the others, must be recognised as absolutely identical to the tripartite universal sphere formed of Virāṭ and the others, so that all distinction between them is resolved [because their nature is identical].*

46. *The totality consisting of viśva, taijasa, and prājña, therefore, is none other than what is expressed by the syllable Om, since no real distinction can be found between the name and the named, and also because, in fact, there is no possibility of knowing any substantial difference between them.*

47. *The letter 'A' represents viśva; the letter 'U' represents taijasa; the letter 'M' represents prājña. This is how the syllable 'Om' is to be understood in the right sequence [of its individual letters].*

Just as the states, as successive externalisations, must be reabsorbed into each other, from the most outward to the least, so the individual parts of the syllable *Om* (*a-u-m*) must be comprehended in such a way that they are resolved one into the other in the right sequence until there is the awareness of universal Being through absorption into the sound of *Om* in its complete and undivided unity.

48. *Thus, before the rise of samādhi, through very intense and constant meditation, all these states must be resolved, from the gross to the subtle, into the ātman, which is pure intelligence (cidātman).*

Having reached universal or qualified Being through the sound of *Om*, one must transcend it through meditation on the syllable *Om* in its 'silent' aspect, the 'soundless' *Brahman* (*aśabdabrahma*), or supreme and unqualified Being, the *ātman* as pure, absolute Being without a second.

49. *The empirical/gross awareness associated with viśva, which corresponds to the letter 'A', must be resolved into the letter 'U'. The dream/subtle awareness associated with taijasa, which corresponds to the letter 'U', must be resolved into the letter 'M'.*

50. *The causal awareness (pure self-consciousness) associated with prājña, which corresponds to the letter 'M', must finally be resolved into the ātman, that is, into pure [unmodified] intelligence. I am the ātman, pure, absolute intelligence, eternal, enlightened, and free, Being without a second.*

51. *I am infinite Bliss. I am Vāsudeva. I am Om. Having thus comprehended and consciously realised, the discriminating mind resolves itself into the witness (sākṣin).*

52. *When the mind is immersed in the pure knowledge of the ātman, then it is not distracted. Thus one remains established in identity with the ātman,*

which is the fullness of knowledge, as infinite and motionless as a vast ocean.

53. *Meditation on the sound of Om leads to the conscious realisation of qualified Being, while meditation on the silent Om leads to the realisation of unqualified Being or the metaphysical Absolute.*

This last form of meditation corresponds to *nirvikalpasamādhi*, pure contemplation, with no trace of differentiation, in which, once the mind and even subjective self-consciousness are in abeyance, there remains the pure non-dual Reality, that is, the *ātman* in its infinite fullness.

54. *Since all this world of becoming is – in its beginning, its middle, and its end – nothing but conflict, it is only by achieving total detachment from everything that one can be established in Reality for ever.*

Upon realisation, renunciation is not a strain or an inhibition, because from the perspective of the supreme Being every contingent thing lacks being and therefore *is not*.

55. *There is nothing further to attain or to know for one who has realised the all-pervading ātman, which is pure bliss, peaceful, and without a second.*

56. *In this way the sage attains the goal of existence and becomes for ever a soul liberated in life. Being established in the ātman, he has transcended the nature of the world (differentiated multiplicity).*

57. *Even if, at the empirical level, he seems to perceive duality, in truth he sees nothing distinct from the*

ātman, which is pure knowledge, because pure Being (cidanvayāt) pervades everything.

58. *Moreover, he recognises [the world of duality] as being nothing but the result of confusion, as when one has a mistaken notion of one's whereabouts or sees a double image of the moon. For him, even his body is a mere appearance that will persist until the prārabdhakarma is exhausted.*

There are three types of *karma*: *prārabdha* is related to actions that have already taken place, and its fruit has matured and produced effects such as the physical body and the mind; *saṁcita* is old *karma* that has not yet borne fruit; *āgāmin*, lastly, is that which, if necessary, will build up in the future.

Once knowledge/realisation has occurred, the prerequisites for the accumulation of *karma* – that is, the ego that acts and the ego that reaps the fruit – are destroyed, and so *saṁcita* is burnt away and *āgāmin* is rendered ineffective; *prārabdhakarma*, on the other hand, persists with its effects of past actions, such as the gross physical body, but no longer binds the being that is liberated. When even this *karma* is exhausted, the *jīva* resolves into the *ātman*.

In reality, one who is liberated in life (*jīvanmukta*) is freed even from this *karma*, because by re-integrating himself into the metaphysical Reality he is no longer identified with the psychosomatic vehicle, which continues to constitute an illusory image of individuality only for non-discriminating minds.

59. *The Śruti says, 'In the same way, the man who has a teacher will assuredly realise Knowledge: his [existence] will last only until he is freed [from the body], after which he will be absorbed [in Brah-*

man].[1] *The persistence of prārabdhakarma is – in the case of one who is liberated – nothing but a mere appearance.*

60-61. The man who has come to know Reality is freed forever. Once the residue of prārabdhakarma has been exhausted, he – being released from all appearances and now transcending the darkness of ignorance, being identical to objectless plenitude, perfectly pure, and beyond the reach of word and thought – attains the supreme state of Viṣṇu.

62. This state is beyond affirmation and negation, beyond the distinction between name and named: it is the absolute bliss and unity of pure knowledge.

These last verses express the condition of one who is realised. In reality, this state transcends the realm of conception, for all definition constitutes a limit.

63. This treatise must be meditated upon very attentively by those who, being qualified, yearn for realisation, having acquired, through discipline, qualities such as profound humility and having also obtained the grace of the guru through fervent devotion.

64. The yogi who is endowed with excellent comprehension and has realised perfect detachment from this world and the next must meditate earnestly and zealously on this knowledge every day at sunset.

Here ends the 'Commentary to Quintuplication' composed by Śrī Sureśvarācārya

[1] *Chāndogya Upaniṣad*, VI, XIV, 2.

THE FIVEFOLD CONVICTION

manīṣāpañcakam

The account given in this composition says that one day an *ācārya*[1] (traditionally identified as Śaṅkara) was walking through the streets of Vārāṇasī when he saw an 'outcaste' (*caṇḍāla*) approaching him. Not wishing to be in this man's presence, the *ācārya* motioned to him to go further off, but he did not budge. In reality he was the Lord Śiva, who had come in this disguise in order to check the *ācārya*'s spiritual maturity and remind him that *Advaita*, the doctrine of Non-duality, is not restricted to a mere act of intellectual understanding but is something that must be lived and integrated into daily life. He invited the *ācārya* to reflect on what he had said, seeking to make him acknowledge, through images that were familiar to him, that no difference can be considered real in relation to the *ātman* and that all apparent distinction is the cause of opposition only with reference to the level of form and not to the level of Essence.

On hearing these words, the *ācārya* realised his mistake and composed these five verses to show that there are no distinctions in the reality of the *Brahman*.

Then Śiva revealed himself and blessed him.

---

[1] *Ācārya* is the term indicating a Master or Teacher who imparts the teaching not only through dialectic and spiritual influence but also through conduct and example.

Traditionally considered as forming part of the composition are the three introductory verses, which are not included, however, in some recensions. The other five verses, which constitute the authentic composition, are known by the name of 'The Fivefold Conviction' (*manīṣāpañcakam*), because each verse ends with the words 'This is my conviction' (*eṣā manīṣā mama*).

1. *One day while the ācārya was walking through the streets of Vārāṇasī, he found himself in front of a man belonging to the lowest caste; but it was Śiva himself, together with his consort Gaurī, who was appearing in this guise. Upon seeing him, the ācārya shouted to him, 'Go away! Keep your distance!' But the Beneficent One, in the form of the caṇḍāla, answered Śaṅkara in his turn:*

2. *'Tell me, noble ascetic, you who are shouting at me to go away and keep my distance, is it this body [of mine], which is sustained by food, that you wish to keep at a proper distance from that body [of yours], which is also sustained by food, or do you wish to separate [my] pure Intelligence from the same Intelligence [which is present in you]?*

3. *'Is there perchance some difference between the sun which is reflected in the waters of the holy Ganges and the sun which is reflected in a puddle of dirty water on a street trodden by caṇḍālas? Again, is there perchance a difference between the space contained in a gold vessel and the space enclosed by a clay pot? Is it not perhaps a serious mistake to believe that there are distinctions – such as thinking of one as a brāhmaṇa and of another as a śvapāka – within our deepest Essence, which, being self-existent Plenitude and pure knowledge, is like a waveless ocean?'*

Śaṅkara answered:

1. *That pure consciousness which shines brightly in the states of waking, dream, and deep sleep, which permeates all bodily forms from Brahmā down to an ant and is the witness of the universe, that same am I, and not an object of knowledge. One who has this firm awareness is a true guru, be he a caṇḍāla or a twice-born. This is my conviction.*

2. *I am Brahman indeed, and this compound universe is a reflection of my consciousness. All this subsists through māyā, characterised by the three attributes. Thus one whose consciousness abides steadfastly in the Supreme, which is eternal, pure, and Fullness supreme, he is a true guru, be he a caṇḍāla or a twice-born. This is my conviction.*

3. *One who has realised, thanks to the Teacher's word, that the whole universe is continuously perishing immerses himself in constant contemplation of the eternal Brahman, with his mind finally brought to peace. In the fire of pure knowledge he will consume the errors he has committed in the past and those that he might commit in the future, and at the same time he will be indifferent to the flux of events that have now matured (prārabdha). This is my conviction.*

4. *The yogi who ever contemplates with a calm mind that awareness which is clearly experienced by all beings – be their nature human, divine, or lower – as the innermost 'I' (ātman), that awareness which, on account of its splendour, causes unconscious objects such as the body, the senses, and the mind, to shine, and which, as the solar disc, is veiled by*

the very objects it illuminates: he is undoubtedly a true guru. This is my conviction.

Being is the unchanging witness of the play of *māyā*, and thus of *māyā/prakṛti*, which veils its authentic nature, the pure Essence on which the whole manifestation is founded.

The 'different' (Plato's word is θάτερον) or 'variety' (to use Kant's expression) is nothing but a reflection of the principial One; it partakes of its essence/*ousía* (οὐσία) but is not the One. One who can see the 'accidental different' as mere phenomenon is a true philosopher. Parmenides puts it like this: 'All those things that mortals have considered, convinced that they were true, will be merely names (ὄνομα) for it.'[1]

5. *That bliss enjoyed by Indra and other divine beings is but a fraction of that ocean [which is Brahman]. The sage experiences it continually in his mind, which is totally at rest. One whose mind has been resolved into that eternal ocean of bliss is verily Brahman and not just a knower of Brahman. Such a being is rare and is worshipped by Indra, Lord of the Gods. This is truly my conviction.*

The encounter with the *caṇḍāla* is understood to symbolise the occasional impact with apparently negative circumstances which, unless they, too, are acknowledged as an aspect of the Divine, can divert the being and regenerate within him the feeling of differentiation. When the absence of duality is fully experienced, even in the world of manifestation – the receptacle of all distinctions of form – every individualised being has to be acknowledged as a

---

[1] Parmenides, *On the Order of Nature*, Fragment 8, 38-39, op. cit.

conscious/existential moment of pure Being and integrated into oneself. True Peace is attained only when totality has been integrated and consciously embraced within oneself.

A HYMN IN TEN VERSES

daśaślkokī

This 'Hymn in ten verses' was composed by Śaṅkara on the occasion of his encounter with the *guru* Govindapāda. When asked who he was, Śaṅkara replied with the ten verses, in each of which, with the exception of the last, he confirms his own identity with the absolute Śiva, that pure, infinite Reality devoid of differentiation, the supreme Truth: *Śivaḥ kevalo 'ham.*

This short but compact work composed by Śaṅkara is an expression of total awareness, unparalleled and devoid of alterity; reflecting the full consciousness of identity with the *ātman*, it has the power to provide a conscious stimulus that is both intense and profound. For a better appreciation it is good to discern in it:

– a penetrating and evocative rhythm that is made apparent by its harmonious, vibrant, and awakening repetition;

– a process of negation at a level of awareness (non-identification, detachment) which extends to the various veiling superimpositions, with the consequent solution of the successive sheaths until the unmoving, infinite Centre of the *ātman* is attained;

– a precise sequence that is comprehensive/integrating and appropriate for the realisation of the harmony between the individual and the universal, between the quantitative/ phenomenal and qualitative/noumenal, until both quantity and quality are transcended and pure non-dual Being is revealed; one cannot realise Non-duality without first comprehending Unity and then transcending it;

– the disclosure of one's real identity in the clarity of Non-duality, where every question dies away and every definition, distinction, and duality is resolved and disappears.

It is said that Śaṅkarācārya, on the point of abandoning the physical form, invited his disciples to meditate on these very verses and to penetrate their essence as absolute Non-duality, which – as is made clear in the last verse – can never find adequate expression in word or concept but only in the total integration of the 'second'.

1. *I am not earth, not water, not fire, not air, not space; I am not even the senses or all of these things together, for [all this] is transient, whereas the One is ever-existent, even in deep sleep. I am therefore that One, absolute and auspicious, who alone abides for ever.*

2. *I am not the social orders or the laws that govern the social orders (varṇas) and the traditional stages of life (āśramas). I am not obliged to practise concentration, meditation, yoga, or the other disciplines. The superimpositions related to notions of 'I' and 'mine' originate in what is not the ātman and are subject to solution [by means of knowledge]. I am therefore that One, absolute and auspicious, who alone abides for ever.*

3. *I am not mother or father, the gods or the different worlds [universal beings/principles and states of existence]. I am not the Vedas or the sacrifices, and I cannot be described as the holy places of pilgrimage. Since, during deep sleep, [all these] become non-existent, like a void, I am that One, absolute and auspicious, who alone abides for ever.*

Between one cycle of manifestation and the next, everything is re-absorbed into the uncaused cause, which is the principial Being. That which exists in one state but not in another cannot be described as real. Since the Witness as such is conscious of existence and non-existence, it alone is Reality, in whose bosom universes appear and disappear like mirages.

4. *I am not the Sāṁkhya teaching or the Śaiva teaching. I am not the Pāñcarātra doctrine, and I do not reflect the Jain view or the Mīmāṁsā teaching or any of the others. Since it is only through specific, effective, and conscious realisation that my nature as the infinitely pure ātman is revealed, I am that One, absolute and auspicious, who alone abides for ever.*

5. *I am not above or below, within or without, at the centre or at the circumference, facing East or facing West. Being all-pervasive like space/ether, I am by nature single and indivisible. I am therefore that One, absolute and auspicious, who alone abides for ever.*

6. *I am not white or black, red or yellow, I am not thin or fat, not short or tall. Since my nature is the pure splendour [of knowledge], I myself am therefore without form. I am that One, absolute and auspicious, who alone abides for ever.*

7. *I am not the teacher or the sacred Text. I am not the disciple or the teaching. I am not 'you' [who are listening to me] or 'I' [who am speaking to you], and I am not even this entire cosmic manifestation. The true nature of the ātman is pure Enlightenment, which admits of no differentiation. I am therefore that One, absolute and auspicious, who alone abides for ever.*

8. *For me there is no waking state, no dream state, and no state of deep sleep. I am not conditioned by the gross plane (viśva), the subtle/luminous plane (taijasa) or the causal plane (prājña). These are of the nature of avidyā, while I am the Fourth, beyond the three [conditioning] states. I am therefore that One, absolute and auspicious, who alone abides for ever.*

9. *Since the ātman alone is all-pervading and all-embracing, it is self-existent. It is also the sole Subject, without 'another', and constitutes the ultimate Truth. I am therefore that One, absolute and auspicious, who alone abides for ever.*

10. *And, in truth, the ātman cannot be defined even as One [with a second]. Indeed, from where could a second that is other than That come forth? That, therefore, is neither absoluteness nor relativity. It cannot be said to be the void or anything at all, for its nature is pure Non-duality. So how can I, then, speak to you of That which the whole of Vedānta proclaims?*

That from which 'word and thought turn back'[1] is the ever-present One-without-a-second: in Non-duality there is no subject or object, no manifestation, and not even a distinction between manifest and un-manifest. Nothing can be said of Non-duality without creating an apparent duality, or without making arbitrary conditions and limitations.

Just as one cannot speak of silence without breaking it, so nothing can be said of pure Being except that it *is*.

[1] See *Taittirīya Upaniṣad*, II, VI, 1.

There is little point in naming Silence: one has to be the Silence that is conscious of every sound/vibration/colour. Yet, on reflection, how could we actually know sound, unless we were already and eternally Silence?

How could we speak of duality without being Non-duality? How could we know without being eternally and absolutely the foundation of knowledge and of the very consciousness of being?

Realisation is the total recognition of one's own nature as non-dual Reality. This does not involve a change of form, and even less a change of substance. It entails a complete reversal of perspective: if the individual, sunk in non-comprehension, observes and interprets a manifestation that is outside him and in opposition to him, one who is realised, being identical to Being/*ātman*, views everything as mere appearance (the 'second') rising and falling on the horizon of the unchanging *ātman*.

THE TEACHING ON KNOWLEDGE OF THE ĀTMAN

ātmajñānopadeśavidhi

'The Teaching on Knowledge of the *Ātman*' is a work that is particularly incisive and essential from the realisative viewpoint, and its very conciseness makes it a specific treatise (*prakaraṇa*) whose verses present a synthetic exposition of the essence of the teaching of *advaita*, which is precisely the knowledge/realisation of the *ātman* (*ātmajñāna*).

In this 'Teaching' Śaṅkara expounds the whole *sādhanā* in a way that is pure *advaita*: the recognition of the *ātman* in that which is superimposed on it, and thus a 'recognition' that is immediate and direct, an enlightenment (*bodhi*) which is true and proper and which instantly dissolves all the dimensions of space, time, and causality.

This work – also known as *Ātmavidyopadeśa* and *Ātmajñānopadeśaprakaraṇa* – is divided into four parts. The first part proceeds to discriminate the *ātman* from the individual veiling sheaths by acknowledging them to be mere objects of perception. The second part deals with the nature of the *ātman* as the supreme Reality which transcends polarity of all kinds (cause/effect, time/space, and so on). The third part examines the states that are superimposed on the *ātman* by means of the analogies of the states of waking, dream, and deep sleep. The final part is concerned with the effective realisation of the Fourth (*Turīya*) as the foundation of all that exists.

PART ONE

Discriminating the ātman from the sheaths

1. Since there is no attainment higher than the realisation of the ātman, let us gird up our loins to expound – for someone who yearns for liberation, who is endowed with profound faith, who has renounced worldly activity and has also eradicated all forms of attachment – a teaching for realising the knowledge of the ātman.

The knowledge of the *ātman* is the highest realisation, but since it transcends the realm of the individual, with its countless ways of extending and developing, as well as the realm of the universal, it is clear that precise qualifications are required of the aspirant.

> 'The Sages have said that for realisation it is necessary to practise four qualifications, without which the attainment of *Brahman* could fail.
>
> 'The first one is discrimination (*viveka*) between the real and the unreal; the second is detachment (*vairāgya*) from the fruit of all actions in this world and in others; the third consists of the group of the six qualities (*śamādi*), such as mental calm, and so on; and the fourth is a firm and yearning aspiration for liberation (*mumukṣutva*).'[1]

[1] Śaṅkara, *Vivekacūḍāmaṇi*, verses 18-19, op. cit.

2. *It is generally well known that whatever represents the object of sight (dṛśya) is quite distinct from the one who sees (draṣṭā).*[1] *Now the question is, Which is the ātman?*

3. *First of all, the body is not the ātman, for it is perceived as having form and other similar characteristics. Indeed, just as pots and other objects, being distinguished precisely on account of their forms and similar attributes, are perceived by means of the sensory organs, such as sight, so the body, being characterised by form and so on, is known as 'this' through the sense of sight and the other faculties.*

4. *Just as fire – which is endowed by nature with the properties of burning and illuminating – is quite different from the wood and other objects which it can burn or illuminate, so it is clearly understood that the ātman, which is the witness/knower, is quite distinct from the body, which is the object of knowledge.*

5. *Furthermore, the ātman must be acknowledged as different from the body for the additional reason that [in relation to the body] there are the states of deep sleep, death, and so on.*

6. *In fact, when the ātman permeates the physical/gross complex of the body, this body – similarly to what happens with a wooden instrument – becomes capable of performing activities and movements. On the other hand, when [conscious-*

[1] Cf. Śaṅkara's 'Introduction' to his commentary (*bhāṣya*) to the *Brahmasūtra*.

ness] departs from the body, then the body lies inert, like a mere piece of wood. This is why it has to be concluded that the ātman is in all respects distinct from the body.[1]

7. *Not even the sensory faculties, such as sight, constitute the ātman, because sight, like a lamp, is a mere instrument that is able to reveal the form of objects.*

8. *Indeed, just as different objects can be perceived through the instrumentality of the lamp, so form is known through the faculty of sight, which therefore constitutes a means.*

9. *The same can be said for the other sensory organs.*

10. *Nor does the empirical mind (manas) constitute the ātman, because it is an object of knowledge and because it, too, is an instrument, just as a lamp is.*

The *ātman*, then, is not composed of the objects of sense, or of the senses themselves, or of the mind which knows them.

It is not the eye that 'sees' the object: it is the mind that receives its form/image by re-presenting it within itself. The sensory faculties act as a means between outer objectivity and the empirical mind, which is able to assume, from time to time, the form of the object of knowledge.[2]

---

[1] Cf. *Gauḍapāda*, *Māṇḍūkyakārikā*, mainly the Chapter 'The extinction of the firebrand', op. cit.

[2] See *Dṛgdṛśyaviveka* (A philosophical investigation into the nature of the 'Seer' and 'seen'). Translation from the Sanskrit and commentary by Raphael. Aurea Vidyā, New York.

The cognitive instrument, whose nature may be sensory, rational, and so on, simply relates the object that is known to the individual subject, but the pure *ātman* transcends both object and subject.

11. Not even the pure intellect (buddhi) can be said to be the ātman, because it, too, is an object of knowledge and is therefore an instrument in the way a lamp is.

For greater clarity we give the diagram (page 211) of the constitution of the individual being in relation to the sheaths or coverings (*kośas*) that enclose the *jīva*.[1] Each sheath represents the condensation/determination of the more inner one, in which it is essentially contained and of which it comprises a given mode of expression: thus, moving from the Centre of the being towards the circumference, there is, as it were, an increase in mass, a slowing-down of vibrational activity, with a consequent reduction in the 'level of freedom' and a relative settling into determined forms of being.

Recognising a given sheath as an object of knowledge leads to the transcendence of the corresponding level of the identification of consciousness and therefore to the penetration of the sheaths closer to the Centre. Withdrawing from a given modality is the result of the conscious attainment and possession of the possibilities contained within that modality.

12. In short, not even the vital force (prāṇa) is the ātman, because in deep sleep there is no awareness [of it or of anything else].

---

[1] To go deeper into the sheaths (*kośas*), see also *Taittirīya Upaniṣad*, II, II, 5.

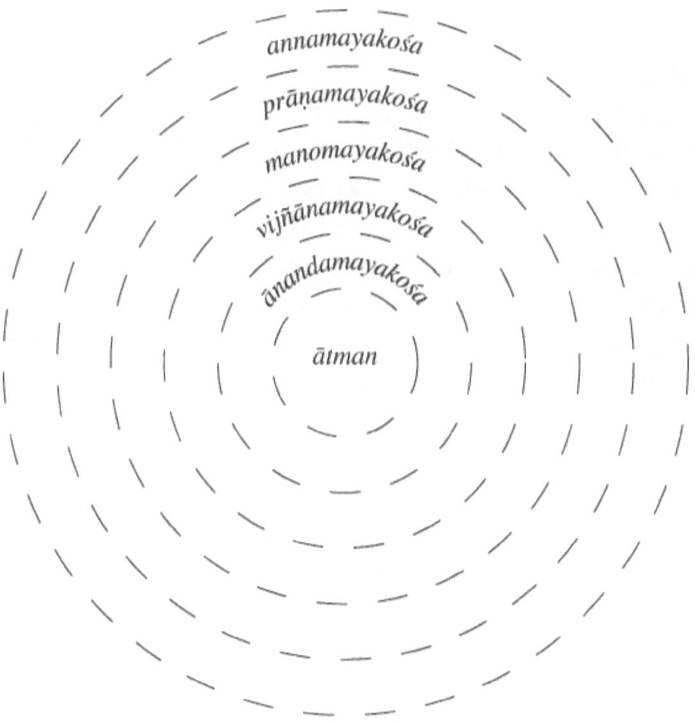

13. *Besides in states that are other [than deep sleep] it cannot be established to whom this awareness belongs, that is, whether it belongs to the vital force [or to something else, such as the senses], which is like being unable to distinguish the servant from the master,*

14. *whereas in the state of deep sleep it can be definitely stated that the vital force [like all the other vehicles/sheaths] is perceived as completely devoid of distinctive knowledge.*

As will be seen, in the fourth part of this work there is a precise correspondence – and therefore a true and just comparison – between the planes of manifestation and the states of waking, dream, and deep sleep, both at the level of the individual and at the universal level. In the movement from the waking state to those of dream and deep sleep, the consciousness is withdrawn from its peripheral determinations and towards the Centre, leaving behind, to their sluggish automatic workings, the various vehicles that correspond to these determinations. During sleep, for example, the body seems to be inert, while the mind may project dream images, and so on. Thus, by manifesting states that are changeable and to some extent contradictory, the various vehicles/states do not constitute that Constant which is the foundation of all that comes later.

> *15. Furthermore, even if it is sometimes presented differently, it must nevertheless be recognised that the absence of perception in the vital force [during deep sleep] is not on account of the cessation of activity on the part of the senses. In fact, since the senses are unable to suspend their specific functions as long as that which governs them (the ātman) is present, like ministers in the presence of the king, they show that they do not depend [solely] on the prāṇa: all these functions, in short, depend exclusively on the ātman, which completely transcends the awareness that is identified with them when, for example, they suspend their own activity, which is what happens during deep sleep.*

The mind is not stimulated by the senses except when it is permeated and activated by consciousness. In this case the external action induces a mental 'resonance' which, by contrast, does not occur when the vehicle is unconscious, as happens in deep sleep. Conversely, in the presence of this consciousness, the specific vehicle cannot fail to reflect its light by expressing itself in ways that are proper and inherent to it.

16. When [the jīva], emerging [from deep sleep], revitalises the various sensory functions, then all the faculties [represented by their respective organs of perception] permeate their own respective object: thus, when the external activity prevails, [the jīva] leaves the state of sleep, and this constitutes the waking state.

17. On the other hand, when [the activity which governs the waking state] comes to an end, [the jīva], gathering all the senses together within itself by means of objective knowledge and also that subjective knowledge which comes from its contact with the vehicle of intellect, experiences dream or deep sleep.

This is the illuminating descent of the *ātman*, whose reflection as the *jīva* activates and enlivens, one by one, the various sheaths. It is always this *jīva* that experiences the states of sleep, dream, and waking.

18. In this way [the ātman] permeates the three states without any discontinuity.

As such, the *ātman* is the witness of the three states.

19. Conversely, the backward and forward movement followed by the individualised mind (manas) has its determining cause in past action.

The mind contains a certain potential content (*vāsanā*) which manifests in relation to contingent conditions. It may be said that the presence of formal contents (*pratyaya*) conditions the container (*citta*) and determines a reaction to every action or stimulus; the external condition, in other words, may be favourable to the development of specific possibilities, to the manifestation of specific qualities; and conversely, the identification with an acting subject, forming as a result of the activity, impresses precise tendencies (*saṁskāras*) on the substance of mind with regard to future activities. This creates a vicious circle (*saṁsāra*): action produces a content which, in turn, finds expression in a given action (*karma*), and so the process goes on.

It is therefore the potential content that, by taking form, brings into manifestation the mind, which expresses itself through its inner projective activity (representation, imagination) and through that which develops externally (action).

20. *[It is for this reason that the jīva] experiences the states of dream and waking. In addition – for the purpose of removing the exhaustion caused by the activity that is determined by the previous two conditions – it also experiences deep sleep.*

21. *What occurs in the waking state also occurs in the states of dream and deep sleep: namely, the prāṇa, in virtue of its particular nature, fulfils the function of maintenance with regard to the gross body, which therefore cannot be mistaken as dead.*

22. *Finally, not even the 'I' (aham) is the ātman. The 'I', in fact, represents a mere object of knowledge, just like a pot or other objects, even though it is identified with the ātman by all those who do not have the clarity to discern the true ātman.*

23. *[Moreover, the 'I' is not the ātman] because it ceases to exist [in deep sleep],*

24. *and because it is characterised by the different and conflicting experiences of pleasure, pain, and so on, as well as by the continual process of becoming, which is exactly what happens to a physical body which is distinguished by features such as being thin or fat, and so on.*

25. *If it were therefore to be asked why the body and other objects are considered as though they were the ātman when they are certainly not the ātman, it has to be acknowledged that this occurs on account of the lack of discrimination applied to the object by the knower.*

The individual is considered to undergo the influence of factors both outer and inner (physical, psychical) as long as he fails to recognise them as representations/objects of knowledge.

If it is easy and immediate to recognise an external object as other than oneself, it is not so easy to recognise an internal object (mental, psycho-subconscious, and so on) in the same way and, more importantly, the ego itself, which synthesises these processes.

Here ends Part One

PART TWO

The nature of the ātman

1. *What, then, is the nature of the ātman? First of all, it is that innermost Essence which is distinct from all the objects which have so far been considered and expounded; it is all-pervasive like space/ether, eternal, without parts or distinctions, devoid of attributes, uncontaminated, having no movements such as those of creating oneself and dissolving oneself, completely lacking all notions of 'I' and 'mine', free from desire, aversion, and inner activity, self-luminous by nature like the brightness of fire and the splendour of the sun. It has no connection with the elements such as ether/space and so on; it has no functions such as the intellect and the others. Being without attributes such as sattva and being distinct from prāṇa and the other vital forces, it [the ātman] is untouched by hunger or thirst, pain or illusion, decrepitude or death, which are respectively features of the prāṇa, the intellect, and the body. The ātman is that which dwells in the heart of all beings and is the witness of their very intellects.*

'This *ātman*, which is within my heart, is smaller than a grain of rice or barley-seed, smaller than a mustard seed or even the kernel of a mustard-seed. This *ātman*, which is within my heart, is bigger than the earth, bigger than the intermediate space (*antarikṣa*), bigger than the sky, bigger than [all] these worlds.'

'In the citadel of the *Brahman* there is this small receptacle shaped like a lotus flower. Within it there is a tiny space/*ākāśa*. What is inside this space is what needs to be sought. That, in truth, is what needs to be known."[1]

2. *Moreover, not even the intellect can be the seat of the all-pervading partless ātman, just as no being, whatever its nature, can constitute the seat of ether/space (ākāśa).*

Just as space/*ākāśa* contains all the elements which it generates but has no other element by which it itself may be contained, so nothing can contain the all-embracing and all-pervading *ātman*.

3. *Again, how can one attribute to the ātman – which is totally distinct from the feeling of 'I' and the idea of 'mine' and is completely devoid of desire, aversion, and volition – the function of the knowing subject, this being defined as the doer of that specific activity which consists of ordinary vision/knowledge?*

4. *If the ātman were the ordinary knowing subject, it would perform a function of perception, and this would give rise to a contradiction [with its avowed immutability], and it would no longer be possible to maintain that the ātman is the witness of all intellects. For example, a certain Devadatta effectively becomes the agent of an activity such as going,*

---

[1] *Chāndogya Upaniṣad*, III, XIV, 3; VIII, I, 1.

coming, and so on, simply by performing those particular activities which are related to specific instruments [such as the organs of movement] or are dependent on them, while other activities are totally independent [of these instruments, but not of Devadatta].

5. In truth there cannot be any activity of perception in *relation to the ātman, for the ātman is unchanging, its nature is that of pure knowledge, and it is totally devoid of any real connection whatsoever with either of the categories of instruments.*

6. *On the other hand, for someone who sees the function of the knowing subject as dependent on specific instruments, and so on, – as happens for the mind (citta), which is comparable to a lamp on account of the forms that it assumes by modifying itself, and also on account of its dependence on other means, and so on, which are its efficient cause – [for such a person the ātman] would become the knower of a limited number of objects, or it would know things one at a time [that is, in succession and not simultaneously], or it would not know at all, or, again, it would merely attain wrong knowledge.*

7. *However, this is not the case with the ātman, for which there is no knowledge that is limited or sequential, no absence of knowledge, and, finally, no false knowledge. This is because there is no modification whatsoever [in the ātman], and also because the ātman does not depend on any other instrument which may constitute its efficient cause,*

which, by contrast, is the case with the mind, which is therefore comparable to a lamp.

Just as a lamp requires a flame for it to be lit and to give light in its turn, so the mind can illuminate objects, both external and internal, only if it is illuminated in its turn by the light of the *ātman*. The mind thus acts as a bridge between pure knowledge and the multiple world of forms.

The *jīvātman* is reflected directly in the *buddhi* and indirectly in the *manas*, which shows that it is the intellect that illumines the empirical mind by bestowing on it both splendour and plasticity.

8. *In what sense, then, can there be said to be any contact between the ātman and the intellect?*

9. *Well, from what has been said, a certain correlation results: a kind of contact between these two [the ātman and the intellect] arises in proportion to the subtlety, self-effulgence, indivisibility [and so on, of the ātman].*

10. *Having understood that the intellect, lacking self-effulgence, seems to become resplendent, like the jewel of a diadem, only in the proximity of a source of light, such as the ātman, whose nature is pure radiance, one may then say that the contact occurring between the ātman and the intellect has the nature of a superimposition.*

11. *On the other hand, between ātman and intellect, both of which are without form, there could not be any contact comparable to that, for example, between wax and wood.*

12. Moreover, as far as the function of a knowing subject is concerned, this function operates only in relation to [and in the presence of] that which is other [than the ātman]. Just as the sun – though devoid of such notions as 'I' and 'mine' and having no will or intentionality – is acknowledged as the illuminator of objects precisely on account of those objects themselves which are manifested thanks to its presence, for the sun itself consists of pure light and performs no activity of any kind (nor, as the illuminator, could it be otherwise), in the same way ignorant people superimpose the properties and function of revealing manifested objects onto the sun, which reveals itself in its true nature of light only in the presence of such objects [although it maintains its nature even when they are absent]. In the same way, the quality of being the knower of knowable objects, such as the intellect, is superimposed on the ātman – which has the nature of pure knowledge, is totally devoid of all activity, has no attributes, and is the witness of the entire content of knowledge – where the ātman can have, at the very most, an [indirect] relationship of proximity with the objects of knowledge, for it nevertheless abides in its nature of pure Essence, ever identical to itself. And this is because the function of knower cannot operate in any other way.

13. How, then, can one speak of the function of agent with reference to the ātman, which is devoid of all activities and attributes? This function, in truth, is defined as purely apparent, as in the case of a magnet.

14. Just as a magnetic mass, by its mere presence, makes iron filings move spontaneously, so the ātman, although devoid of all activity whatsoever, constitutes the illuminator of the acting subject.

15. Consequently, any talk of activity [with reference to the ātman] is due to the fact that it bestows light/vitality on the subject of the action.

Everything in the universe – and therefore everything in the different acting beings of all orders and degrees – can manifest, express themselves, and move because there is that ultimate foundation which is the attributeless *ātman/Brahman*, which therefore transcends subject, object, and the very knowledge which makes them known.

16-17. The 'agents' of action are defined as all those instruments/vehicles which, being illuminated and rendered active by consciousness, permeate their respective objects.

18. It is therefore only in a secondary sense that one can speak of activity with regard to the ātman, because the ātman is totally changeless and attributeless.

'The condition of agent cannot belong to the *ātman*, [even in the apparent state of individualised self] as its intrinsic nature: indeed, if this were the case, a serious result would be the absolute impossibility of liberation. In fact, on the hypothesis that the condition of agent constituted the authentic nature of the *ātman*, liberation from this nature of agent would become impossible, just as fire [can never be liberated from its intrinsic constituted property] by heat. Moreover, from one who has not been emancipated from the condition of agent, there cannot even be the attainment of the supreme human goal, which consists of the highest bliss, since a condition of being the agent is by its very nature a part of suffering ... the condition characterised by the [real or potential] function of agent does not belong intrinsically to the nature of the *ātman*, but is attributed to it through the superimposition of properties which, in fact, pertain to the vehicles. In this context, there is the passage from the *Śruti* which states, 'It is *as if* it thought, *as if* it acted.' (*Bṛhadāraṇyaka Upaniṣad*, IV, III, 7).

19. Thus it can no longer be asked, 'How can the ātman be known through the intellect?, because, like the self-effulgent sun, it is the ātman itself that illuminates the intellect.

20. Just as the sun by its very nature [as a source of light] cannot itself be illuminated, so the ātman cannot be perceived by means of the intellect.

21. Moreover, since the intellect is an object of knowledge, it clearly cannot become the subject/knower, and this is also why the ātman cannot be known by means of the intellect.

22. Again, if [the intellect] were to assume the function of the knowing subject, then, because it is [at the same time] an object of knowledge, it would not have the capacity to know, exactly as is the case with two lamps [which cannot illuminate each other].

No temporal instrument, which corresponds to *prakṛti* – including knowledge itself (*sattva*) as a means of knowing – can comprehend or know the *ātman*, which is the fundamental cause of everything. And the *ātman* has no need of knowledge, or of consciousness itself, in order to know itself or be aware of itself. Of the *ātman*, all that can be said is that it *is*, without adding anything further. (See verse 4 of Part Three of the present work).

Here ends Part Two

PART THREE

The states superimposed on the ātman

1. *The analogical conditions of waking, dream, and deep sleep are now dealt with: they constitute states which characterise the mind in its entirety. Such states are spoken of particularly in relation to being transcended, so that the full revelation of the ātman can occur.*

The states of sleep, dream, and waking are the modifications which are superimposed on the *ātman* and which characterise specific modalities of knowledge.

In the waking state there is the projection of an external objective duality in which one has the experience of the phenomenal world by means of the empirical mind (*manas*) and the sensory apparatus. In this condition the steadfast consciousness of the *ātman* permeates the whole of the individual complex in the unending process of relationship and polarity.

In the dream state there is the projection/superimposition of an inner subjective duality in which one experiences the dream or mental world by means of the various subtle vehicles.

In the state of deep or dreamless sleep there is no dual projection, and both object and subject rest in their causal/unmanifest state. There is, therefore, no egoic experience or awareness while the consciousness of the *jīvātman*, which has withdrawn even from the subtle determinations, permeates only the sattvic vehicle of plenitude, resting thus in a state of purely being the witness.

A correspondence can be found between the above-mentioned conditions and the states of consciousness, at both the individual and the universal orders:

Plane	Order Universal	Order Individual	State Analogical
Causal	*Īśvara*	*prājña*	deep sleep
Subtle	*Hiraṇyagarbha*	*taijasa*	dream
Gross	*Virāṭ*	*viśva* or *vaiśvānara*	waking

> 2. *Of these, the waking state is defined as that in which the various sensory organs, such as sight, being upheld in their functions by light and so on, fulfil their specific activities by permeating their respective objects. In such conditions even the mind experiences activity in the manner of an instrument.*

In the waking state the mind, in its entirety, acts as a mean between the *jīva* and outer empirical objectivity.

> 3. *Being permeated by the [first reflection of the] consciousness of the innermost ātman, of which it is a superimposition, and thus appearing endowed with its own consciousness, the intellect (buddhi) is modified, assuming the forms of both seer (subject) and seen (object). Why is the term 'ātman' then qualified by the adjective 'innermost'? Well, this is solely for the purpose of showing that nothing which gives an appearance of continuity within its own existence is the ātman.*

It is useful to summarise what has been expounded in the present verse, because it is important in relation to the purposes of understanding: the *ātman/Brahman*, as the foundation of all that exists, gives the *jīva* – its ray of light – the possibility of manifesting at the universal causal level and, with one of its rays of consciousness, at the lower level of *viśva* and *taijasa*, or the sensible plane.

> 4. *Thus the intellect and the other vehicles/sheaths constitute the instruments or means of expression. Although they are objects of knowledge, like pots and so on, on account of their contact with the innermost ātman they are considered as the ātman itself with regard to objects external to them, just as warmth seems to effectively belong to water which has been heated through contact with fire. This notwithstanding, the ātman can never become the non-ātman through its proximity with these objects, just as fire can never become cold through its contact with water.*

The various sheaths/vehicles receive light from the *ātman* and reflect it by reason of their transparency or block it through their opaqueness. However, they are nothing but condensations and therefore modifications of form that are superimposed on the substratum, or foundation, represented by the *ātman*, which, through its unique a-causal nature, cannot be enmeshed by any kind of superimposition.

> 5. *But, as happens for the intellect and other faculties – there being within the ātman no further beings – the ātman remains for ever and in all ways the most internal, and it could not be otherwise: this is why the ātman merits the adjective 'innermost'.*

This makes it abundantly clear that there is no end to the essential nature of the ātman.

6. *Thus the intellect, which appears to be self-effulgent since it is permeated by a ray of consciousness from the innermost ātman, is modified as it splits into the subject/seer and the object that is seen; and coming into contact [through the sensory organs] with the various objects and so on, it assumes the form of these objects of knowledge, just as molten copper takes the forms of the moulds into which it is poured.*

Both the imaginative representation and the outer sensory perception, which characterises the waking state, induce in the mind the scissure/polarisation into subject/object.

7. *Thus, when this is the situation, this is the waking state for the ātman (jīva), although the ātman has the nature of pure knowledge and is witness of both (subject and object), all-pervading like space/ākāśa, time, and so on, without parts and unchangeable.*

8. *Then when the intellect – permeated and imbued with the impressions of the forms [of external objects], but yet having no effective contact with them – assumes the form of both [seer and seen], like a pot that holds the impressions of flowers, it (in the form of representative seeds and under the influence of ignorance, causal connection, and actions undertaken) comes to a halt like an inert object [in the presence of the ātman]: this experience constitutes what is defined as the dream state superimposed on the ātman, which, apparently identified with the mind (the subtle plane), seems to move, like the reflection of the moon on the surface of water.*

The projecting power of the mind represents the inert state of the contents of the mind, which, even when it is detached from the senses and the body, expresses such potentialities within itself. In other words, the waking state induces a movement which persists in the dream state, too.

But the dual movement, which is produced by the 'field of forces' between the 'poles' of empirical experience/knowledge, is within the mind, which is an object of knowledge for the *jīva*.

9. *Lastly, when the ātman (jīva) – being detached from the manifest expression that is contained in the forms of the mental impressions, and being gathered into itself as pure Intelligence, [which has] in fact the nature of the Void [because it is devoid of superimpositions] – resolves itself into featureless [causal] unity, this condition constitutes the state of deep sleep (the causal plane), where the mind is like the banyan tree in seed form.*

With the ontological state (the causal state) there is the One-many, from where the process of manifestation begins, a process represented by the world of names and forms (multiplicity). Beyond the ontological state, which is already movement and quality, there is the *Brahman*/*ātman*, which imparts *esse*[1] to the causal principle and to all that comes from it. It needs to be remembered that the *upādhis*/vehicles are the effects of *prakṛti* and have a mortal nature, while the *jīva*, and hence the *ātman*, is of an immortal nature.

Here ends Part Three

[1] *esse*: a term denoting 'essence' in scholastic philosophy.

PART FOUR

Realisation of the Fourth

1. *In truth, the ātman has the nature of pure, absolute Intelligence and is totally free of effect, cause, and ignorance, as well as desire and activity. The ātman is as transparent as clear water and has no support other than itself.*

2. *The relative states [waking, dream, and deep sleep] are features of the mind, but in no way of the ātman, on account of its absolute immutability.*

3. *Having comprehended and transcended these [three] states, one must realise the Fourth, which is the ātman.*

4. *Now, to be the Fourth [in relation to the relativity of the other three superimposed states] means that the ātman is essentially an absolute unity of pure intelligence, like a single homogeneous mass of shining gold.*

5. *This notwithstanding, [the ātman] is not in the least opposed to the other states. In fact, it is none other than [their] witness, and this solely through its essential presence as pure intelligence.*

In the waking state one is conscious of the empirical subject and the empirical object. In the dream state one is aware of the subject and object that are projected by the mind. Lastly, in deep sleep there is only awareness of unity. Thus in all three states there is consciousness, for these states are modifications that are superimposed one after the other.

In the three states, the consciousness remains unchanged. Beyond the three states, there is only the *ātman*/*Brahman* as the foundational cause of the whole quantitative and qualitative universe, and of it one can only say *neti*, *neti*.

6. *On the other hand, if [the Fourth] were to represent a further relative state, one would inevitably reach a void, because in such an eventuality the absolute Reality constituted by the ātman could never be known and realised. Moreover, [the theory of the void is unacceptable] because it is not reasonable to maintain that superimposed objects can subsist in the absence of a substratum.*

To maintain the idea of the void would be equivalent to postulating a composite nocturnal universe that is independent of the dreamer and, as an absurdity, an unlimited quantity of self-contradictory realities, or a projection that has no substratum. Moreover, to posit a fifth or sixth state beyond the Fourth would lead to a process without end.

7. *How, then, can these [three relative states] constitute a valid means of revealing and realising the absoluteness of the ātman? Simply by becoming aware of the pure absolute ātman within these relative states [as their absolute witness].*

How can the relative lead to the Absolute? In effect, the relative cannot lead to the Absolute, for the finite cannot realise the Infinite[1]. The relative, the finite, and so on, are mere movement which has no aseity, so that, once the veil of *māyā* is removed, the limitlessness of the *ātman* reveals itself by itself. 'You are That' is the highest *vākya* of *Vedānta.*

8. *How can one realise it? Only by consciously acknowledging the continuity of the presence of the witness in all the three states.*

9. *Nor could it be objected that in deep sleep there is cessation of this continuity [of awareness]; in fact, it is well known that in this state it is only the existence of 'objects of knowledge' that can be denied. How? [By stating] 'During deep sleep I did not know or experience anything', but it is absolutely impossible to deny the existence of knowledge itself [which knows precisely this]. This proves the immutability and eternity of pure knowledge, and this proof is actually given through the conscious acknowledgement of its continuity in all the states.*

10. *From this it follows that [the pure knowledge that is comparable to the ātman] cannot be proved [or refuted] by purely logical means. Indeed, for all those beings which do not have absolute independent existence there is a corresponding limitation and hence the possibility of becoming objects of proof through inference, but proof of the existence*

[1] The Infinite has neither size (big or small) nor duration (succession of moments, long or short); the Infinite is beyond all size and duration because it is neither space nor time, even though these may be extended to the unlimited/limitless. *Gauḍapāda*, *Māṇḍūkyakārikā*, Raphael's commentary to *kārikā* 97, Chapter IV. Aurea Vidyā, New York.

of the ātman does not depend on any logical reasoning. It is precisely for this reason, therefore, that it is established that the ability to prove [the ātman] belongs only to one who is the ātman itself.

11. *Then if [it were objected that] the ātman is proved by the Scriptures, [one must acknowledge that] the Scriptures are in no way intended to prove the existence of the ātman: their sole purpose is to lead to the realisation of the identity of the ātman with the Brahman through the negation of those attributes which do not pertain to the ātman but have been superimposed on it. [The Scriptures constitute a means of knowledge], not in the sense of proving a thesis but of revealing a meaning [that would otherwise be] unknown [or evident, as it consists precisely in this identity] in two terms*[1]*, the direct meaning of each being well known, however, inasmuch as the ātman is self-evident.*

12. *Remembering 'so'ham – I am That' [in all the states], having no cessation of continuity or any relationship with merit or demerit, one realises that the ātman comprehends and transcends the three states, is eternal, pure, free, changeless, single, and identical to one's own essential nature.*

The *karma/dharma* relating to merit and demerit pertains to the individual and not to the all-embracing *ātman*.

Conscious comprehension leads to the transcendence of the various planes of existence and the conditions inherent in them: one can realise *Brahman* inasmuch as one is *Brahman*. It is therefore necessary to effect a threefold 'comprehension':

[1] The two terms are 'You' and 'That' from the *mahāvākya* 'tat tvam asi'. See the 'Introduction' to *Vākyavṛtti* in this very volume.

the first phase leads to the reintegration of the individualised state into the state of the intelligible *jīva*; the second realises the *jīva* within the principial state of *Īśvara*; the third and definitive comprehension leads to the total solution of the *jīva* into the pure non-dual *Brahman/ātman*.

13. *It is only through its own experience (anubhava) that the sage can recognise that he has attained realisation.*

14. *In this way, by virtue of the grace bestowed by the Teacher, the sage awakens from the deep sleep of ignorance and is immediately liberated from multifarious transmigratory existence.*

15. *This is 'The Teaching on the knowledge of the ātman'. It is only by comprehending it that one attains the goal of existence, and in no other way.*

16. *This is the exposition of Vedānta; this is the exposition of Vedānta.*

May this 'Teaching' therefore awaken, in those who realise *paravairāgya* in order to comprehend and to be, the supra-intelligible state of the *ātman*, the 'Fire that consumes everything', the source of total peace and complete liberation: 'the *ātman* has no support other than itself'.

Here ends Part Four

Here ends the 'Teaching on the knowledge of the ātman composed by the venerable Śaṅkarācārya, the teacher exalted among the wandering paramahaṁsa ascetics

THE FIVEFOLD REALISATION OF ŚIVA

śivapañcākṣaram

In this short work Śaṅkara expounds some cornerstones of *advaita* realisation.

In the first verse he provides a synthesis regarding detachment from the empirical plane: the being that becomes conscious of itself as the *ātman* cannot continue to identify itself with its own psychosomatic vehicle or even with anything that belongs to it and has any relationship to it. Even the intellect (*buddhi*), though it is a vehicle that is relatively pure and suitable for receiving knowledge, must be put on one side, because even it is not one's true nature.

The second verse gives us an explanation of Śaṅkara's teaching on *māyā* (*māyāvāda*). His teaching does not totally deny the existence of the world but gives it its rightful place in the order of things, that is, in the order of relative and not absolute existence. Being a victim of confusion, the individual attributes absoluteness, and therefore truth, to what is only relative; that is, he takes non-being for Being, the unreal for the Real, or – to use Śaṅkara's expression – the snake for the rope. This is the origin of his conflictual situation, which is incomplete and destined to remain so, whatever his external circumstances.

However, just as a word or a gesture is enough to let the wayfarer understand that the snake is, in reality, superimposed on the rope, so for man, too – provided that he has the requisite qualification and aspiration – simply hearing the teaching is enough to awaken him to the full awareness of being the *ātman*. When the disciple learns that he is not the body, that he doesn't really have parents, wife, children, property, teachers or disciples, that he is not in truth immersed in the swirl of events, and so on, but that he is the witness of all these, then his consciousness will spontaneously *recognise itself* as being beyond the whole process of becoming/relativity/appearance, thus resolving himself into the absolute Śiva.

The third verse shows how the universe is an allegorical 'dream' of the Lord *Īśvara*.

Sleep is the natural basis of dreams and of the ephemeral experiences which the individual believes he has in dreams. The universe is completely contained in *Mahat* (the great Mind), from which it arises and into which it is re-absorbed. But beyond *Mahat* and beyond the principial unity there is the non-dual state of the *ātman*. To use Plato's terms, beyond the 'One *and* the many' (becoming) and beyond the 'One-many' (Being) there is the One-One, or the One-Good, which is the metaphysical foundation of Being and of becoming or non-being.

The fourth verse considers the embodied being and states that, in its essential nature, it is beyond the world of becoming and beyond its very experiences in *saṁsāra*. Birth, growth, and death concern the form/appearance, the phenomenon, the *upādhis*, and not the eternal and unchanging *ātman*.

1. *I am not the body, the senses, or the [empirical] mind. I am not the sense of 'I', the totality of the vital energies, or even the intellect. I am far from identifying myself with wife, children, possessions, and all kinds of wealth. I am the innermost ātman, the eternal witness. I am Śiva!*

2. *Just as a rope appears as a snake because [its nature as] rope is hidden, so the ātman appears as jīva when its true nature as ātman is ignored. In truth, when the error is removed by affirming [the illusory nature of the snake], then one recognises it to be a rope. In the same way, when I am told that I possess no body, [I appreciate that] I am not a jīva but [the ātman itself]. I am Śiva!*

'Seeing' the snake instead of the rope results from an error of perspective or a change in sensory perception. When the error is removed, one discovers that there is only the rope, and the sensory illusion vanishes without a trace. This is the superimposition (*adhyāropa* or *adhyāsa*) spoken of by Śaṅkara in other contexts.

3. *In truth, all this [universe], which is not absolute reality, appears, through an illusion, as ātman, whose nature is reality, knowledge, and fullness. However, it [the universe] has the same existence as a dream which is born from the confusion produced by sleep. Pure, complete, eternal, and alone, I am Śiva!*

4. *I have no birth, no growth, no death even. All quality pertains to prakṛti and is therefore said to concern [only] bodies. Likewise, the function of agent, too, and of others, refers only to the sense of 'I' (ahaṁkāra) and has no relationship at all to me, for I am the ātman, which is pure Being. I am Śiva!*

5. *Thus there exists no other universe that is independent of me. Objectivity [seems to be] external and real, but it is only a projection of māyā, which, like the image seen in a mirror, is revealed through me, who am pure Non-duality. I am Śiva!*

A SHORT EXPOSITION OF THE SENTENCE

laghuvākyavṛtti

In this work Śaṅkara examines the *mahāvākya* '*Aham Brahmāsmi* – I am *Brahman*'.

The four most important *mahāvākyas* ('great sentences') are found in the four *Vedas*:

1. *Prajñānam brahma*, *Brahman* is pure knowledge (*Aitareya Upaniṣad*, III, 3) from the *Ṛg Veda*.
2. *Tat tvam asi*, You are That (*Chāndogya Upaniṣad*, VI, VIII, 7)[1] from the *Sāma Veda*.
3. *Ahaṁ Brahmāsmi*, I am *Brahman* (*Bṛhadāraṇyaka Upaniṣad*, I, IV, 10) from the *Yajur Veda*.
4. *Ayam ātmā brahma*, This *ātmā* is *Brahman* (*Māṇḍūkya Upaniṣad*, II) from the *Atharva Veda*.

The *mahāvākyas*, through which the sages (*ṛṣis*) expressed their direct experience of identity with the supreme Reality, are the synthetic expression of the Teaching of *Vedānta*. They may be considered as *mantras* (sacred formulas or words) that are able to confer and establish certain states of consciousness; if they are 'comprehended' by the seeker they can reveal, at a stroke, the supreme reality.

[1] This *mahāvākya* was taken up repeatedly by Śaṅkara, who saw it as the foundation of *Advaita Vedānta* and elucidated it in many of his works; in particular, see his commentary to the *Chāndogya Upaniṣad*.

The instrument for making use of them is not the discursive mind (*manas*) but super-conscious intuition (*buddhi*). It is a question, in fact, of awakening our deepest awareness to the acknowledgement that we are 'That' (the *Brahman*). This method, which is peculiarly *advaita*, seeks to show the disciple a direct way of awakening.

According to *Advaita Vedānta*, the things that cover our real nature are the *upādhis*, which, as a result of *avidyā*, are superimposed on the pure witness of the limitless modifications of the three *guṇas* of *prakṛti* or manifesting nature.

> 'The witness is not touched by the properties of things, because it is distinct from them, because it has no modifications and is indifferent, like a lamp that lights a room but is not touched by the properties of the room.'[1]

1. *The physical body is made of materiality; the subtle body is made of desires; the organs of perception and movement are connected to the mind and the vital energy.*

Śaṅkara succinctly describes the constitution of being in its individual expression.

Thus we have the five sheaths (*kośas*):

- *annamayakośa*
- *prāṇamayakośa*
- *manomayakośa*
- *buddhimayakośa* or *vijñānamayakośa*
- *ānandamayakośa*

To these bodies/aggregates must be added the organs of perception (*jñānendriya*) – hearing, touch, sight, taste,

[1] Śaṅkara, *Vivekacūḍāmaṇi*, 505, op. cit.

smell – and the organs of action (*karmendriya*) – speech, hands, feet, organs of generation and excretion.

> 2. *Ignorance (ajñāna) [creates the] causal [body]; the witness illuminates the intellect (the bodies or sheaths). A ray of consciousness, united to the intellect, becomes the agent of good and evil.*

Avidyā or *ajñāna* (ignorance related to the nature of Being) forms the body or energetic amalgam of the causes, which, in turn, bring about the precipitation of the effects/vehicles or energetic compounds referred to in the first verse.

Behind the causal body, and therefore behind all the sheaths, is the witness (*ātman*) which illumines everything. A ray of the *ātman*, united to the intellect (*buddhi*), forms the *jīva*, the living soul, which imparts life to the various bodies. In turn, a spark of the *jīva* creates the 'individualised or embodied agent', which, by means of the *guṇas*, does good or evil.

Avidyā is the equivalent of *māyā* at the individual level. *Māyā* is that phenomenon which corresponds to the world of names and forms. Form, characterised by the *guṇas*, covers, hides, and limits the inherent reality.

Thus *avidyā* creates the germ/seed for the formation of bodies and for identification with the effects. This is the state of Narcissus, who, seeing his reflection (or projecting his own image), falls in love with his likeness/the object, creates an identity with it, and loses himself, forgetting his original state.

> 3. *In truth, he (the agent) transmigrates (saṁsaret) unceasingly in the two worlds through the impulse of karma. One should very carefully distinguish*

pure Intelligence from its reflection, which is linked to the intellect.

See verse 4 of the *Śivapañcākṣaram*.

Throughout these brief Treatises it is frequently stated that the ultimate witness, the *ātman*, transcends the three states and so is beyond all manifestation, being immutable, unborn, and of the nature of the *Brahman*.

4. *The activities and relationships of the ray of [egoic] consciousness exist only in the waking state (jāgrat) and the dream state (svapna). When the ray of consciousness is in the state of deep sleep (suṣupti), the light of the consciousness (bodhābhāsa) [of the jīva] illuminates [only] the causal state.*

The *jīva* operates on the principial and universal plane; and with a ray of its awareness it operates on the plane of forms.

5. *Even in the waking state the peace of the mind is illuminated by pure Being, just as the ray of consciousness (the jīva) and the activities of the mind are also illuminated.*

All the activities of the mind, and hence of the *jīva* itself, are ever illuminated by the pure *ātman* (See the diagram on page 37).

These subtle bodies, having been already made, during life, into mere instruments of relationship, become – when the realised person abandons the physical/gross form – 'ash' immediately. In rare cases the realised being can even, at a stroke, resolve the entire vehicular *mass* into *energy* and fly towards the undivided Unity; then even the physical body at once disintegrates completely without leaving any trace.

To clarify the whole picture we offer this diagram as a summary:[1]

Sheaths/bodies	States/planes	Analogies
ānandamaya	*prājña* (causal)	*suṣupti* (sleep)
buddhimaya *manomaya* *prāṇamaya*	*taijasa* (subtle)	*svapna* (dream)
annamaya	*viśva* (gross)	*jāgrat* (waking)

It should be remembered that the hyper-physical or subtle world is *qualified* by the tendencies or qualities which the various *jīva*s habitually express. This implies that the subtle world and the gross world are the effect or result of our creations, our qualifications, our imaginations.

> 6. *Water boiling on the fire and being united with the heat becomes a source of heat for the body; in the same way the mind, made radiant by pure intelligence (cit) and united with its reflection, illuminates other [objects].*

Just as water on the fire gains heat and becomes capable of warming the body, so the mind, when illuminated by pure Intelligence (*cit*), can in turn illuminate external objects.

The knowledge of external objects is given by the mind when it is illuminated by the *jīva*.

[1] For an exhaustive exposition of the three states/planes with the five sheaths/bodies, see Śaṅkara, *Vivekacūḍāmaṇi*, 71-209 and *Dṛgdṛśyaviveka*, op. cit.

7. *In form the notions of good and evil are activities of the mind; pure intelligence illuminates these activities together with their objects.*

'If heat and cold, good and ill could by chance touch someone's shadow, in what could he be touched, being distinct from his shadow?

'The witness (*sākṣin*) is not touched by the properties of things, because it is distinct from them, because it has no modifications and is indifferent, as a lamp that lights a room is not touched by the properties of the room.'[1]

8. *Absolute pure intelligence (citiḥ) is distinct from the notion of good and evil and from [sensory] form; in truth, it stands behind the notion of form, taste, and so on.*

9. *The modifications of the mind vary from moment to moment, but not so the pure intelligence. This is joined to the mind like a thread to pearls.*

10. *Just as the thread hidden by the pearls is seen between one pearl and the next, so the pure intelligence covered by the modifications of the mind [shows] between one modification and the next.*

11. *In the interval between one mental modification and the next, there shines the pure unmodified essence of consciousness.*

12. *In this way, one who yearns for the realisation of the Brahman should practise suppressing the modification [of thought] in stages of one, two, three … seconds at a time.*

---

[1] Śaṅkara, *Vivekacūḍāmaṇi*, 504-505, op. cit.

The last three verses are of the utmost importance, because they show:

1. The position of consciousness that needs to be realised in order to uncover pure reality;

2. The technique to use to assist the uncovering of the real witness in us;

3. When the *ātman* reveals itself.

If we wished to express it all in a few words, we could say that the universe is a continuum/discontinuum that can be interrupted at any moment. Between one quantum of light and the next, there is the 'void'.

Between one musical note and the next, there is 'silence'.

Between one idea (modification) and the next, there is the 'all-pervasive Silence'.

If we manage to *expand* the 'space' of silence between one thought-modification and the next, we have realised spatial limitlessness. If we manage to insert ourselves between one photon and the next, then we have left the earthly three-dimensional realm.

We would like to give a somewhat relevant example: it is customary to say that a disciple who is a novice must realise himself, keep the mind silent, and free himself from his ego, but as long as such things are being said it will always be the ego that is chattering and 'thought-modifications' that are expressing themselves. Liberation has to be realised in the 'void', in the realm of Essence and not in the realm of phenomenal existence. Liberation happens when the 'Yes' and the 'No', the 'Is' and the 'Is not' of the mind have vanished into the Unmodified.

This 'void', which is *fullness*, is the *śūnya* of Buddhism.[1]

[1] Of particular interest in this respect are Raphael's words in the Appendix to Chapter 2 of Book II in the *Brahmasūtra*. Aurea Vidyā, New York.

13. *This jīva [covered by the guṇas] which are in movement recognises Brahman without modifications, [by realising] thus: 'I am Brahman'. Such is the message of this treatise.*

The *jīva* is not separated from its Source; the moment the one is free from the modifications of *māyā*, one dissolves like the all-pervasive *ātman*.

14. *Consciousness qualified by 'I am' is [ever] one with Brahman. Those modifications which are self-evident are to be strenuously suppressed.*

15. *If one can [gain] complete suppression [of the modifications of the mind], [then one has] perfect concentration (samādhi), which is the final goal of those who know. If this is not possible, [then in order to re-discover] one's own Essence, one needs to gradually control [the modifications] with great faith.*

If one has the ability to completely resolve the modifications of the mind or the superimpositions upon the pure *ātman*, one will find oneself in the state of *samādhi*. If this is not possible, because the *vāsanā*s are still powerful, one must continue to practise, through one's own efforts, continually, steadily, and with great faith.

16. *Having comprehended the teaching, one should meditate, with faith, on its essential nature, using [all] the faculties of the intellect to the very limit of one's possibilities.*

The disciple who has truly comprehended the *mantra* 'I am *Brahman*' should never allow the mind to move from this principle until the Identity is realised.

17. [One should] meditate on That (Brahman), speak of That, enlightening one another, and yearn for identity with Brahman: this the sages have comprehended [and taught].

To practise meditation on the *Brahman* with a seed and without a seed, to enlighten each other (as disciples), to yearn intensely for identity with the *ātman*: this is what the knowers of *Brahman* have taught.

18. With the firm conviction of one's identity with Brahman, like one's conviction of identity with the body, one attains the goal. One [who has attained the goal] is liberated, beyond all doubt, and can die at any moment.

If the human being finds himself in the condition of being severed from his Essence, then the only aim left to him is to dissolve this condition.

In life there is no purpose other than to 're-discover oneself', 'fulfil oneself', 're-unite oneself', be Unity. Every action, every movement, every externalisation or objectivisation, every inclination represents nothing but alienation, avoidance, and a movement away from what one really is.

One who is liberated, realised, finding himself in the Centre or Pole of Being, no longer takes part in the becoming of things, but reflects the non-activity or immobility of Heaven.

'I do not act any longer, nor do I cause others to act. I do not experience, nor do I cause others to experience.

I do not see, nor do I cause others to see. I am the resplendent and transcendent *ātman*."[1]

[1] Śaṅkara, *Vivekacūḍāmaṇi*, 507, op. cit.

SANSKRIT TEXT

prātaḥsmaraṇastotram ||

prātaḥ smarāmi hṛdi saṁsphurad ātmatattvaṁ
saccitsukhaṁ paramahaṁsagatiṁ turīyam |
yat svapnajāgarasuṣuptim avaiti nityaṁ
tad brahma niṣkalam ahaṁ na ca bhūtasaṅghaḥ || 1 ||

prātar bhajāmi manasāṁ vacasām agamyaṁ
vāco vibhānti nikhilā yadanugraheṇa |
yan neti neti vacanair nigamā avocuḥ
tad devadevam ajam acyutam āhur agryam || 2 ||

prātar namāmi tamasaḥ param arkavarṇaṁ
pūrṇaṁ sanātanapādaṁ puruṣottamākhyam |
yasminn idaṁ jagad aśeṣam aśeṣamūrtau
rajjvā bhujaṅgama iva pratibhāsitaṁ vai || 3 ||

ślokatrayam idaṁ puṇyaṁ lokatrayavibhūṣaṇam |
prātaḥkāle paṭhed yas tu sa gacchet paramaṁ padam || 4 ||

ātmabodhaḥ ||

tapobhiḥ kṣīṇapāpāṇāṁ śāntānāṁ vītarāgiṇāṁ |
mumukṣūṇām apekṣyo 'yam ātmabodho vidhīyate || 1 ||

bodho 'nyasādhanebhyo hi sākṣānmokṣaikasādhanam |
pākasya vahnivaj jñānaṁ vinā mokṣo na sidhyati || 2 ||

avirodhitayā karma nā 'vidyāṁ vinivartayet |
vidyāvidyāṁ nihanty eva tejastimirasaṅghavat || 3 ||

paricchinna ivājñānāt tannāśe sati kevalaḥ |
svayaṁ prakāśate hy ātmā meghāpāye 'ṁśumān iva || 4 ||

ajñānakaluṣaṁ jīvaṁ jñānābhyāsād vinirmalam |
kṛtvā jñānaṁ svayaṁ naśyej jalaṁ katakareṇuvat || 5 ||

saṁsāraḥ svapnatulyo hi rāgadveṣādisaṅkulaḥ |
svakāle satyavad bhāti prabodhe saty asad bhavet || 6 ||

tāvat satyaṁ jagad bhāti śuktikārajataṁ yathā |
yāvan na jñāyate brahma sarvādhiṣṭhānam advayam || 7 ||

upādāne 'khilādhāre jaganti parameśvare |
sargasthitilayānyānti budbudānīva vāriṇi || 8 ||

saccidātmany anusyūte nitye viṣṇau prakalpitāḥ |
vyaktayo vividhās sarvā hāṭake kaṭakādivat || 9 ||

yathākāśo hṛṣīkeśo nānopādhigato vibhuḥ |
tadbhedād bhinnavad bhāti tannāśe kevalo bhavet || 10 ||

nānopādhivaśād eva jātivarṇāśramādayaḥ |
ātmany āropitās toye rasavarṇādibhedavat || 11 ||

pañcīkṛtamahābhūtasaṁbhavaṁ karmasañcitam ।
śarīraṁ sukhaduḥkhānāṁ bhogāyatanam ucyate ॥ 12 ॥

pañcaprāṇamanobuddhir daśendriyasamanvitam ।
apañcīkṛtabhūtotthaṁ sūkṣmāṅgaṁ bhogasādhanam ॥ 13 ॥

anādyavidyānirvācyā kāraṇopādhir ucyate ।
upādhitritayād anyam ātmānam avadhārayet ॥ 14 ॥

pañcakośādiyogena tattanmaya iva sthitaḥ ।
śuddhātmā nīlavastrādiyogena sphaṭiko yathā ॥ 15 ॥

vapus tuṣādibhiḥ kośair yuktaṁ yuktyāvaghātataḥ ।
ātmānam antaraṁ śuddhaṁ vivicyāt taṇḍulaṁ yathā ॥ 16 ॥

sadā sarvagato 'py ātmā na sarvatrāvabhāsate ।
buddhāv evāvabhāseta svaccheṣu pratibimbavat ॥ 17 ॥

dehendriyamanobuddhiprakṛtibhyo vilakṣaṇam ।
tadvṛttisākṣiṇaṁ vidyād ātmānaṁ rājavat sadā ॥ 18 ॥

vyāpṛteṣv indriyeṣv ātmā vyāpārīvāvivekinām ।
dṛśyate 'bhreṣu dhāvatsu dhāvann iva yathā śaśī ॥ 19 ॥

ātmacaitanyam āśritya dehendriyamanodhiyaḥ ।
svakriyārtheṣu vartante sūryalokaṁ yathā janāḥ ॥ 20 ॥

dehendriyaguṇān karmāṇy amale saccidātmani ।
adhyasyanty avivekena gagane nīlatādivat ॥ 21 ॥

ajñānān mānasopādheḥ kartṛtvādīni cātmani ।
kalpyante 'mbugate candre calanādi yathāmbhasaḥ ॥ 22 ॥

rāgecchāsukhaduḥkhādi buddhau satyaṁ pravartate ।
suṣuptau nāsti tannāśe tasmād buddhes tu nātmanaḥ ॥ 23 ॥

prakāśo 'rkasya toyasya śaityam agner yathoṣṇatā ।
svabhāvaḥ saccidānandanityanirmalatātmanaḥ ॥ 24 ॥

ātmanaḥ saccidaṁśaś ca buddher vṛttir iti dvayam ।
saṁyojya cāvivekena jānāmīti pravartate ॥ 25 ॥

ātmano vikriyā nāsti buddher bodho na jātv iti ।
jīvaḥ sarvamalaṁ jñātvā jñātā draṣṭeti muhyati ॥ 26 ॥

rajjusarpavad ātmānaṁ jīvo jñātvā bhayaṁ vahet ।
nāhaṁ jīvaḥ parātmeti jñātaś cen nirbhayo bhavet ॥ 27 ॥

ātmāvabhāsayaty eko buddhyādīnīndriyāṇy api ।
dīpo ghaṭādivat svātmā jaḍais tair nāvabhāsyate ॥ 28 ॥

svabodhe nānyabodhecchā bodharūpatayātmanaḥ ।
na dīpasyānyadīpecchā yathā svātmaprakāśane ॥ 29 ॥

niṣidhya nikhilopādhīn neti netīti vākyataḥ ।
vidyād aikyaṁ mahāvākyair jīvātmaparamātmanoḥ ॥ 30 ॥

avidyākaṁ śarīrādi dṛśyaṁ budbudavat kṣaram ।
etad vilakṣaṇaṁ vidyād ahaṁ brahmeti nirmalam ॥ 31 ॥

dahānyatvān na me janmajarākārśyalayādayaḥ ।
śabdādiviṣayaiḥ saṅgo nirindriyatayā na ca ॥ 32 ॥

amanatvān na me duḥkharāgadveṣabhayādayaḥ ।
aprāṇo hy amanāḥ śubhra ity ādiśrutiśāsanāt ॥ 33 ॥

nirguṇo niṣkriyo nityo nirvikalpo nirañjanaḥ ।
nirvikāro nirākāro nityamukto ’smi nirmalaḥ ॥ 34 ॥

aham ākāśavat sarvaṁ bahirantargato ’cyutaḥ ।
sadā sarvasamaḥ śuddho nissaṅgo nirmalo ’calaḥ ॥ 35 ॥

nityaśuddhavimuktaikam akhaṇḍānandam advayam ।
satyaṁ jñānam anantaṁ yat paraṁ brahmāham eva tat ॥ 36 ॥

evaṁ nirantarābhyastā brahmaivāsmīti vāsanā ।
haraty avidyāvikṣepān rogān iva rasāyanam ॥ 37 ॥

viviktadeśa āsīno virāgo vijitendriyaḥ ।
bhāvayed ekam ātmānaṁ tam anantam ananyadhīḥ ॥ 38 ॥

ātmany evākhilaṁ dṛśyaṁ pravilāpya dhiyā sudhīḥ ।
bhāvayed ekam ātmānaṁ nirmalākāśavat sadā ॥ 39 ॥

rūpavarṇādikaṁ sarvaṁ vihāya paramārthavit ।
paripūrṇacidānandasvarūpeṇāvatiṣṭhate ॥ 40 ॥

jñātṛjñānajñeyabhedaḥ pare nātmani vidyate ।
cidānandaikarūpatvād dīpyate svayam eva hi ॥ 41 ॥

evam ātmāraṇau dhyānamathane satataṁ kṛte ।
uditāvagatir jvālā sarvājñānendhanaṁ dahet ॥ 42 ॥

aruṇeneva bodhena pūrvaṁ santamase hṛte ।
tata āvirbhaved ātmā svayam evāṁśumān iva ॥ 43 ॥

ātmā tu satataṁ prāpto 'py aprāptavad avidyayā ।
tannāśe prāptavad bhāti svakaṇṭhābharaṇaṁ yathā ॥ 44 ॥

sthāṇau puruṣavad bhrāntyā kṛtā brahmaṇi jīvatā ।
jīvasya tāttvike rūpe tasmin dṛṣṭe nivartate ॥ 45 ॥

tattvasvarūpānubhavād utpannaṁ jñānam añjasā ।
ahaṁ mameti cājñānaṁ bādhate digbhramādivat ॥ 46 ॥

samyag vijñānavān yogī svātmany evākhilaṁ jagat ।
ekaṁ ca sarvam ātmānam īkṣate jñānacakṣuṣā ॥ 47 ॥

ātmaivedaṁ jagat sarvam ātmano 'nyan na vidyate ।
mṛdo yadvad ghaṭādīni svātmānaṁ sarvam īkṣate ॥ 48 ॥

jīvanmuktas tu tad vidvān pūrvopādhiguṇāṁs tyajet ।
saccidānanadarūpatvād bhaved bhramara kīṭavat ॥ 49 ॥

tīrtvā mohārṇavaṁ hatvā rāgadveṣādirākṣasān ।
yogī śāntisamāyukta ātmārāmo virājate ॥ 50 ॥

bhāyānityasukhāsaktiṁ hitvātmasukhanirvṛtaḥ ।
ghaṭasthadīpavat svasthaḥ svāntareva prakāśate ॥ 51 ॥

upādhistho 'pi taddharmair alipto vyomavan muniḥ ।
sarvavin mūḍhavat tiṣṭhed asakto vāyuvac caret ॥ 52 ॥

upādhivilayād viṣṇau nirviśeṣaṁ viśen muniḥ ।
jale jalaṁ viyad vyomni tejas tejasi vā yathā ॥ 53 ॥

yallābhān nāparo lābho yatsukhān nāparaṁ sukham |
yajjñānān nāparaṁ jñānaṁ tad brahmety avadhārayet || 54 ||

yad dṛṣṭvā nāparaṁ dṛśyaṁ yad bhūtvā na punar bhāvaḥ |
yaj jñātvā nāparaṁ jñeyaṁ tad brahmety avadhārayet || 55 ||

tiryag ūrdhvam adhaḥ pūrṇaṁ saccidānandam advayam |
anantaṁ nityam ekaṁ yat tad brahmety avadhārayet || 56 ||

atadvyāvṛttirūpeṇa vedāntair lakṣyate 'dvayam |
akhaṇḍānandam ekaṁ yat tad brahmety avadhārayet || 57 ||

akhaṇḍānandarūpasya tasyānandalavāśritāḥ |
brahmādyās tāratamyena bhavanty ānandino 'khilāḥ || 58 ||

tadyuktam akhilaṁ vastu vyavahāras tadanvitaḥ |
tasmāt sarvagataṁ brahma kṣīre sarpir ivākhile || 59 ||

anaṇv asthūlam ahrasvam adīrgham ajam avyayam |
arūpaguṇavarnākhyaṁ tad brahmety avadhārayet || 60 ||

yadbhāsā bhāsyate 'rkādi bhāsyair yat tu na bhāsyate |
yena sarvam idaṁ bhāti tad brahmety avadhārayet || 61 ||

svayamantarbahirvyāpya bhāsayann akhilaṁ jagat |
brahma prakāśate vahniprataptāyasapiṇḍavat || 62 ||

jagadvilakṣaṇaṁ brahma brahmaṇo 'nyan na kiñcana |
brahmānyad bhāti cen mithyā yathā marumarīcikā || 63 ||

dṛśyate śrūyate yad yad brahmaṇo 'nyan na tad bhavet |
tattvajñānāc ca tad brahma saccidānandam advayam || 64 ||

sarvagaṁ saccidātmānaṁ jñānacakṣur nirīkṣate |
ajñānacakṣur nekṣeta bhāsvantaṁ bhānum andhavat || 65 ||

śravaṇādibhir uddīpta jñānāgniparitāpitaḥ |
jīvas sarvamalān muktaḥ svarṇavad dyotate svayam || 66 ||

hṛdākāśodito hy ātmā bodhabhānus tamo 'pahṛt |
sarvavyāpī sarvadhārī bhāti bhāsayate 'khilam || 67 ||

digdeśakālādyanapekṣya sarvagaṁ
śītādihṛn nityasukhaṁ nirañjanam |
yas svātmatīrthaṁ bhajate viniṣkriyaḥ
sa sarvavit sarvagato 'mṛto bhavet || 68 ||

ity ātmabodhaḥ samāptaḥ ||

daśaślokīstutiḥ ||

tapoyajñadanādibhiḥ śuddhabuddhir
virakto nṛpadau pade tucchabuddhyā |
parityajya sarvaṁ yad āpnoti tattvaṁ
paraṁ brahma nityaṁ tad evāham asmi || 1 ||

dayāluṁ guruṁ brahmaniṣṭhaṁ praśāntaṁ
samārādhya matyā vicārya svarūpaṁ |
yad āpnoti tattvaṁ nididhyāsya vidvān
paraṁ brahma nityaṁ tad evāham asmi || 2 ||

yad ānandarūpaṁ prakāśasvarūpaṁ
nirastaprapañcaṁ paricchedaśūnyam |
ahaṁbrahmavṛttyaikagamyaṁ turīyaṁ
paraṁ brahma nityaṁ tad evāham asmi || 3 ||

yad ajñānato bhāti viśvaṁ samastaṁ
vinaṣṭaṁ ca sadyo yad ātmaprabodhe |
manovāgatītaṁ viśuddhaṁ vimuktaṁ
paraṁ brahma nityaṁ tad evāham asmi || 4 ||

niṣedhe kṛte netinetītivākyaiḥ
samādhisthitānāṁ yad ābhāti pūrṇaṁ |
avasthātrayātītam ekaṁ turīyaṁ
paraṁ brahma nityaṁ tad evāham asmi || 5 ||

yadānandaleśais tad ānandiviśvaṁ
yadābhānasattve tad ābhāti sarvam |
yadālocanārūpaman tat samastaṁ
paraṁ brahma nityaṁ tad evāham asmi || 6 ||

anantaṁ vibhuṁ sarvayoniṁ nirṭhaṁ
śivaṁ saṅgahīnaṁ yad oṁkāragamyam |
nirākāramatyujjvalaṁ mṛtyuhīnaṁ
paraṁ brahma nityaṁ tad evāham asmi || 7 ||

yadānandasindhau nimagnaḥ pumān syād
avidyāvilāsaḥ samastaḥ prapañcaḥ |
yadā na sphuraty adbhutaṁ yannimittaṁ
paraṁ brahma nityaṁ tad evāham asmi || 8 ||

svarūpānusandhānarūpāṁ stutiṁ yaḥ
paṭhed ādarād bhaktibhāvo manuṣyaḥ |
śṛṇotīha vā nityam udyuktacitto
bhaved viṣṇur atraiva vedapramāṇāt || 9 ||

vijñānanāvaṁ parigṛhya kaścit
tared yad ajñānamayaṁ bhavābdhim |
jñānāsīnā yo hi vicchidya tṛṣṇāṁ
viṣṇoḥ padaṁ yāti sa eva dhanyaḥ || 10 ||

jīvanmuktānandalaharī ||

pure paurān paśyan narayuvatinānākṛtimayān
suveṣān svarṇālaṅkaraṇakalitāṁś citrasadṛśān |
svayaṁ sākṣād draṣṭety api ca kalayaṁs taiḥ saha raman
munir na vyāmohaṁ bhajati gurudīkṣākṣatatamāḥ || 1 ||

vane vṛkṣān paśyan dalaphalabharān namrasuśikhān |
ghanacchāyācchannān bahula kalakūjaddvijagaṇān |
bhajanghasre rātrāv avanitalatalpaika śayano
munir na vyāmohaṁ bhajati gurudīkṣākṣatatamāḥ || 2 ||

kadācit prāsāde kvacid api ca saudheṣu dhaninām
kadā kāle śaile kvacid api ca kūleṣu saritām |
kuṭīre dāntānāṁ munijanavarāṇām api vasan
munir na vyāmohaṁ bhajati gurudīkṣākṣatatamāḥ || 3 ||

kvacid bālaiḥ sārdhaṁ karatalajatālaiḥ saha sitaiḥ
kvacit tāruṇyālaṅkṛtanaravadhūbhiḥ saha raman |
kvacid vṛddhaiś cintākulitahṛdayaiś cāpi vilapan
munir na vyāmohaṁ bhajati gurudīkṣākṣatatamāḥ || 4 ||

kadācid vidvadbhir vividiṣubhir atyantaniratаiḥ
kadācit kāvyālaṅkṛtirasarasālaiḥ kavivaraiḥ |
kadācit sattarkair anumitiparais tārkikavaraiḥ
munir na vyāmohaṁ bhajati gurudīkṣākṣatatamāḥ || 5 ||

kadā dhyānābhyāsaiḥ kvacid api saparyāṁ vikasitaiḥ
sugandhaiḥ satpuṣpaiḥ kvacid api dalair eva vimalaiḥ |
prakurvan devasya pramuditamanāḥ saṁnatiparo
munir na vyāmohaṁ bhajati gurudīkṣākṣatatamāḥ || 6 ||

śivāyāḥ śambhor vā kvacid api ca viṣṇor api kadā
gaṇādhyakṣasyāpi prakaṭatapanasyāpi ca kadā |
paṭhan vai nāmāliṁ nayana racitānanda salilo
munir na vyāmohaṁ bhajati gurudīkṣākṣatatamāḥ || 7 ||

kadā gaṅgāmbhobhiḥ kvacid api ca kūpotthitajalaiḥ
kvacit kāsārotthaiḥ kvacid api saduṣṇaiś ca śiśiraiḥ |
bhajan snānaṁ bhūtyā kvacid api ca karpūranibhayā
munir na vyāmohaṁ bhajati gurudīkṣākṣatatamāḥ || 8 ||

kadācij jāgṛtyāṁ viṣayakaraṇaiḥ saṁvyavaharan
kadācit svapnasthān api ca viṣayān eva ca bhajan |
kadācit sauṣuptaṁ sukham anubhavann eva satataṁ
munir na vyāmohaṁ bhajati gurudīkṣākṣatatamāḥ || 9 ||

kadā 'py āśāvāsāḥ kvacid api ca divyāmbaradharaḥ
kvacit pañcāsyotthāṁ tvacam api dadhānaḥ kaṭitaṭe |
manasvī niḥsaṅgaḥ sujanahṛdayānandajanako
munir na vyāmohaṁ bhajati gurudīkṣākṣatatamāḥ || 10 ||

kadācit sattvasthaḥ kvacid api rajovṛttisugatas
tamovṛttiḥ kvāpi tritayarahitaḥ kvāpi ca punaḥ |
kadācit saṁsārī śrūtipathavihārī kvacid aho
munir na vyāmohaṁ bhajati gurudīkṣākṣatatamāḥ || 11 ||

kadācin maunasthaḥ kvacid api ca vāgvādanirataḥ
kadācit svānande hasati rabhasā tyaktavacanaḥ |
kadācil lokānāṁ vyavahṛtisamālokanaparo
munir na vyāmohaṁ bhajati gurudīkṣākṣatatamāḥ || 12 ||

kadācic chalīnāṁ vikacamukhapadmeṣu kabalān
kṣipaṁs tāsāṁ kvāpi svayam api ca gṛhyan svamukhataḥ |
tadadvaitaṁ rūpaṁ nijaparavihīnaṁ prakaṭayan
munir na vyāmohaṁ bhajati gurudīkṣākṣatatamāḥ || 13 ||

kvacic chaivaiḥ sārdhaṁ kvacid api ca śālaiḥ saha raman
kadā viṣṇor bhaktaiḥ kvacid api ca sauraiḥ saha vasan |
kadā gāṇāpatyair gatasakalabhedo 'dvayatayā
munir na vyāmohaṁ bhajati gurudīkṣākṣatatamāḥ || 14 ||

nirākāraṁ kvāpi kvacid api ca sākāram amalaṁ
nijaṁ śaivaṁ rūpaṁ vividhaguṇabhedena bahudhā |
kadā 'ścaryaṁ paśyan kim idam iti hṛṣyann api kadā
munir na vyāmohaṁ bhajati gurudīkṣākṣatatamāḥ || 15 ||

kadā 'dvaitaṁ paśyann akhilam api satyaṁ śivamayaṁ
mahāvākyārthānām avagatisamabhyāsavaśataḥ |

gatadvaitābhāsaḥ śiva śiva śivety eva vilapan
munir na vyāmohaṁ bhajati gurudīkṣākṣatatamāḥ || 16 ||

imāṁ muktāvasthāṁ paramaśivasaṁsthāṁ gurukṛpā-
sudhāpāṅgavyāpyāṁ sahaja sukhavāpyām anudinam |
muhur majjan majjan bhajati sukṛtaiś cen naravaraḥ
sadā yogī tyāgī kavir iti vadantīha kavayaḥ || 17 ||

yātipañcakam ||

vedāntavākyeṣu sadā ramanto
    bhikṣānnamātreṇa ca tuṣṭimantaḥ |
viśokam antaḥkaraṇe carantaḥ
    kaupīnavantaḥ khalu bhāgyavantaḥ || 1 ||

mūlaṁ taroḥ kevalam āśrayantaḥ
    pāṇidvayaṁ bhoktum amatrayantaḥ |
kanthām iva śrīm api kutsayantaḥ
    kaupīnavantaḥ khalu bhāgyavantaḥ || 2 ||

dehābhimānaṁ parihṛtya dūrāt
    ātmānam ātmany avalokayantaḥ |
nāntar na madhyaṁ na bahiḥ smarantaḥ
    kaupīnavantaḥ khalu bhāgyavantaḥ || 3 ||

svānandabhāve parituṣṭimantaḥ
    saṁśānta sarvendriyavṛttimantaḥ |
ahar niśaṁ brahmaṇi ye ramantaḥ
    kaupīnavantaḥ khalu bhāgyavantaḥ || 4 ||

brahmākṣaraṁ pāvanam uccarantaḥ
    patiṁ paśūnāṁ hṛdi bhāvayantaḥ |
bhikṣāśanā dikṣu paribhramantaḥ
    kaupīnavantaḥ khalu bhāgyavantaḥ || 5 ||

dhanyāṣṭakam ||

taj jñānaṁ praśamakaraṁ yad indriyāṇāṁ
taj jñeyaṁ yad upaniṣatsu niścitārtham |
te dhanyā bhuvi paramārthaniścitehāḥ
śeṣās tu bhramanilaye paribhramanti || 1 ||

ādau vijitya viṣayān madamoharāga-
dveṣādiśatrugaṇam āhṛtayogarājyāḥ |
jñātvā mataṁ samanubhūya parātmavidyā-
kāntāsukhaṁ vanagṛhe vicaranti dhanyāḥ || 2 ||

tyaktvā gṛhe ratim adhogatihetubhūtām
ātmecchayopaniṣadartharasaṁ pibantaḥ |
vītaspṛhā viṣayabhogapade viraktā
dhanyāś caranti vijaneṣu vimuktasaṅgāḥ || 3 ||

tyaktvā mamāham iti bandhakare pade dve
mānāvamānasadṛśāḥ samadarśinaś ca |
kartāram anyam avagamya tadarpitāni
kurvanti karmaparipākaphalāni dhanyāḥ || 4 ||

tyaktvaiṣaṇātrayam avekṣitamokṣamārgā
bhaikṣāmṛtena parikalpitadehayātrāḥ |
jyotiḥ parāt parataraṁ paramātmasaṁjñaṁ
dhanyā dvijā rahasi hṛdy avalokayanti || 5 ||

nāsan na san na sadasan na mahan na cāṇu
na strī pumān na ca na puṁsakam ekabījam |
yair brahma tat samam upāsitam ekacittair
dhanyā virejur itare bhavapāśabaddhāḥ || 6 ||

ajñānapaṅkaparimagnam apetasāraṁ
duḥkhālayaṁ maraṇajanmajarāvasaktam |
saṁsārabandhanam anityam avekṣya dhanyā
jñānāsinā tadavaśīrya viniścayanti || 7 ||

śāntair ananyamatibhir madhurasvabhāvaiḥ
ekatvaniścitamanobhir apetamohaiḥ | |
sākaṁ vaneṣu viditātmapadasvarūpais
tad vastu samyag aniśaṁ vimṛśanti dhanyāḥ || 8 ||

dakṣiṇāmūrtistotram ||

viśvaṁ darpaṇadṛśyamānanagarītulyaṁ nijāntargataṁ
paśyann ātmani māyayā bahir ivodbhūtaṁ yathā nidrayā | yaḥ
sākṣāt kurute prabodhasamaye svātmānam evādvayaṁ
tasmai śrīgurumūrtaye nama idaṁ śrīdakṣiṇāmūrtaye || 1 ||

bījasyāntar ivāṅkuro jagad idaṁ prāṅ nirvikalpaṁ punar
māyākalpitadeśakālakalanāvaicitryacitrīkṛtam |
māyāvīva vijṛmbhayaty api mahāyogīva yaḥ svecchayāḥ
tasmai śrīgurumūrtaye nama idaṁ śrīdakṣiṇāmūrtaye || 2 ||

yasyaiva sphuraṇaṁ sadātmakam asatkalpārthagaṁ bhāsate
sākṣāt tat tvam asīti vedavacasā yo bodhayaty āśritān |
yat sākṣāt karaṇād bhaven na punar āvṛttir bhavāmbhonidhau
tasmai śrīgurumūrtaye nama idaṁ śrīdakṣiṇāmūrtaye || 3 ||

nānācchidraghaṭodarasthitamahādīpaprabhābhāsvaram
jñānaṁ yasya tu cakṣurādikāraṇadvārā bahiḥ spandate |
jānāmīti tam eva bhāntam anubhāty etat samastaṁ jagat
tasmai śrīgurumūrtaye nama idaṁ śrīdakṣiṇāmūrtaye || 4 ||

dehaṁ prāṇam apīndriyāṇy api calāṁ buddhiṁ śūnyaṁ viduḥ
strībālān ghajaḍopamās tv aham iti bhrāntā bhṛśaṁ vādinaḥ |
māyāśaktivilāsakalpitamahāvyāmohasahāriṇe
tasmai śrīgurumūrtaye nama idaṁ śrīdakṣiṇāmūrtaye || 5 ||

rāhugrastadivākarendusadṛśo māyāsamācchādanāt
sanmātraḥ kara-ṇopasaṁharaṇato yo 'bhūt suṣuptaḥ pumān |
prāg asvāpsam iti prabodhasamaye yaḥ pratyabhijñāyate
tasmai śrīgurumūrtaye nama idaṁ śrīdakṣiṇāmūrtaye || 6 ||

bālyādiṣv api jāgradādiṣu tathā sarvāsv avasthāsv api
vyāvṛttāsv anuvartamānam aham ity antaḥ sphurantaṁ sadā |
svātmānaṁ prakaṭī karoti bhajatāṁ yo mudrayā bhadrayā
tasmai śrīgurumūrtaye nama idaṁ śrīdakṣiṇāmūrtaye || 7 ||

viśvaṁ paśyati kāryakāraṇatayā svasvāmisaṁbandhataḥ
śiṣṭācārya-tayā tathaiva pitṛputrādyātmanā bhedataḥ I
svapne jāgrati vā ya eṣa puruṣo māyāparibhrāmitas
tasmai śrīguru-mūrtaye nama idaṁ śrīdakṣiṇāmūrtaye II 8 II

bhūr ambhāṁsy analo 'nilo 'mbaramaharnātho himāṁśuḥ pumān
ity ābhāti carācarātmakam idaṁ yasyaiva mūrtyaṣṭakam I
nānyat kiṁcana vidyate vimṛśatāṁ yasmāt parasmād vibhos
tasmai śrīgurumūrtaye nama idaṁ śrīdakṣiṇāmūrtaye II 9 II

sarvātmatvam iti sphuṭīkṛtam idaṁ yasmād amuṣmiṁs tave
tenāsya śravaṇāt tadarthamananād dhyānāc ca saṁkīrtanāt I
sarvātmatvamahāvibhūtisahitaṁ syād īśvaratvaṁ svataḥ
sidhyet tat punar aṣṭadhā pariṇataṁ caiśvaryam avyāhatam II 10 II

vākyavṛttiḥ ||

śrīgaṇeśāya namaḥ ||

sargasthitipralayahetum acintyaśaktiṁ
viśveśvaraṁ viditaviśvam anantamūrtim |
nirmuktabandhanam apārasukhāmburaśiṁ
śrīvallabhaṁ vimalabodhaghanam namāmi || 1 ||

yasya prasādād aham eva viṣṇur
mayy eva sarvaṁ parikalpitaṁ ca |
itthaṁ vijñānāmi sadātmarūpaṁ
tasyāṅghripadmaṁ praṇato 'smi nityam || 2 ||

tāpatrayārkasantaptaḥ kaścid udvignamānasaḥ |
śamādisādhanair yuktaṁ sadguruṁ paripṛcchati || 3 ||

anāyāsena yenāsmān mucyeyaṁ bhavabandhanāt |
tan me saṁkṣipya bhagavaṅ kevalaṁ kṛpayā vada || 4 ||

gurur uvāca |
sādhvī te vacanavyaktiḥ pratibhāti vadāmi te |
idaṁ tad iti vispaṣṭaṁ sāvadhānamanāḥ śṛṇu || 5 ||

tattvamasyādivākyotthaṁ yaj jīvaparamātmanoḥ |
tādātmaviṣayaṁ jñānaṁ tad idaṁ muktisādhanam || 6 ||

śiṣya uvāca |
ko jīvaḥ kaḥ paraḥ cātmā tādātmyaṁ vā kathaṁ tayoḥ |
tattvamasyādivākyaṁ vā kathaṁ tat pratipādayet || 7 ||

gurur uvāca |
atra brūmaḥ samādhānaṁ ko 'nyo jīvas tvam eva hi |
yas tvaṁ pṛcchasi māṁ ko 'haṁ brahmaivāsi na saṁśayaḥ || 8 ||

śiṣya uvāca ।
padārtham eva jānāmi nādyāpi bhagavan sphuṭam ।
ahaṁ brahmeti vākyārthaṁ pratipadye kathaṁ vada ॥ 9 ॥

gurur uvāca ।
satyam āha bhavān atra vigānaṁ naiva vidyate ।
hetuḥ padārthabodho hi vākyārthāvagater iha ॥ 10 ॥

antaḥkaraṇatadvṛttisākṣicaitanyavigrahaḥ ।
ānandarūpaḥ satyaḥ saṅ kiṁ nātmānaṁ prapadyase ॥ 11 ॥

satyānandasvarūpaṁ dhīsākṣiṇaṁ bodhavigraham ।
cintayātmatayā nityaṁ tyaktvā dehādigaṁ dhiyam ॥ 12 ॥

rūpādimān yataḥ piṇḍas tato nātmā ghaṭādivat ।
viyadādimāhābhūtavikāratvāc ca kumbhavat ॥ 13 ॥

anātmā yadi piṇḍo 'yam uktahetubalān mataḥ ।
karāmalakavatsākṣād ātmānaṁ pratipādaya ॥ 14 ॥

ghaṭadraṣṭā ghaṭād bhinnaḥ sarvathā na ghaṭo yathā ।
dehadraṣṭā tathā deho nāham ity avadhāraya ॥ 15 ॥

evam indriyadṛṅ nāham indriyāṇīti niścinu ।
manobuddhis tathā prāṇo nāham ity avadhāraya ॥ 16 ॥

saṁghato 'pi tathā nāham iti dṛśyavilakṣaṇam ।
draṣṭāram anumānena nipuṇaṁ saṁpradhāraya ॥ 17 ॥

dehendriyādayo bhāvā hānādivyāpṛtikṣamāḥ ।
yasya sannidhimātreṇa so 'ham ity avadhāraya ॥ 18 ॥

anāpannavikāraḥ sannayaskāntavad eva yaḥ ।
buddhyādīṁś calayet pratyak so 'ham ity avadhāraya ॥ 19 ॥

ajaḍātmavad ābhānti yat sannidyāj jaḍā api ।
dehendriyamanaḥprāṇāḥ so 'ham ity avadhāraya ॥ 20 ॥

agaman me mano 'nyatra sampratam ca sthirīkṛtam ।
evaṁ yo vetti dhīvṛttiṁ so 'ham ity avadhāraya ॥ 21 ॥

svapnajāgarite suptiṁ bhāvābhāvau dhiyāṁ tathā ।
yo vetty avikriyaḥ sākṣāt so 'ham ity avadhāraya ॥ 22 ॥

ghaṭāvabhāsako dīpo ghaṭād anyo yatheṣyate ।
dehāvabhāsako dehī tathāhaṁ bodhavigrahaḥ ॥ 23 ॥

putravittādayo bhāvā yasya śeṣatayā priyāḥ ।
draṣṭā sarvapriyatamaḥ so 'ham ity avadhāraya ॥ 24 ॥

parapremāspadatayā mā nābhuvam ahaṁ sadā ।
bhūyāsam iti yo draṣṭā so 'ham ity avadhāraya ॥ 25 ॥

yaḥ sākṣilakṣaṇo bodhas tvaṁpadārthaḥ sa ucyate ।
sākṣitvam api boddhṛtvam avikāritayātmanaḥ ॥ 26 ॥

dehendriyamanaḥprāṇāhaṁkṛtibhyo vilakṣaṇaḥ ।
projjhitāśeṣaṣaḍbhāvavikāras tvaṁpadābhidhaḥ ॥ 27 ॥

tvamartham evaṁ niścitya tadarthaṁ cintayet punaḥ ।
atadvyāvṛttirūpeṇa sākṣād vidhimukhena ca ॥ 28 ॥

nirastāśeṣasaṁsāradoṣo 'sthūlādilakṣaṇaḥ ।
adṛśyatvādiguṇakaḥ parākṛtatamomalaḥ ॥ 29 ॥

nirastātiśayānandaḥ satyaprajñānavigrahaḥ ।
sattāsvalakṣaṇaḥ pūrṇaḥ parātmātmeti gīyate ॥ 30 ॥

sarvajñātvaṁ pareśatvaṁ tathā saṁpūrṇaśaktitā ।
vedaiḥ samarthyate yasya tad brahmety avadhāraya ॥ 31 ॥

yajjñānāt sarvavijñānaṁ śrutiṣu pratipāditam ।
mṛdādyanekadṛṣṭāntais tad brahmety avadhāraya ॥ 32 ॥

yadānantyaṁ pratijñāya śrutis tatsiddhaye jagau ।
tatkāryatvaṁ prapañcasya tad brahmety avadhāraya ॥ 33 ॥

vijijñāsyatayā yac ca vedānteṣu mumukṣubhiḥ ।
samarthyate 'tiyatnena tad brahmety avadhāraya ॥ 34 ॥

jīvātmanā praveśaś ca niyantṛtvaṁ ca tān prati ।
śrūyate yasya vedeṣu tad brahmety avadhāraya ॥ 35 ॥

karmaṇāṁ phaladātṛtvaṁ yasyaiva śrūyate śrutau ।
jīvānāṁ hetukartṛtvaṁ tad brahmety avadhāraya ॥ 36 ॥

tattvaṁpadārthau nirṇītau vākyārthaś cintyate 'dhunā ।
tādātmyam atra vākyārthas tayor eva padārthayoḥ ॥ 37 ॥

saṁsargo vā viśiṣṭo vā vākyārtho nātra saṁmataḥ ।
akhaṇḍaikarasatvena vākyārtho viduṣāṁ mataḥ ॥ 38 ॥

pratyagbodho ya ābhāti so 'dvayānandalakṣaṇaḥ ।
advayānandarūpaś ca pratyagbodhaikalakṣaṇaḥ ॥ 39 ॥

ittham anyonyatādātmyapratipattir yadā bhavet ।
abrahmatvaṁ tvamarthasya vyāvarteta tadaiva hi ॥ 40 ॥

tadarthasya ca pārokṣyaṁ yady eva kiṁ tataḥ śṛṇu ।
pūrṇānandaikarūpeṇa pratyagbodho 'vatiṣṭhate ॥ 41 ॥

tattvamasyādivākyaṁ ca tādātmyapratipādane ।
lakṣyau tattvaṁpadārthau dvāv upādāya pravartate ॥ 42 ॥

hitvā dvau śabdau vākyau hi vākyaṁ vākyārthabodhane ।
yathā pravartate 'smābhis tathā vyākhyātam ādarāt ॥ 43 ॥

ālambanatayābhāti yo 'smatpratyayaśabdayoḥ ।
antaḥkaraṇasaṁbhinnabodhaḥ sa tvaṁpadābhidhaḥ ॥ 44 ॥

māyopādhir jagadyoniḥ sarvajñātvādilakṣaṇaḥ ।
pārokṣyaśabalaḥ satyādyātmakas tatpadābhidhaḥ ॥ 45 ॥

pratyakparokṣataikasya sadvitīyatvapūrṇatā ।
virudhyate yatas tasmāl lakṣaṇā saṁpravartate ॥ 46 ॥

mānāntaravirodhe tu mukhyārthasya parigrahe ।
mukhyārthenāvinābhūte pratītir lakṣaṇocyate ॥ 47 ॥

tattvamasyādivākyeṣu lakṣaṇā bhāgalakṣaṇā ।
so 'yam ityādivākyasthapadayor iva nāparā ॥ 48 ॥

ahaṁ brahmeti vākyārthabodho yāvad dṛḍhībhavet ।
śamādisahitas tāvad abhyasec chravaṇādikam ॥ 49 ॥

śrutyācāryaprasādena dṛḍho bodho yadā bhavet ।
nirastāśeṣasaṁsāranidānaḥ puruṣas tadā ॥ 50 ॥

viśīrṇakāryakaraṇo bhūtasūkṣmair anāvṛtaḥ ।
vimuktakarmanigaḍaḥ sadya eva vimucyate ॥ 51 ॥

prārabdhakarmabhogena jīvanmukto yadā bhavet ।
kiñcit kālam anārabdhakarmabandhasya saṁkṣaye ॥ 52 ॥

nirastātiśayānandaṁ vaiṣṇavaṁ paramaṁ padam ।
punar āvṛttirahitaṁ kaivalyaṁ pratipadyate ॥ 53 ॥

iti paramahaṁsaparivrājaka
acāryaśrīmacchaṅkarācāryaviracitā
vākyavṛttiḥ samāptā ॥

upadeśapañcaratnam ||

vedo nityam adhīyatāṁ taduditaṁ karma svanuṣṭhīyatāṁ
teneśasya vidhīyatām apacitiḥ kāmye matis tyajyatām |
pāpaudhaḥ paridhuyatāṁ bhavasukhe doṣo 'nusandhīyatām
ātmecchā vyavasīyatāṁ nijagṛhā stūrṇaṁ vinirgamyatām || 1 ||

saṅgaḥ satsu vidhīyatāṁ bhagavato muktir dṛḍhā dhīyatāṁ
śāntyādiḥ paricīyatāṁ dṛḍhataraṁ karmāśu saṁtyajyatām |
sadvidvān upasarpyatāṁ pratidinaṁ tatpādukā sevyatāṁ
brahmaikākṣaram arthyatāṁ śrutiśirovākyaṁ samākarṇyatām || 2 ||

vākyārthaś ca vicāryatāṁ śrutiśiraḥ pakṣaḥ samāśrīyatāṁ
dustarkāt suviramyatāṁ śrutimatas tarke 'nusandhīyatām |
brahmāsmīti vibhāvyatām ahar ahar gaveḥ parityajyatāṁ
deho 'haṁmati rujjñyatāṁ budhajanair vadaḥ parityajyatām || 3 ||

kṣuddhyādhiś ca cikitsyatāṁ pratidinaṁ bhikṣauṣadhaṁ bhujyatāṁ
svādvannaṁ na tu yācyatāṁ vidhivaśāt prāptena saṁtuṣyatāṁ |
śītoṣṇādi viṣahyatāṁ na tu vṛthā vākyaṁ samuccāryatām
audāsīnyam abhīpsyatāṁ janakṛpānaiṣṭhuryam utsṛjyatām || 4 ||

ekānte sukham āsyatāṁ paratare cetaḥ samādhīyatāṁ
pūrṇātmā satyam īkṣyatāṁ jagad idaṁ tadbādhitaṁ dṛśyatām |
prākkarma pravilāpyatāṁ citibalān nāpy uttaraiḥ śliṣyatāṁ
prārabdha tv iha bhujyatām atha parabrahmātmanā sthīatām || 5 |

anātmaśrīvigarhaṇam ||

labdhāvidyā rājamānyā tataḥ kiṁ
prāptā saṁpatprābhavāḍhyā tataḥ kim |
bhuktā nārī sundarāṅgī tataḥ kiṁ
yena svātmā naiva sākṣātkṛto 'bhūt || 1 ||

keyūrādyair bhūṣito vā tataḥ kiṁ
kauśeyādyair āvṛto vā tataḥ kim |
tṛpto mṛṣṭānnādinā vā tataḥ kiṁ
yena svātmā naiva sākṣātkṛto 'bhūt || 2 ||

dṛṣṭā nānā cārudeśās tataḥ kiṁ
puṣṭāś ceṣṭā bandhuvargās tataḥ kim |
naṣṭaṁ dāridryādiduḥkhaṁ tataḥ kiṁ
yena svātmā naiva sākṣātkṛto 'bhūt || 3 ||

snātaṁ tīrthe jahnujādau tataḥ kiṁ
dānaṁ dattaṁ dvyaṣṭasaṁkhyaṁ tataḥ kim |
japtā mantrāḥ koṭiśo vā tataḥ kiṁ
yena svātmā naiva sākṣātkṛīto 'bhūt || 4 ||

gotraṁ samyagbhūṣitaṁ vā tataḥ kiṁ
gātraṁ bhasmāc chāditaṁ vā tataḥ kim |
rudrākṣādiḥ saṁdhṛto vā tataḥ kiṁ
yena svātmā naiva sākṣātkṛto 'bhūt || 5 ||

annair viprās tarpitā vā tataḥ kiṁ
yajñair devās toṣitā vā tataḥ kim |
kīrtyāvyāptāḥ sarvalokās tataḥ kiṁ
yena svātmā naiva sākṣātkṛto 'bhūt || 6 ||

kāyaḥ kliṣṭaś copavāsais tataḥ kiṁ
labdhāḥ putrāḥ svīyapatnyās tataḥ kim |
prāṇāyāmaḥ sādhito vā tataḥ kiṁ
yena svātmā naiva sākṣātkṛto 'bhūt || 7 ||

yuddhe śatrur nirjito vā tataḥ kiṁ
bhūyo mitraiḥ pūrito vā tataḥ kim ।
yogaiḥ prāptāḥ siddhayo vā tataḥ kiṁ
yena svātmā naiva sākṣātkṛto 'bhūt ॥ 8 ॥

abdhiḥ padbhyāṁ laṅghito vā tataḥ kiṁ
vāyuḥ kumbhe sthāpito vā tataḥ kim ।
meruḥ pāṇāv uddhṛto vā tataḥ kiṁ
yena svātmā naiva sākṣātkṛto 'bhūt ॥ 9 ॥

kṣvelaḥ pīto dugdhavad vā tataḥ kiṁ
vahnir jagdho lājavad vā tataḥ kim ।
prāptaś cāraḥ pakṣivat khe tataḥ kiṁ
yena svātmā naiva sākṣātkṛto 'bhūt ॥ 10 ॥

baddhāḥ samyakpāvakādyās tataḥ kiṁ
sākṣādviddhā lohavaryās tataḥ kim ।
labdho nikṣepo 'ñjanādyais tataḥ kim
yena svātmā naiva sākṣātkṛto 'bhūt ॥ 11 ॥

bhupendratvaṁ prāptam urvyāṁ tataḥ kiṁ
devendratvaṁ saṁbhṛtaṁ vā tataḥ kim ।
muṇḍīndratvaṁ copalabdhaṁ tataḥ kiṁ
yena svātmā naiva sākṣātkṛto 'bhūt ॥ 12 ॥

mantraiḥ sarvaiḥ stambhito vā tataḥ kiṁ
bāṇair lakṣyo bhedito vā tataḥ kim ।
kālajñānaṁ cāpi labdhaṁ tataḥ kiṁ
yena svātmā naiva sākṣātkṛto 'bhūt ॥ 13 ॥

kāmātaṅkaḥ khaṇḍito vā tataḥ kiṁ
kopāveśaḥ kuṇṭhito vā tataḥ kim ।
lobhāśleṣo varjito vā tataḥ kiṁ
yena svātmā naiva sākṣātkṛto 'bhūt ॥ 14 ॥

mohadhvāntaḥ poṣito vā tataḥ kiṁ
jāto bhūmau nirmado vā tataḥ kim ।
mātsaryārtir mīlitā vā tataḥ kiṁ
yena svātmā naiva sākṣātkṛto 'bhūt ॥ 15 ॥

dhātur lokaḥ sādhito vā tataḥ kiṁ
viṣṇor loko vīkṣito vā tataḥ kim ।

śaṁbhor lokaḥ śāsito vā tataḥ kiṁ
yena svātmā naiva sākṣātkṛto 'bhūt ‖ 16 ‖

yasyedaṁ hṛdaye samyag anātmaśrīvigarhaṇam |
sadodeti sa evātmasākṣātkārasya bhājanam ‖ 17 ‖

anye tu māyika jagadbhrāntivyāmohamohitāḥ |
na teṣāṁ jāyate kvāpi svātmasākṣātkṛtir bhuvi ‖ 18 ‖

bhaja govindam ||

dvādaśamañjarikāstotram ||

bhaja govindaṁ bhaja govindaṁ bhaja govindaṁ mūḍhamate |
saṁprāpte sannihite kāle na hi na hi rakṣati ḍukṛñkaraṇe ||

mūḍha jahīhi dhanāgamatṛṣṇāṁ kuru sadbuddhiṁ manasi vitṛṣṇām |
yal labhase nijakarmopāttaṁ vittaṁ tena vinodaya cittam || 1 ||

nārīstanabharanābhīdeśaṁ dṛṣṭvā mā gā mohāveśam |
etan māṁsavasādivikāraṁ manasi vicintaya vāraṁ vāram || 2 ||

nalinīdalagatajalam atitaralaṁ tadvaj jīvitam atiśayacapalam |
viddhi vyādhyabhimānagrastaṁ lokaṁ śokahataṁ ca samastam || 3 ||

yāvad vittopārjanasaktas tāvan nijaparivāro raktaḥ |
paścāj jīvati jarjaradeh vārtāṁ ko 'pi na pṛcchati gehe || 4 ||

yāvat pavano nivasati dehe tāvat pṛcchati kuśalaṁ gehe |
gatavati vāyau dehāpāye bhāryā bibhyati tasmin kāye || 5 ||

bālas tāvat krīḍāsaktas taruṇas tāvat taruṇīsaktaḥ |
vṛddhas tāvac cintāsaktaḥ pare brahmaṇi ko 'pi na saktaḥ || 6 ||

artham anarthaṁ bhāvaya nityaṁ nāsti tataḥ sukhaleśaḥ satyam |
putrād api dhanabhājāṁ bhītiḥ sarvatraiṣā vihitā rītiḥ || 7 ||

kā te kāntā kas te putraḥ saṁsāro 'yam atīva vicitraḥ |
kasya tvaṁ kaḥ kuta āyāta tattvaṁ cintaya tad iha bhrātaḥ || 8 ||

satsaṅgatve nissaṅgatvaṁ nissaṅgatve nirmohatvam |
nirmohatve niścalatattvaṁ niścalatattve jīvanmuktiḥ || 9 ||

vayasi gate kaḥ kāmavikāraḥ śuṣke nīre kaḥ kāsāraḥ |
kṣīṇe vitte kaḥ parivāro jñāte tattve kaḥ saṁsāraḥ || 10 ||

mā kuru dhanajanayauvanagarvaṁ harati nimeṣāt kālaḥ sarvam ।
māyāmayam idam akhilaṁ hitvā brahmapadaṁ tvaṁ praviśa viditvā ॥ 11 ॥

dinam api rajanī sāyaṁ prātaḥ śiśiravasantau punar āyātaḥ ।
kālaḥ krīḍati gacchaty āyuḥ tad api na muñcaty āśāvāyuḥ ॥ 12 ॥

dvādaśamañjarikābhir aśeṣaḥ kathito vaiyākaraṇsyaiṣaḥ ।
upadeśo 'bhūd vidyānipunaiḥ śrīmacchaṅkarabhagavaccaraṇaiḥ ॥

iti śrīguruśaṅkaravijaye śrīmacchaṅkarabhagavatpāda
vaiyākaraṇasaṁvāde paramahaṁsaparivrājakācāryavarya
śrīmacchaṅkarācāryopadiṣṭadvādaśamañjarikāstotram ॥

caturdaśamañjarikāstotram ||

kā te kāntādhanagatacintā vātula kiṁ tava nāsti niyantā |
trijagati sajjanasaṁgatir ekā bhavati bhavārṇavataraṇe naukā || 1 ||

jaṭilo muṇḍī luñcitakeśaḥ kāṣāyāmbarabahukṛtaveṣaḥ |
paśyann api ca na paśyati mūḍho hy udaranimittaṁ bahukṛtaveṣaḥ || 2 ||

aṅgaṁ galitaṁ palitaṁ muṇḍaṁ daśanavihīnaṁ jātaṁ tuṇḍam |
vṛddho yāti gṛhītvā daṇḍaṁ tad api na muñcaty āśāpiṇḍam || 3 ||

agre vahniḥ pṛṣṭe bhānū rātrau cubukasamarpitajānuḥ |
karatalabhikṣas tarutalavāsaḥ tad api na muñcaty āśāpāśaḥ || 4 ||

kurute gaṅgāsāgaragamanaṁ vrataparipālanam athavā dānam |
jñānavihīnaḥ sarvamatena muktiṁ na bhajati janmaśatena || 5 ||

suramandiratarumūlanivāsaḥ śayyā bhūtalam ajinaṁ vāsaḥ |
sarvaparigrahabhogatyāgaḥ kasya sukhaṁ na karoti virāgaḥ || 6 ||

yogarato vā bhogarato vā saṅgarato vā saṅgavihīnaḥ |
yasya brahmaṇi ramate cittaṁ nandati nandati nandaty eva || 7 ||

bhagavadgītā kiñcid adhītā gaṅgājalalavakaṇikā pītā |
sakṛd api yena murārisamarcā kriyate tasya yamena na carcā || 8 ||

punar api jananaṁ punar api maraṇaṁ punar api jananījaṭhare śayanam |
iha saṁsāre bahudustāre kṛpayā 'pāre pāhi murāre || 9 ||

rathyākarpaṭaviracitakanthaḥ puṇyāpuṇyavivarjitapanthaḥ |
yogī yoganiyojitacitto ramate bālonmattavad eva || 10 ||

kas tvaṁ ko 'haṁ kuta āyātaḥ kā me jananī ko me tātaḥ |
iti paribhāvaya sarvam asāraṁ viśvaṁ tyaktvā svapnavicāram || 11 ||

tvayi mayi cānyatraiko viṣṇur vyarthaṁ kupyasi mayy asahiṣṇuḥ |
sarvasminn api paśyātmānaṁ sarvatrotsṛja bhedājñānam || 12 ||

śatrau mitre putre bandhau mā kuru yatnaṁ vigrahasandhau ।
bhava samacittaḥ sarvatra tvaṁ vāñchasy acirād yadi viṣṇutvam ॥ 13 ॥

kāmaṁ krodhaṁ lobhaṁ mohaṁ tyaktvā 'tmānaṁ bhāvaya ko 'ham ।
ātmajñānavihīnā mūḍhāḥ te pacyante narakanigūḍhāḥ ॥ 14 ॥

geyaṁ gītānāmasahasraṁ dhyeyaṁ śrīpatirūpam ajasram ।
neyaṁ sajjanasaṅge cittaṁ deyaṁ dīnajanāya ca vittam ॥ 15 ॥

mūḍhaḥ kaścana vaiyākarano ḍukṛñkaraṇādhyayanadhurīṇaḥ ।
śrīmacchaṅkarabhagavacchiṣyair bodhita āsīc choditakaraṇaḥ ॥

iti śrīguruśaṅkaravijaye śrīmacchaṅkarabhagavatpāda
vaiyākaraṇasaṁvāde paramahaṁsaparivrājakācāryavarya
śrīmacchaṅkarācāryājñaptaśiṣyopanyastacaturdaśamañjarikāstotram ॥

upakṛtaślokāḥ ।

sukhataḥ kriyate rāmābhogaḥ paścād dhanta śarīre rogaḥ ।
yady api loke maraṇaṁ śaraṇaṁ tad api na muñcati pāpācaraṇaṁ ॥ 16 ॥

prāṇāyāmaṁ pratyāhāraṁ nityānityavivekavicāram ।
jāpyasameta samādhividhānaṁ kurv avadhānaṁ mahadavadhānam ॥ 17 ॥

gurucaraṇāmbujanirbharabhaktaḥ saṁsārād acirād bhava muktaḥ ।
sendriyamānasaniyamād evaṁ drakṣyasi nijahṛdayasthaṁ devam ॥ 18 ॥

sadācāraḥ ||

saccidānandakandāya jagadaṅkurahetave |
sadoditāya pūrṇāya namo 'nantāya viṣṇave || 1 ||

sarvavedāntasiddhāntagrathitaṁ nirmalaṁ śivam |
sadācāraṁ pravakṣyāmi yogināṁ jñānasiddhaye || 2 ||

prātaḥ smarāmi devasya savitur bharga ātmanaḥ |
vareṇyaṁ tad dhiyo yo naś cidānande pracodayāt || 3 ||

anvayavyatirekābhyāṁ jāgratsvapnasuṣuptiṣu |
yad ekaṁ kevalaṁ jñānaṁ tad evāhaṁ paraṁ bṛhat || 4 ||

jñānājñānavilāso 'yaṁ jñānājñāne ca paśyati |
jñānājñāne parityajya jñānam evāvaśiṣyate || 5 ||

atyantamalino deho dehī cātyantanirmalaḥ |
asaṅgo 'ham iti jñātvā śaucam etat pracakṣate || 6 ||

manmano mīnavan nityaṁ krīḍaty ānandavāridhau |
susnātas tena pūtātmā samyagvijñānavāriṇā || 7 ||

athāghamarṣaṇaṁ kuryāt prāṇāpānanirodhataḥ |
manaḥ pūrṇe samādhāya magna kumbho yathārṇave || 8 ||

layavikṣepayoḥ sandhau manas tatra nirāmiṣam |
sa sandhiḥ sādhito yena sa mukto nātra saṁśayaḥ || 9 ||

sarvatra prāṇināṁ dehe japo bhavati sarvadā |
haṁsa so 'ham iti jñātvā sarvabandhaiḥ pramucyate || 10 ||

tarpaṇe svasukhenaiva svendriyāṇāṁ pratarpaṇam |
manasā mana ālokya svayam ātmā prakāśate || 11 ||

ātmani svaprakāśāgnau cittam ekāhutiṁ kṣipet ।
agnihotrī sa vijñeya itare nāmadhārakāḥ ॥ 12 ॥

deho devālayaḥ prokto dehī devo nirañjanaḥ ।
arcitaḥ sarvabhāvena svānubhūtyā virājate ॥ 13 ॥

maunaṁ svādhyayanaṁ dhyānaṁ dhyeyaṁ brahmānucintanam ।
jñāneneti tayoḥ samyaṅ niṣedhāntaḥ pradarśanam ॥ 14 ॥

atītānāgataṁ kiñcin na smarāmi na cintaye ।
rāgadveṣavinā prāptaṁ bhuñjāmy atra śubhāśubham ॥ 15 ॥

abhayaṁ sarvabhūtānāṁ jñānam āhur manīṣiṇaḥ ।
nijānande spṛhā nānye vairāgyasyāvadhir mataḥ ॥ 16 ॥

vedāntaiḥ śravaṇaṁ kuryān mananaṁ copapattibhiḥ ।
yogenābhyāsanaṁ nityaṁ tato darśanam ātmanaḥ ॥ 17 ॥

śabdaśakter acintyatvāc chabdād evāparokṣadhīḥ ।
suṣuptaḥ puruṣo yadvat śabdenaivānubudhyate ॥ 18 ॥

ātmānātmavivekena jñānaṁ bhavati nirmalam ।
guruṇā bodhitaḥ śiṣyaḥ śabdabrahmātivartate ॥ 19 ॥

na tvaṁ deho nendriyāṇi na prāṇo na mano na dhīḥ ।
vikāritvād vināśitvād dṛśyatvāc ca ghaṭo yathā ॥ 20 ॥

viśuddhaṁ kevalaṁ jñānaṁ nirviśeṣaṁ nirañjanam ।
yad ekaṁ paramānandaṁ tat tvam asy advayaṁ param ॥ 21 ॥

śabdasyādyantayoḥ siddhaṁ manaso 'pi tathaiva ca ।
madhye sākṣitayā nityaṁ tad eva tvaṁ bhramaṁ jahi ॥ 22 ॥

sthūlavairājyayor aikyaṁ sūkṣmahairaṇyagarbhayoḥ ।
ajñānamāyayor aikyaṁ pratyagvijñānapūrṇayoḥ ॥ 23 ॥

cinmātraikarase viṣṇau brahmātmaikasvarūpake ।
bhrama eva jagaj jātaṁ rajjvāṁ sarpabhramo yathā ॥ 24 ॥

tārkikāṇāṁ ca jīveśau vācyāv etau vidur budhāḥ ।
lakṣyau ca sāṁkhyayogābhyāṁ vedāntair aikyatānayoḥ ॥ 25 ॥

kāryakāraṇavācyāṁśau jīveśau yau jahac ca tau |
ajahac ca tayor lakṣyau cidaṁśāv ekarūpiṇau || 26 ||

karmaśāstre kuto jñānaṁ tarke naivāsti niścayaḥ |
sāṁkhyayogau dvidhāpannau śābdikā śabdatatparāḥ || 27 ||

anye pākhaṇḍinaḥ sarve jñānavārtāsu durbalāḥ |
ekaṁ vedāntavijñānaṁ svānubhūtyā virājate || 28 ||

ahaṁ mamety ayaṁ bandho nāhaṁ mameti muktatā |
bandho mokṣo guṇair bhāti guṇāḥ prakṛtisaṁbhavāḥ || 29 ||

jñānam ekaṁ sadā bhāti sarvāvasthāsu nirmalam |
mandabhāgyā na jānanti svarūpaṁ kevalaṁ bṛhat || 30 ||

saṅkalpasākṣiṇaṁ jñānaṁ sarvalokaikajīvanam |
tad asmīti ca yo veda sa mukto nātra saṁśayaḥ || 31 ||

pramātā ca pramāṇaṁ ca prameyaṁ pramitis tathā |
tasya bhāsāvabhāseta mānaṁ jñānāya tasya kim || 32 ||

arthākārā bhaved vṛttiḥ phalenārthaḥ prakāśate |
arthajñānaṁ vijānāti sa evārthaḥ paraḥ smṛtaḥ || 33 ||

vṛttivyāpyatvam evāstu phalavyāptiḥ kathaṁ bhavet |
svaprakāśasvarūpatvāt siddhatvāc ca cidātmanaḥ || 34 ||

arthād arthe yathā vṛttir gantuṁ calati cāntare |
anādhārā nirvikārā sā daśā sonmanī smṛtā || 35 ||

cittaṁ cic ca vijānīyāt takāra rahitaṁ yadā |
takāro viṣayādhyāso japārāgav yathā maṇau || 36 ||

jñeyavastuparityāgāj jñānaṁ tiṣṭhati kevalam |
tripuṭī kṣīṇatām eti brahmanirvāṇam ṛcchati || 37 ||

manomātram idaṁ sarvaṁ cinmano jñānamātrakam |
ajñānabhramam ity āhur vijñānaṁ paramaṁ padam || 38 ||

ajñānaṁ cānyathā jñānaṁ māyām etāṁ vadanti te |
īśvaraṁ māyinaṁ vidyān māyātītaṁ nirañjanam || 39 ||

sadānande cidākāśe māyāmeghas taḍin manaḥ ǀ
ahaṁtā garjanaṁ tatra dhārāsāro hi yat tamaḥ ǁ 40 ǁ

mahāmohāndhakāre 'smin devo varṣati līlayā ǀ
asyā vṛṣṭer virāmāya prabodhaika samīraṇaḥ ǁ 41 ǁ

jñānaṁ dṛgdṛśyayor bhānaṁ vijñānaṁ dṛśyaśūnyatā ǀ
ekam evādvayaṁ brahma neha nānā 'sti kiñcana ǁ 42 ǁ

kṣetrakṣetrajñayor jñānaṁ taj jñānaṁ jñānam ucyate ǀ
vijñānaṁ cobhayor aikyaṁ kṣetrajñaparamātmanoḥ ǁ 43 ǁ

parokṣaṁ śāstrajaṁ jñānaṁ vijñānaṁ cātmadarśanam ǀ
ātmano brahmaṇaḥ samyagupādhidvayavarjitam ǁ 44 ǁ

tvamartho viṣayajñānaṁ vijñānaṁ tatpadāśrayam ǀ
padayor aikya bodhas tu jñānavijñānasaṁjñakam ǁ 45 ǁ

ātmānātmavivekas tu jñānam āhur manīṣiṇaḥ ǀ
ajñānaṁ cānyathā loke vijñānaṁ tanmayaṁ jagat ǁ 46 ǁ

anvayavyatirekābhyāṁ sarvatraikaṁ prapaśyati ǀ
yat tu tadvṛttijaṁ jñānaṁ vijñānaṁ jñānamātrakam ǁ 47 ǁ

ajñānadhvaṁsakaṁ jñānaṁ vijñānaṁ cobhayātmakam ǀ
jñānavijñānaniṣṭeyaṁ tat sad brahmaṇi cārpaṇam ǁ 48 ǁ

bhoktā sattvaguṇaḥ śuddho bhogānāṁ sādhanaṁ rajaḥ ǀ
bhogyaṁ tamoguṇaṁ prāhur ātmā caiṣā prakāśakaḥ ǁ 49 ǁ

brahmādhyayanasaṁyukto brahmacaryarataḥ sadā ǀ
sarvaṁ brahmeti yo veda brahmacārī sa ucyate ǁ 50 ǁ

gṛhastho guṇam adhyasthaḥ śarīraṁ gṛham ucyate ǀ
guṇāḥ kurvanti karmāṇi nāhaṁ karteti buddhimān ǁ 51 ǁ

kim ugraiś ca tapobhiś ca yasya jñānamayaṁ tapaḥ ǀ
harṣāmarṣavinirmukto vānaprasthaḥ sa ucyate ǁ 52 ǁ

dehānyāso hi saṁnyāso naiva kāṣāyavāsasā ǀ
nā 'haṁ deho mahātmeti niścayo 'jñānalakṣaṇam ǁ 53 ǁ

sadācāram imaṁ nityaṁ ye ’nusandadhate budhāḥ |
saṁsārasāgarāc chīdhraṁ mucyante nātra saṁśayaḥ || 54 ||

brahmajñānavālī ||

asaṅgo 'ham asaṅgo 'ham asaṅgo 'haṁ punaḥ punaḥ |
saccidānandarūpo 'ham aham evāham avyayaḥ || 1 ||

nityaśuddhavimukto 'haṁ nirākāro 'ham avyayaḥ |
bhūmānandasvarūpo 'ham aham evāham avyayaḥ || 2 ||

nityo 'haṁ niravadyo 'haṁ nirākāro 'ham acyutaḥ |
paramānandarūpo 'ham aham evāham avyayaḥ || 3 ||

śuddhacaitanyarūpo 'ham ātmarāmo 'ham eva ca |
akhaṇḍānandarūpo 'ham aham evāham avyayaḥ || 4 ||

pratyakcaitanyarūpo 'haṁ śānto 'haṁ prakṛteḥ paraḥ |
śāśvatānandarūpo 'ham aham evāham avyayaḥ || 5 ||

tattvātītaḥ parātmā 'haṁ madhyātītaḥ paraḥ śivaḥ |
māyātītaḥ paraṁ jyotir aham evāham avyayaḥ || 6 ||

nānārūpavyatīto 'haṁ cidākāro 'ham acyutaḥ |
sukharūpasvarūpo 'ham aham evāham avyayaḥ || 7 ||

māyātatkāryadehādi mama nāsty eva sarvadā |
svaprakāśaikarūpo 'ham aham evāham avyayaḥ || 8 ||

guṇatrayavyatīto 'haṁ brahmādīnāṁ ca sākṣyaham |
anantānandarūpo 'ham aham evāham avyayaḥ || 9 ||

antaryāmisvarūpo 'haṁ kūṭasthaḥ sarvago 'smy aham |
sarvasākṣisvarūpo 'ham aham evāham avyayaḥ || 10 ||

dvandvādisākṣirūpo 'ham acalo 'haṁ sanātanaḥ |
sarvasākṣisvarūpo 'ham aham evāham avyayaḥ || 11 ||

prajñānaghana evāhaṁ vijñānaghana eva ca ǀ
akartāham abhoktāham aham evāham avyayaḥ ǁ 12 ǁ

nirādhārasvarūpo 'haṁ sarvādhāro 'ham eva ca ǀ
āptakāmasvarūpo 'ham aham evāham avyayaḥ ǁ 13 ǁ

tāpatrayavinirmukto dehatrayavilakṣaṇaḥ ǀ
avasthātrayasākṣyasmy aham evāham avyayaḥ ǁ 14 ǁ

dṛgdṛśyau dvau padārthau staḥ parasparavilakṣaṇau ǀ
dṛg brahma dṛśyaṁ māyeti sarvavedāntaḍiṇḍimaḥ ǁ 15 ǁ

ahaṁ sākṣīti yo vidyād vivicyaivaṁ punaḥ punaḥ ǀ
sa eva muktaḥ so vidvān iti vedāntaḍiṇḍimaḥ ǁ 16 ǁ

ghaṭakuṇyādikaṁ sarvaṁ mṛttikamātram eva ca ǀ
tadvad brahma jagat sarvam iti vedāntaḍiṇḍimaḥ ǁ 17 ǁ

brahma satyaṁ jagan mithyā jīvo brahmaiva nāparaḥ ǀ
anena vedyaṁ sac chāstram iti vedāntaḍiṇḍimaḥ ǁ 18 ǁ

antarjyotī bahirjyotiḥ pratyagjyotiḥ parāt param ǀ
jyotirjyotiḥ svayaṁjyotiḥ ātmajyotiḥ śivo 'smy aham ǁ 19 ǁ

śivo 'ham śivo 'ham ||

manobuddhyahaṅkāracittāni nāhaṁ
na ca śrotajihve na ca ghrāṇanetre |
na ca vyomabhūmī na tejo na vāyuś
cidānandarūpaḥ śivo 'haṁ śivo 'ham || 1 ||

na ca prāṇasaṁjño na ca pañcavāyur
na vā saptadhātur na vā pañcakośaḥ |
na vākpāṇipādau na copasthapāyū
cidānandarūpaḥ śivo 'haṁ śivo 'ham || 2 ||

na me dveṣarāgau na me lobhamohau
mado naiva me naiva mātsaryabhāvaḥ |
na dharmo na cārtho na kāmo na mokṣaḥ
cidānandarūpaḥ śivo 'haṁ śivo 'ham || 3 ||

na puṇyaṁ na pāpaṁ na saukhyaṁ na duḥkhaṁ
na mantro na tīrthaṁ na vedā na yajñāḥ |
nāhaṁ bhojanaṁ naiva bhojyaṁ na bhoktā
cidānandarūpaḥ śivo 'haṁ śivo 'ham || 4 ||

na mṛtyur na śaṅkā na me jātibhedaḥ
pitā naiva me naiva mātā ca janma |
na bandhur na mitraṁ gurur naiva śiṣyaḥ
cidānandarūpaḥ śivo 'haṁ śivo 'ham || 5 ||

ahaṁ nirvikalpo nirākārarūpo
vibhutvāc ca sarvatra sarvendriyāṇām |
na cāsaṅgataṁ naiva mātā na meyaḥ
cidānandarūpaḥ śivo 'haṁ śivo 'ham || 6 ||

pañcīkaraṇam ||

oṁ | pañcīkṛtapañcamahābhūtāni tatkāryaṁ ca sarvaṁ virāḍ ity ucyate | etat sthūlaśarīram ātmanaḥ | indriyair arthopalabdhir jāgaritam | tadubhayābhimānyātmā viśvaḥ | etat trayam akāraḥ || 1 ||

apañcīkṛtapañcamahābhūtāni pañcatanmātrāṇi tatkāryaṁ ca pañca prāṇāḥ daśendriyāṇi mano buddhiś ceti saptadaśakaṁ liṅgaṁ bhautikaṁ hiraṇyagarbha ity ucyate | etat sūkṣmaśarīram ātmanaḥ || 2 ||

karaṇeṣūpasaṁhṛteṣu jāgaritasaṁskārajaḥ pratyayaḥ saviṣayaḥ svapna ity ucyate | tadubhayābhimanyātmā taijasaḥ | etat trayam ukāraḥ || 3 ||

śarīradvayakāraṇam ātmājñānaṁ sābhāsam avyākṛtam ity ucyate | etat kāraṇaśarīram ātmanaḥ | tac ca san nāsan nāpi sadasan na bhinnaṁ nāpi bhinnābhinnaṁ kutaścin na niravayavaṁ na sāvayavaṁ nobhayaṁ kiṁ tu kevalabrahmātmaikatvajñānāpanodayam || 4 ||

sarvaprakārajñānopasaṁhāre buddheḥ kāraṇātmā 'vasthānaṁ suṣuptiḥ | tadubhayābhimānyātmā prājñaḥ | etat trayaṁ makāraḥ || 5 ||

akāra ukāra ukāro makāre makāra oṁkāra oṁkāro 'hamy eva | aham ātmā sākṣī kevalaś cinmātrasvarūpaḥ nājñānaṁ nāpi tatkāryaṁ kiṁ tu nityaśuddhabuddhamuktasatyasvabhāvaṁ paramānandādvayaṁ pratyagbhūtacaitanyaṁ brahmaivāham asmīty abhedenāvasthānaṁ samādhiḥ || 6 ||

"tat tvam asi" "brahmāsmi" "prajñānam ānandaṁ brahma" "ayam ātmā brahma" ity ādi śrutibhyaḥ | iti pañcīkaraṇaṁ bhavati || 7 ||

iti śrīśaṅkarācāryaviracitaṁ pañcīkaraṇam ||

śrīsureśvarācāryakṛta
pañcīkaraṇavārttikam ||

oṁkāraḥ sarvavedānāṁ sāras tattvaprakāśakaḥ |
tena cittasamādhānaṁ mumukṣūṇāṁ prakāśyate || 1 ||

āsīd ekaṁ paraṁ brahma nityamuktam avikriyam |
tat svamāyāsamāveśād bījam avyākṛtātmakam || 2 ||

tasmād ākāśam utpannaṁ śabdatanmātrarūpakam |
sparśātmakas tato vāyus tejo rūpātmakaṁ tataḥ || 3 ||

āpo rasātmikās tasmāt tābhyo gandhātmikā mahī |
śabdaikaguṇam ākāśaṁ śabdasparśaguṇo marut || 4 ||

śabdasparśarūpaguṇais triguṇaṁ teja ucyate |
śabdasparśarūparasaguṇair āpaś caturguṇāḥ || 5 ||

śabdasparśarūparasagandhaiḥ pañcaguṇa mahī |
tebhyaḥ samabhavat sūtraṁ bhūtaṁ sarvātmakaṁ mahat || 6 ||

tataḥ sthūlāni bhūtāni pañca tebhyo virāḍ abhūt |
pañcīkṛtāni bhūtāni sthūlānīty ucyate budhaiḥ || 7 ||

pṛthivyādīni bhūtāni praty ekaṁ vibhajed dvidhā |
ekaikaṁ bhāgam ādāya caturdhā vibhajet punaḥ || 8 ||

ekaikaṁ bhāgam ekasmin bhūte saṁveśayet kramāt |
tataś cākāśabhūtasya bhāgāḥ pañca bhavanti hi || 9 ||

vāyvādibhāgāś catvāro vāyvādiṣv evam ādiśet |
pañcīkaraṇam etat syād ity āhus tattvavedinaḥ || 10 ||

pañcīkṛtāni bhūtāni tatkāryaṁ ca virāḍ bhavet |
sthūlaṁ śarīram etat syād aśarīrasya cātmanaḥ || 11 ||

adhidaivatam adhyātmam adhibhūtam iti tridhā |
ekaṁ brahma vibhāgena bhramād bhāti na tattvataḥ || 12 ||
indriyair arthavijñānaṁ devatānugrahānvitaiḥ |
śabdādiviṣayaṁ jñānaṁ taj jāgaritam ucyate || 13 ||

śrotram adhyātmam ity uktaṁ śrotavyaṁ śabdalakṣaṇam |
adhibhūtam tad ity uktaṁ diśas tatrādhidaivatam || 14 ||

tvag adhyātmam iti proktaṁ spraṣṭavyaṁ sparśalakṣaṇam |
adhibhūtam tad ity uktaṁ vāyus tatrādhidaivatam || 15 ||

cakṣur adhyātmam ity uktaṁ draṣṭavyaṁ rūpalakṣaṇam |
adhibhūtam tad ity uktam āditYo 'trādhidaivatam || 16 ||

jihvā 'dhyātmaṁ tayā "svādyam adhibhūtaṁ rasātmakam |
varuṇo devatā tatra jihvāyām adhidaivatam || 17 ||

ghrāṇam adhyātmam ity uktaṁ ghrātavyaṁ gandhalakṣaṇam |
adhibhūtam tad ity uktaṁ pṛthivy atrādhidaivatam || 18 ||

vāg adhyātmam ity proktaṁ vaktavyaṁ śabdalakṣaṇam |
adhibhūtam tad ity uktam agnis tatrādhidaivatam || 19 ||

hastāv adhyātmam ity uktam ādātavyaṁ ca yad bhavet |
adhibhūtam tad ity uktam indras tatrādhidaivatam || 20 ||

pādāv adhyātmam ity uktaṁ gantavyaṁ tatra yad bhavet |
adhibhūtaṁ tad ity uktaṁ viṣṇus tatrādhidaivatam || 21 ||

pāyur indriyam adhyātmaṁ visargas tatra yo bhavet |
adhibhūtaṁ tad ity uktaṁ mṛtyus tatrādhidaivatam || 22 ||

upasthendriyam adhyātmaṁ stryādyānandasya kāraṇam |
adhibhūtaṁ tad ity uktam adhidaivaṁ prajāpatiḥ || 23 ||

mano 'dhyātmam iti proktaṁ mantavyaṁ tatra yad bhavet |
adhibhūtaṁ tad ity uktaṁ candras tatrādhidaivatam || 24 ||

buddhir adhyātmam ity uktaṁ boddhavyaṁ tatra yad bhavet |
adhibhūtaṁ tad ity uktam adhidaivaṁ bṛhaspatiḥ || 25 ||

ahaṁkāras tathā 'dhyātmam ahaṁkartavyam eva ca |
adhibhūtaṁ tad ity uktaṁ rudras tatrādhidaivatam || 26 ||

cittam adhyātmam ity uktaṁ cetavyaṁ tatra yad bhavet |
adhibhūtaṁ tad ity uktaṁ kṣetrajño 'trādhidaivatam || 27 ||

tamo 'dhyātmam iti proktaṁ vikāras tatra yo bhavet |
adhibhūtaṁ tad ity uktam īśvaro 'trādhidaivatam || 28 ||

bāhyāntāḥkaraṇair evaṁ devatānugrahānvitaiḥ |
svaṁ svaṁ ca viṣayajñānaṁ taj jāgaritam ucyate || 29 ||

yeyaṁ jāgaritāvasthā śarīraṁ kāraṇāśrayam |
yas tayor abhimānī syād viśva ity abhidhīyate || 30 ||

viśvaṁ vairajarūpeṇa paśyed bhedanivṛttaye |
jñānendriyāṇi pañcaiva pañca karmendriyāṇi ca || 31 ||

śrotratvanṁnayanaghrāṇajihvā dhīndriyapañcakam |
vākpāṇipādapāyūpasthāḥ karmendriyapañcakam || 32 ||

mano buddhir ahaṁkāraś cittaṁ ceti catuṣṭayam |
sanṁkalpākhyaṁ manorūpaṁ buddhir niścayarūpiṇī || 33 ||

abhimānātmakas tadvad ahaṁkāraḥ prakīrtitaḥ |
anusaṁdhānarūpaṁ ca cittam ity abhidhīyate || 34 ||

prāṇo 'pānas tathā vyāna udānākhyas tathaiva ca |
samānaś ceti pañcaitāḥ kīrtitaḥ prāṇavṛttayaḥ || 35 ||

khaṁvāyvagnyambukṣitayo bhūtasūkṣmāṇi pañca ca |
avidyākāmakarmāṇi linṁgaṁ puryaṣṭakaṁ viduḥ || 36 ||

etat sūkṣmaśarīraṁ syān māyikaṁ pratyagātmanaḥ |
kāraṇoparame jāgratsaṁskārotthaṁ prabodhavat || 37 ||

grāhyagrāhakarūpeṇa sphuraṇaṁ svapna ucyate |
abhimānī tayor yas tu taijasaḥ parikīrtitaḥ || 38 ||

hiraṇyagarbharūpeṇa taijasaṁ cintayed budhaḥ |
caitanyābhāsakhacitaṁ śarīradvayakāraṇam || 39 ||

ātmājñānaṁ tad avyaktam avyākṛtam itīryate ।
na san nāsan na sadasad bhinnābhinnaṁ na cātmanaḥ ॥ 40 ॥

na sabhāgaṁ na nirbhāgaṁ na cāpy ubhayarūpakam ।
brahmātmaikatvavijñānaheyaṁ mithyātvakāraṇāt ॥ 41 ॥

jñānānām upasaṁhāro buddheḥ kāraṇatāsthitiḥ ।
vaṭabīje vaṭasyeva suṣuptir abhidhīyate ॥ 42 ॥

abhimānī tayor yas tu prājña ity abhidhīyate ।
jagatkāraṇarūpeṇa prajñātmānaṁ vicintayet ॥ 43 ॥

viśvataijasasuṣuptavirāṭsūtrākṣarātmabhiḥ ।
vibhinnam iva saṁmohād ekaṁ tattvaṁ cidātmakam ॥ 44 ॥

viśvādikatrayaṁ yasmād vairajāditrayātmakam ।
ekatvenaiva saṁpaśyed anyābhāvaprasiddhaye ॥ 45 ॥

oṁkāramātram akhilaṁ viśvaprājñādilakṣaṇam ।
vācyavācakatābhedād bhedenānupalabdhitaḥ ॥ 46 ॥

akāramātraṁ viśvaḥ syād ukāras taijasaḥ smṛtaḥ ।
prājño makāra ity evaṁ paripaśyet krameṇa tu ॥ 47 ॥

samādhikālāt prāg evaṁ vicintyātiprayatnataḥ ।
sthūlasūkṣmakramāt sarvaṁ cidātmani vilāpayet ॥ 48 ॥

akāraṁ puruṣaṁ viśvam ukāre pravilāpayet ।
ukāraṁ taijasaṁ sūkṣmaṁ makāre pravilāpayet ॥ 49 ॥

makāraṁ kāraṇaṁ prājñaṁ cidātmani vilāpayet ।
cidātmāhaṁ nityaśuddhabuddhamuktasadadvayaḥ ॥ 50 ॥

paramānandasaṁdohavāsudevo 'ham om iti ।
jñātvā vivecakaṁ cittaṁ tat sākṣiṇi vilāpayet ॥ 51 ॥

cidātmani vilīnaṁ cet tac cittaṁ naiva cālayet ।
pūrṇabodhātmanā 'sīta pūrṇācalasamudravat ॥ 52 ॥

evaṁ samāhito yogī śraddhābhaktisamanvitaḥ ।
jitendriyo jitakrodhaḥ paśyed ātmānam advayam ॥ 53 ॥

ādimadhyāvasaneṣu duḥkhaṁ sarvam idaṁ yataḥ I
tasmāt sarvāṁ parityajya tattvaniṣṭho bhavet sadā II 54 II

yaḥ paśyet sarvagaṁ śāntam ānandātmānam advayam I
na tena kiṁcid āptavyaṁ jñātavyaṁ vāvaśiṣyate II 55 II

kṛtakṛtyo bhaved vidvān jīvanmukto bhaved sadā I
ātmany evārūḍhabhāvo jagad etan na vīkṣate II 56 II

kadācid vyavahāre tu dvaitaṁ yady api paśyati I
bodhātmavyatirekeṇa na paśyati cidanvayāt II 57 II

kiṁ tu paśyati mithyaiva dinṁmohenduvibhāgavat I
pratibhāsaḥ śarīrasya tadā ''prārabdhasaṁkṣayāt II 58 II

tasya tāvad eva ciram ity ādi śrutir abravīt I
prārabdhasyānuvṛttis tu muktasyābhāsamātrataḥ II 59 II

sarvadā mukta eva syāj jñānatattvaḥ pumān asau I
prārabdhabhogaśeṣasya saṁkṣaye tad anantaram II 60 II

avidyātimirātītaṁ sarvābhāsavivarjitam I
ānandam amalaṁ śuddhaṁ manovācām agocaram II 61 II

vācyavācakanirmuktaṁ heyopadeyavarjitam I
prajñānaghanam ānandaṁ vaiīṇavaṁ padam aśnute II 62 II

idaṁ prakaraṇaṁ yatnāj jñātavyaṁ bhagavattamaiḥ I
amānitvādiniyamair gurubhaktiprasādataḥ II 63 II

imāṁ vidyāṁ prayatnena yogī saṁdhyāsu sarvadā I
samabhyased ihāmutrabhogānāsaktadhīḥ sudhīḥ II 64 II

iti śrīmatsureśvarācāryaviracitaṁ
pañcīkaraṇavārttikaṁ saṁpūrṇam II

manīśāpañcakam ||

sat tyācāryasya gamane kadācin muktidāyakam |
kāśīkṣetraṁ prati saha gāryā mārge tu śaṅkaraṁ ||
antyaveṣadharaṁ dṛṣ vā gaccha gaccheti cābravīt |
śankaraḥ go 'pi cāṇḍālastaṁ pūnaḥ prāha śaṅkaraṁ || 1 ||

annamayād annamayaṁ hy atha vā caitanyam eva caitanyāt |
dvijavara dūrīkartuṁ vācchasi kiṁ brūhigaccha gaccheti || 2 ||

kiṁ gaṅgāṁ buni bimbite 'mbaramanau caṇḍālavāṭīpayaḥ
pūre cāntaram asti kāñcanaghatīm ṛtkumbhayor vāmbare |
pratyagvastuni nistaraṅgasahajānandāvabodhāmbudhau
vipro 'yaṁ svapaco 'yam ity api mahān ko 'yaṁ vibhedabramḥ || 3 ||

śaṅkara uvāca —
jāgratsvapnasuṣuptiṣusphu atarā yā saṁvidujjṛmbhate
yā brahmādipipīlikāntatanuṣu protā jagatsākṣiṇī |
sa iva ahaṁ na ca dṛśyavastv iti dṛḍhaprajñāsti yasyā pi cec
caṇḍālo 'stu sa tu dvijo 'stu gurur ity eṣā manīṣā mama || 1 ||

brahma iva aham idam jagac ca sakalaṁ ccinmāttravistāritaṁ
sarvaṁ ca itad avidyayā triguṇayāśeṣaṁ mayā kalpitaṁ |
itthaṁ yasya dṛḍhā matiḥ sukhatare nityepare nirmale
caṇḍālo 'stu sa tu dvijo 'stu gurur ity eṣā manīṣā mama || 2 ||

śvaśvannaśvaram eva viśvam akhilaṁ niścitya vācā guror
nityaṁ brahma nirantaraṁ vimṛśatā nirvyājaśāntātmanā |
bhūtam bhāvi ca duṣkṛtaṁ pradahatā saṁninmaye pāvake
prārabdhaya samarpitaṁ svavapurityeṣā manīṣā mama || 3 ||

yā tiriyaṅ naradevatābhir ity antaḥ sphuṭā gṛhyate
yad bhāsā hṛdayākṣadehaviṣayā bhānti svato 'cetanāḥ |
tāṁ bhāsyaiḥ pihitārkamaṇḍalanibhāṁ sphūrtiṁ sadā bhāvayan
yogī nirvṛtamānaso hi gurur ity eṣā manīṣā mama || 4 ||

yat saukhyām budhileśaleśata ime śakrādayo nirvṛtā
 yac citte nitaraṁ praśāntakalane labdhvā munir nirvṛtaḥ |
yasmin nityasukhāmbuddhau galitadhīr iva na brahmavidyaḥ
 kaścit sa surendravanditapado nūnaṁ manīṣā mama || 5 ||

daśaślokī ||

na bhūmir nna toyaṁ na tejo na vāyur
nna khaṁ nendriyaṁ na teṣāṁ samūhaḥ |
anaikāntikatvāt suṣuptyekasiddhaḥ
tad eko 'vaśiṣṭaḥ śivaḥ kevalo 'ham || 1 ||

na varṇā na varṇāśramācāradharmā
na me dhāraṇādhyānayogādayo 'pi |
anātmāśrayāhaṁmamādyāsahānāḥ
tad eko 'vaśiṣṭaḥ śivaḥ kevalo 'ham || 2 ||

na mātā pitā ca na devā na lokāḥ
na vedā na yajñā na tīrthaṁ bruvanti |
suṣuptau nirastātiśūnyātmakatvāt
tad eko 'vaśiṣṭaḥ śivaḥ kevalo 'ham || 3 ||

na sāṁkhyaṁ na śaivaṁ na tat pāñcarātraṁ
na jainaṁ na mīmāṁsakāder mataṁ vā |
viśiṣṭānubhūtyā viśuddhātmakatvāt
tad eko 'vaśiṣṭaḥ śivaḥ kevalo 'ham || 4 ||

na cordhvaṁ na cādho na cāntar nna bāhyaṁ
na madhyaṁ na tiryaṅ na pūrva parā dik |
viyadvyāpakatvād akhaṇḍaikarūpaḥ
tad eko 'vaśiṣṭaḥ śivaḥ kevalo 'ham || 5 ||

na śuklaṁ na kṛṣṇaṁ na raktaṁ na pītaṁ
na kubjaṁ na pīnaṁ na hrasvaṁ na dīrgham |
arūpaṁ tathā jyotirākārakatvāt
tad eko 'vaśiṣṭaḥ śivaḥ kevalo 'ham || 6 ||

na śāstā na śāstraṁ na śiṣyo na śikṣā
na ca tvaṁ na cāhaṁ na cāyaṁ prapañcaḥ |
svarūpāvabodho vikalpāsahiṣṇuḥ
tad eko 'vaśiṣṭaḥ śivaḥ kevalo 'ham || 7 ||

na jāgran na me svapnako vā suṣuptir
na viśvo na vā taijasaḥ prājñako vā ।
avidyātmakatvāt trayāṇāṁ turīyaṁ
tad eko 'vaśiṣṭaḥ śivaḥ kevalo 'ham ॥ 8 ॥

api vyāpakatvād dhi tattvaprayogāt
svataḥsiddhabhāvād ananyāśrayatvāt ।
jagat tuccham etat samastaṁ tad anyat
tad eko 'vaśiṣṭaḥ śivaḥ kevalo 'ham ॥ 9 ॥

na caikaṁ tad anyaṁ dvitīyaṁ kutaḥ syān
na vā kevalatvaṁ na cā 'kevalatvam ।
na śūnyaṁ na cā 'śūnyam advaitakatvāt
kathaṁ sarvavedāntasiddhaṁ bravīmi ॥ 10 ॥

ātmajñānopadeśavidhi ||

prathamaḥ khaṇḍaḥ || 1 ||

athātmajñānopadeśavidhiṁ vyākhyāsyāmo mumukṣave śraddadhanāya yataye vītarāgāyātmalābhāt paralābhābhāvāt || 1 ||

draṣṭur dṛśyo 'nya iti prasiddho loke 'thā ka ātmeti || 2 ||

dehas tāvad ātmā na bhavati rūpādimattenopalabhyamānatvād yathā ghaṭādayo rūpādimantaś cakṣurādikaraṇair upalabhyanta evaṁ deho 'pi rūpādimāṁś cakṣurādikaraṇair upalabhyate 'yam iti || 3 ||

yathā dāhyaprakāśyakaṣṭhādivyatirikto dāhaprakāśako 'gnis tathā dṛśyād draṣṭā vyatirikta ātmā siddhaḥ || 4 ||

etasmād api kāraṇād dehavyatirikta ātmā svāpamaraṇādidarśanāt || 5 ||

yasmiṅ kāle dehaṁ saṁvyāpya vartata ātmā kaṣṭhādivat tadā deho vyavahārayogyo bhavati yadā dehād apasarpati tadā dehaḥ kaṣṭhādisadṛśo bhavati | tasmād dehavyatirikta ātmā siddhaḥ || 6 ||

cakṣur apy ātmā na bhavati rūpagrahaṇasādhanatvāt pradīpavat || 7 ||

yathā pradīpena karaṇena rūpam upalabhyate tathā cakṣuṣāpi karaṇena rūpam upalabhyate || 8 ||

evam evetarāṇy api karaṇāni || 9 ||

mano 'py ātmā na bhavati dṛśyatvāt karaṇatvāc ca pradīpavat || 10 ||

buddhir apy ātmā na bhavati dṛśyatvāt karaṇatvāt pradīpavat || 11 ||

prāṇo 'py ātmā na bhavati suṣuptau caitanyābhāvāt || 12 ||

prāṇasyetarasmiṅ kāle bhṛtyasvāminor iva saṁkīrṇayor na jñāyate kasyedaṁ caitanyam iti || 13 ||

suṣupte tu punar vijñānarahitaḥ prāṇa upalabhyate || 14 ||

karaṇoparamād vijñānābhāvaḥ prāṇasyeti cen na svāmini vyāpriyamāṇe karaṇoparamābhāvād rājapuruṣavad ata eva na prāṇasya itāni | yaḥ svāpenoparatas tasya itāni karaṇāny uparatāni || 15 ||

yadāsau bahirnirgatya karaṇāny adhitiṣṭhati tadā sarvāṇi karaṇāni svasvaviṣaye pravartante | yadā jāgratiṣṭhatinimittaṁ karmodbhūtaṁ bhavati tadā svāpād uparato bhavati || 16 ||

tatkṣaye sarvāṇi karaṇāni gṛhitvā buddhyupādhisaṁparkajanitaviṣayavijñānena svapnaṁ suṣuptaṁ vā gacchati || 17 ||

evaṁ sthānatrayam anavarataṁ gacchati || 18 ||

karmanimittaṁ cedaṁ manaso gamanāgamanam || 19 ||

svapnajāgarite gacchati punaḥ sthānadvayanimittakarmodbhūtaśramānopadanāya suṣuptim api gacchati || 20 ||

prāṇo 'pi taddharmavaśād eva śarīraṁ palayan vartate svapnasuṣuptayor jāgarita iva mṛtibhrāntiparihārāya || 21 ||

aham apy ātmā na bhavati sarvair ātmatvenābhimato 'pi pratyagātmavivekarahitair dṛśyatvād ghaṭādivad eva || 22 ||

vyābhicārāt || 23 ||

sukhaduḥkhādyanekaviśiṣṭatvāc ca saṁsāraviśiṣṭatvāc ca kṛśatvasthūlatvādidharmaviśiṣṭadehavat || 24 ||

yady evaṁ dehādiṣv anātmatvam ātmaśaṅkā kuta iti ced draṣṭur dṛśyavivekābhāvāt || 25 ||

iti prathamaḥ khaṇḍaḥ ||

dvitīyaḥ khaṇḍaḥ || 2 ||

atha sa ātmā ka ity uktebhyaḥ sarvebhyo vyatirikta āntaratama ākāśavatsarvagataḥ sūkṣmo nityo niravayavo nirguṇo nirajano gamanāgamanādikriyārahito 'haṁkāramamakārecchādveṣaprayatnarahitaḥsva yaṁjyotiḥsvabhāvo 'gnyuṣṇavatsavitṛprakāśavadākāśādibhūtarahito buddhyādikaraṇarahitaḥ sattvādiguṇarahitaḥ prāṇādivāyubhedarahito 'śanāyāpipāsāśokamohajarāmaraṇ aprāṇabudd iśarīra dharmarahito yaḥ sarvaprāṇihṛdi sthitaḥ sarvabuddher draṣṭā sa ātmeti || 1 ||

sarvabuddhiviśiṣṭatvenopalabhyamānatvāt sarvaprāṇihṛdistha ity ucyate na punaḥ sarvagatasya niravayavasyātmano buddhyādhāratvaṁ saṁbhavati yathākāśasya na kaścit padārtha ādhāro bhavati || 2 ||

kathaṁ punar ahaṁkāra mamakārecchādveṣaprayatnarahitasyātmano draṣṭṛtvam ity ucyate | draṣṭṛtvaṁ nāma darśanakriyākartṛtvam || 3 ||

yadi darśanakriyāṁ karotīty ātmā draṣṭā syāt tadāśeṣabuddhidraṣṭṛtvaṁ nopapadyate virodhād | yathā devadattasya kriyānurodhena yutāyutasiddha karaṇādisavyapekṣayā gamanāgamanā dikriyākartṛtvam || 4 ||

nobhayaprakārakaraṇasaṁbandharahitasyāvikriyasya dṛgrūpasyātmano darśanakriyā syāt || 5 ||

yasya tu punaḥ karaṇādisavyapekṣayā draṣṭṛtvaṁ tasyālpaviṣa yadraṣṭṛtvaṁ kramadraṣṭṛtvam adraṣṭṛtvam anyathādraṣṭṛtvaṁ syāt | pariṇāmitvāt karaṇādinimittasavyapekṣatvāc ca cittapradīpavad eva || 6 ||

naivam ātmano 'lpaviṣayadraṣṭṛtvaṁ kramadraṣṭṛtvam adraṣṭṛtvam anyathādraṣṭṛtvaṁ ceṣyate vikriyābhāvāt karaṇādinimittanirapekṣatvāc ca vyatirekena cittapradīpavat || 7 ||

kathaṁ buddhyātmanoḥ saṁyoga ity ucyate || 8 ||

ito 'pi sambandhaḥ sambhavati | sūkṣmatvāt svacchatvān niravayavatvāc cobhayoḥ saṁbandhayogyatā bhavati || 9 ||

tatra śuddhaprakāśasvarūpa ātmā sphaṭikamaṇikalpā ca buddhir aprakāśasvarūpā satī prakāśasannidhimātreṇa prakāśasvarūpā bhavatīti kṛtvā buddhyātmanor ādhyāsikaḥ saṁyoga ity ucyate || 10 ||

na punar amūrtayor buddhyātmanor jatukāṣṭhavat saṁśleṣaḥ saṁbhavati || 11 ||

anyāpekṣatvāc ca draṣṭṛtvasya yathāhaṁkāramamakārecchāprayatnarahitasyādityasya prakāśasvarūpasannidhimātreṇāvikri yamāṇena prakāśena prakāśakatvam anyathā prakāśakatvābhavāt tasyaivaṁ prakāśasvarūpa sannidhisattāmātreṇa vartamānasyādityasya prakāśakatvam adhyāropyate 'jñaiḥ prakāśyābhivyaktyapekṣayaivam eva sarvavikriyāviśeṣarahitasyātmano dṛgrūpasya caitanyasvarūpeṇāvyatiriktena sarvapratyayasākṣiṇo dṛśyasannidhimātreṇa draṣṭṛtvam upacaryate buddhyādidṛśyābhivyaktyapekṣayā 'nyathā draṣṭṛtvābhāvāt || 12 ||

*t*asya kathaṁ sarvavikriyāviśeṣarahitasyātmanaḥ kartṛtvam ity ucyate cumbakavadbhrāmakavat || 13 ||

yathā cumbako bhrāmakaḥ svarūpasannidhisattāmātreṇa lohasya prerako bhavaty evam eva sarvavikriyārahito 'py ātmā kārakāvabhāsako bhavati || 14 ||

tatra kārakāvabhāsakatvaṁ nāma kartṛtvopacaranimittam || 15 ||

buddhyādīni kārakāṇy ucyante || 16 ||

tāni caitanyāvabhāsitāni svasvaviṣayeṣu pravartante || 17 ||

tatraivaṁ sati sarvavikriyāviśeṣarahitasyātmanaḥ kartṛtvam upacaryante || 18 ||

evam ātmānaṁ kathaṁ buddhyā vijānīyād iti tan na śakyate vaktum | buddher avabhāsakatvād ādityajyotirvat || 19 ||

yathādityo rūpeṇa na prakāśyate tathātmā na dṛśyate buddhyā || 20 ||

etasmād apy ātmā na dṛśyate buddhyā buddher vedyāyā veditṛtvānupapatteḥ || 21 ||

yadi tasyāpi vedyāyā veditṛtvaṁ syāt tadā vedyatā na syāt prakāśayor iva || 22 ||

iti dvitīyaḥ khaṇḍaḥ ||

tṛtīyaḥ khaṇḍaḥ || 3 ||

tatra jāgratsvapnasuṣuptāni upanyasyantebuddher avasthāviśeṣaṇāni | teṣāṁ parityagārtham ātmaviśuddhipratipādanāya ca || 1 ||

tatra jāgran nāma cakṣurādīni karaṇāny ādityādyanugṛhitāni svasvaviṣayeṣu pravartante tatra buddhir api karaṇavyāpāram anubhavati || 2 ||

pratyagātmani pratyagātmacaitanyavajjātobhayātmikā buddhir draṣṭṛdṛśyākārā vipariṇamate | tatra pratyagātmeti kasmād ātmā viśiṣyate | vyabhicāriṇām anātmatvakhyāpanārtham || 3 ||

tatra buddhyādīni karaṇāni | ghaṭādivaddṛśyabhūtāny api bāhyāpekṣayā tāratamyakrameṇa pratyagātmasaṁyogād ātmano bhavanty udakasyāgnisaṁyoga ivoṣṇatvaṁ na tv ātmanas tatsaṁyogād anātmatvaṁ sambhavaty udakasaṁyogād ivāgner anuṣṇatvam || 4 ||

na tv ātmanaḥ pratyagātmatvaṁ kadācid api vyabhicaraty ātmābhyantare vastvantarābhāvād buddhyādīnām ivāta evātmā pratyagātmaviśeṣaṇārha evaṁ ca saty avyabhicāritvam ātmatvaṁ khyāpitaṁ bhavati || 5 ||

tatra pratyagātmacaitanyavajjvālitadhīr draṣṭṛdṛśyākārā vipariṇamate dṛśyādyuparaktā satī dṛśyākārā mūṣāṇiṣiktadrutatāmrādivat || 6 ||

tatraivaṁ sati tadubhayasākṣiṇaḥ kālākāśādivatsarvagatasya niravayavasyāvikriyasya dṛgrūpasyātmano jāgaraṇam iva bhavati || 7 ||

atha punaḥ sa dhīḥ rūpādyākāravāsanāvāsitā rūpādyantareṇa puṣpapuṭikevobhayātmikā | vidyākālakarmabhiḥ preṣyamāṇā saṁskārarūpā dṛśyatvenaivāvatiṣṭhate taddarśanaṁ svapna iva bhavati tadanukāritvād ātmano jalacandravat || 8 ||

atha punaḥ sa dhīḥ sphuraṇarahitā vāsanārūpeṇa svarūpaśūnyeva caitanyagrastā sāmānyarūpeṇa vyavatiṣṭhate tatsuṣuptaṁ vaṭakaṇikāyām iva vṛkṣaḥ || 9 ||

iti tṛtīyaḥ khaṇḍaḥ ||

caturthaḥ khaṇḍaḥ || 4 ||

tatra cinmātrasvarūpa evātmā kāryakaraṇā 'vidyākāmakarmavinirmuktaḥ salilavat svacchaḥ svātmastho bhavati || 1 ||
etāni buddher avasthāviśeṣaṇāni nātmano 'vikriyatvāt || 2 ||

etāni parityajya turīya ātmeti pratipattavyaḥ || 3 ||

tatra turīyatvaṁ nāma suvarṇaghanavadvijñāna ghanatvam || 4 ||

tathāpi caitanyasvarūpasannidhimātreṇa sākṣimātratvaṁ na tv avasthāntaram || 5 ||

tatrāvasthāntare ātmatattvapratipattyabhāvāc chūnyatvaprāpteḥ | kalpitānāṁ ca nirāspadatvānupapatteś ca || 6 ||

katham etāny ātmaviśuddhipratipattihetūny eteṣu hi satsu svātmaviśuddhir avagamyate || 7 ||

katham avagamyate | ity ucyata iteṣu hi tṛṣv api sthāneṣu draṣṭṛtvāvyabhicārāt || 8 ||

suṣupte vyabhicaratīti cet tan na tatrāpi dṛśyam eva nivārayati sarvalokaḥ katham | nāham atra suṣupte kicid apy upalabdhavān iti na dṛṣṭim | tasyās tarhi sarvatrāvyabhicārāt kūṭasthanityatā siddhā || 9 ||

ata eva na pramāṇāpekṣā 'siddhasya hi vastunaḥ paricchittiḥ pramāṇāpekṣā ca na tv ātmana ātmanaś cet pramāṇāpekṣasiddhiḥ kasya pramātṛtvaṁ syād | yasya pramātṛtvaṁ sa evātmeti niścīyate || 10 ||

nanv āgamenātmā paricchidyate nāgamenāpy ātmany adhyaropitātaddharmanivartanadvāreṇa brahmātmanor ekatvapratipattiṁ prati pramāṇatvaṁ pratipadyate nirjñātapadārthadvayasyānirjñātārthābhivyañjakatvena na tu phalarūpeṇa svataḥsiddhatvād ātmanaḥ || 11 ||

so 'ham iti smṛtyā pratisaṁdhānāt puṇyāpuṇyasaṁbandhā bhāvāc ca sthānatrayavyatiriktatvaṁ nityatvaṁ śuddhatvaṁ buddhatvaṁ muktatvam avikriyatvam apariluptadṛksvarūpatvam ekatvaṁ cātmanaḥ || 12 ||

svānubhavenaiva mama siddham iti jānāti vidvān || 13 ||

ācāryaprasādād ajñānanidrāprabuddhaḥ sakalasaṁsāravimukto vidvān || 14 ||

eṣa ātmajñānopadeśavidhir evaṁ jñātvā kṛtakṛtyo bhavati nanyatheti || 15 ||

evaṁ vedāntānuśāsanaṁ vedāntānuśāsanam || 16 ||

iti caturthaḥ khaṇḍaḥ ||

iti śrīmatparamahaṁsaparivrājaka
acāryabhagavacchaṅkaraviracitātmājñānopadeśavidhiḥ
samāptaḥ ||

śivapañcākṣaram ||

nāhaṁ deho nendriyāṇy antaraṅgaṁ
    nāhaṁkāraḥ prāṇavargo na buddhiḥ |
dārāpatyakṣetravittādidūraḥ
    sākṣī nityaḥ pratyagātmā śivo 'ham || 1 ||

rajjvajñānād bhāti rajjur yathāhiḥ
    svātmājñānād ātmano jīvabhāvaḥ |
āptoktyā hi bhrāntināśe sa rajjur
    jīvo nāhaṁ deśikoktyā śivo 'ham || 2 ||

ābhātīdaṁ viśvam ātmany asatyaṁ
    satyajñānānandarūpe vimohāt |
nidrāmohāt svapnavat tan na satyaṁ
    śuddhaḥ pūrṇo nitya ekaḥ śivo 'ham || 3 ||

nāhaṁ jāto na pravṛddho na neṣṭo
    dehasyoktāḥ prākṛtāḥ sarvadharmāḥ |
kartṛtvādiś cinmayasyāsti nāhaṁ
    kārasyaiva hy ātmano me śivo 'ham || 4 ||

matto nānyat kiṁcid atrāsti viśvaṁ
    satyaṁbāhyaṁ vastu māyopakøptam |
ādarśāntarbhāsamānasya tulyaṁ
    mayy advaite bhāti tasmāc chivo 'ham || 5 ||

laghuvākyavṛttiḥ

sthūlo māṁsamayo dehaḥ sūkṣmaḥ syād vāsanāmayaḥ |
jñānakarmendriyaiḥ sārdhaṁ dhīprāṇau tac charīragau || 1 ||

ajñānaṁ kāraṇaṁ sākṣī bodhas teṣāṁ vibhāsakaḥ |
bodhābhāso buddhigataḥ kartā syāt puṇyapāpayoḥ || 2 ||

sa eva saṁsaret karmavaśāl lokadvaye sadā |
bodhābhāsāc chuddhabodhaṁ vivicyād atiyatnataḥ || 3 ||

jāgarasvapnayor eva bodhābhāsaviḍambanā |
suptau tu tal laye śuddhabodho jāḍyaṁ prakāśayet || 4 ||

jāgare 'pi dhiyas tūṣṇīṁbhāvaḥ śuddhena bhāsyate |
dhīvyāpāraś ca tadbhasyāś cidābhāsena saṁyutāḥ || 5 ||

vahnitaptajalaṁ tāpayuktaṁ dehasya tāpakam |
cidbhāsyā dhīs tadābhāsayuktānyaṁ bhāsayet tathā || 6 ||

rūpādau guṇadoṣādivikalpā buddhigāḥ kriyāḥ |
tāḥ kriyā viṣayaiḥ sārdhaṁ bhāsayantī citir matā || 7 ||

rūpāc ca guṇadoṣābhyāṁ viviktā kevalā citiḥ |
saivānuvartate rūparasādīnāṁ vikalpane || 8 ||

kṣaṇe kṣaṇe 'nyathābhūtā dhīvikalpāś citir na tu |
muktāsu sūtravadbuddhivikalpeṣu citiḥ sthitā || 9 ||

muktābhir āvṛtaṁ sūtraṁ muktayor madhya īkṣate |
tathāvṛtā vikalpaiś citspaṣṭā madhye vikalpayoḥ || 10 ||

naṣṭe pūrvavikalpe tu yāvad anyasya nodayaḥ |
nirvikalpacaitanyaṁ tu spaṣṭaṁ tāvad vibhāsate || 11 ||

ekadvitrikṣaṇenaivaṁ vikalpasya nirodhanam |
krameṇābhyasyatāṁ yatnād brahmānubhavakāṁkṣibhiḥ || 12 ||

savikalpaka jīvo 'yaṁ brahma syān nirvikalpakam |
ahaṁ brahmeti vākyena so 'yam artho 'bhidhīyate || 13 ||

vikalpakacid yo 'haṁ brahmaikaṁ nirvikalpakam |
svataḥsiddhā vikalpās te niroddhavyāḥ prayatnataḥ || 14 ||

śakyaḥ sarvanirodhaś cet samādhir jñāninām priyaḥ |
tadaśaktau kṣaṇaṁ rudhvā śraddheyā brahmatā 'tmanaḥ || 15 ||

śraddhālur brahmatāṁ svasya cintayed buddhivṛttibhiḥ |
vākyavṛttyā yathāśakti jñātvā hy abhyasyatāṁ sadā || 16 ||

taccintanaṁ tatkathanaṁ tatparasparabodhanam |
etad ekaparatvaṁ ca brahmābhyāsaṁ vidur budhāḥ || 17 ||

dehātmadhīvad brahmātmadhīdārḍhye kṛtakṛtyatā |
yadā tadāyaṁ mriyatāṁ mukto 'sau nātra saṁśayaḥ || 18 ||

PUBLICATIONS

Aurea Vidyā Collection

1. Raphael, ***The Threefold Pathway of Fire***, Thoughts that Vibrate for an Alchemical, Æsthetical, and Metaphysical ascesis
Retail ISBN 978-1-931406-00-0
Amazon 978-1-931406-00-0
Apple etal. 978-1-931406-46-8 forthcoming

2. Raphael, ***At the Source of Life***, Questions and Answers concerning the Ultimate Reality
Retail ISBN 978-1-931406-01-7
Amazon 979-8-576124-75-6
Apple etal. 978-1-931406-32-1

3. Raphael, ***Beyond the illusion of the ego***, Synthesis of a Realizative Process
Retail ISBN 978-1-931406-03-1
Amazon 978-1-931406-03-1
Apple etal. 978-1-931406-18-5 forthcoming

4. Raphael, ***Tat tvam asi***, That thou art, The Path of Fire According to the Asparśavāda
Retail ISBN 978-1-931406-02-4
Amazon 979-8-583067-52-7
Apple etal. 978-1-931406-34-5

5. Gauḍapāda, ***Māṇḍūkyakārikā***, The Metaphysical Path of *Vedānta**
Retail ISBN 978-1-931406-04-8
Amazon 978-1-931406-04-8
Apple etal. 978-1-931406-45-1 forthcoming

6. Raphael, ***Orphism and the Initiatory Tradition***
Retail ISBN 979-8-539590-78-9
Amazon 978-1-931406-05-5
Apple etal. 978-1-931406-35-2

7. Śaṅkara, ***Ātmabodha***, Self-knowledge*
Retail ISBN 978-1-931406-06-2
Amazon 978-1-931406-06-2
Apple etal. 978-1-931406-53-6 forthcoming

8. Raphael, ***Initiation into the Philosophy of Plato***
Retail ISBN 978-1-931406-07-9
Amazon 978-1-466486-98-0
Apple etal. 978-1-931406-52-9

9. Śaṅkara, ***Vivekacūḍāmaṇi***, The Crest-jewel of Discernment*
Retail ISBN 978-1-931406-08-6
Amazon 978-1-931406-08-6
Apple etal. 978-1-931406-48-2 forthcoming

10. ***Dṛdṛśyaviveka***, A philosophical investigation into the nature of the 'Seer' and the 'seen'*
Retail ISBN 978-1-931406-09-3
Amazon 979-8-669178-69-7
Apple etal. 978-1-931406-28-4

11. Parmenides, ***On the Order of Nature***, Περί φύσεως, For a Philosophical Ascesis*
Retail ISBN 978-1-931406-10-9
Amazon 979-8-698821-95-3
Apple etal. 978-1-931406-22-2

12. Raphael, ***The Science of Love***, From the desire of the senses to the Intellect of Love
Retail ISBN 978-1-931406-12-3
Amazon 978-1-931406-12-3
Apple etal. 978-1-931406-54-3 forthcoming

13. Vyāsa, ***Bhagavadgītā***, The Celestial Song*
Retail ISBN 978-1-931406-13-0
Amazon 979-8-562809-02-5
Apple etal. 978-1-931406-50-5

14. Raphael, ***The Pathway of Fire according to the Qabbālāh*** (Ehjeh 'Ašer 'Ehjeh), I am That I am
Retail ISBN 978-1-931406-14-7
Amazon 978-1-931406-14-7
Apple etal. 978-1-931406-49-9 forthcoming

15. Patañjali, ***The Regal Way to Realization***, Yogadarśana*
Retail ISBN 978-1-931406-15-4
Amazon 978-1-931406-15-4
Apple etal. 978-1-931406-20-8

16. Raphael, ***Beyond Doubt***, Approaches to Non-duality
Retail ISBN 978-1-931406-16-1
Amazon 979-8-657281-16-3
Apple etal. 978-1-931406-25-3

17. Bādarāyaṇa, ***Brahmasūtra****
Retail ISBN 978-1-931406-17-8
Amazon 978-1-931406-17-8
Apple etal. 978-1-931406-47-5 forthcoming

18. Śaṅkara, ***Aparokṣānubhūti***, Self-realization*
Retail ISBN 978-1-931406-23-9
Amazon 978-1-931406-19-2
Apple etal. 978-1-931406-30-7

19. Raphael, ***The Pathway of Non-Duality***, Advaitavāda
Retail ISBN 978-1-931406-21-5
Amazon 979-8-552322-16-9
Apple etal. 978-1-931406-24-6

20. ***Five Upaniṣads***, Īśa, Kaivalya, Sarvasāra, Amṛtabindu, Atharvaśira*
Retail ISBN 978-1-931406-26-0
Amazon 978-1-931406-26-0
Apple etal. 978-1-931406-29-1

21. Raphael, ***The Philosophy of Being,*** A conception of life for coming out of the turmoil of individual and social conflict
Retail ISBN 978-1-931406-27-7
Amazon 979-8-630006-39-4
Apple etal. 978-1-931406-31-4

22. Raphael, ***Awakening***

Retail ISBN 978-1-931406-44-4
Amazon 979-8-716953-07-9
Apple etal. 978-1-931406-33-8

23. Raphael, ***Essence and Purpose of Yoga***, The Initiatory Pathways to the Transcendent

Retail ISBN 978-1-931406-36-9
Amazon 978-1-931406-61-1
Apple etal. 978-1-931406-62-8

24. Śaṅkara, ***Short Works***, Treatises and Hymns*

Retail ISBN 978-1-931406-71-0
Amazon 978-1-931406-55-0
Apple etal. 978-1-931406-56-7

Related Publications

A brief biography, ***Śaṅkara***
Aurea Vidyā. New York.

Retail ISBN 978-1-931406-11-6
Amazon 978-1-931406-11-6

Forthcoming Publications

Māṇḍūkya Upaniṣad, with the Gauḍapāda's *kārikā*s and the Commentary of Śaṅkara*

Retail ISBN 978-1-931406-37-6
Amazon 978-1-931406-57-4
Apple etal. 978-1-931406-58-1

Upaniṣads*

Retail ISBN 978-1-931406-38-3
Amazon 978-1-931406-59-8
Apple etal. 978-1-931406-60-4

Self-knowledge, The Harmonization of Psychic Energy. Edited by the Kevala Group

Retail ISBN 978-1-931406-40-6
Amazon 978-1-931406-63-5
Apple etal. 978-1-931406-64-2

Uttaragītā*

Retail ISBN 978-1-931406-68-0
Amazon 978-1-931406-69-7
Apple etal. 978-1-931406-70-3

Sanskrit Glossary

Retail ISBN 978-1-931406-67-3
Amazon 978-1-931406-65-9
Apple etal. 978-1-931406-66-6

* Translation from Sanskrit or Greek and Commentary by Raphael.

Aurea Vidyā is the Publishing House of the Parmenides Traditional Philosophy Foundation, a Not-for-Profit Organization whose purpose is to make Perennial Philosophy accƒessible.

The Foundation goes about its purpose in a number of ways: by publishing and distributing Traditional Philosophy texts with Aurea Vidyā, by offering individual and group encounters, by providing a Reading Room and daily Meditations at its Center.

* * *

Those readers who have an interest in Traditional Philosophy are welcome to contact the Foundation at:
parmenides.foundation@earthlink.net.

www.ingramcontent.com/pod-product-compliance
Lightning Source LLC
Chambersburg PA
CBHW030239170426
43202CB00007B/51